GOING CO-OP

Going Co-op

*The Complete Guide to Buying and
Owning Your Own Apartment*

WILLIAM COUGHLAN, JR.,
MONTE FRANKE

Beacon Press   Boston

Grateful acknowledgment is made to the National Association of Housing Co-ops for permission to reprint the list appearing in Appendix 1.

The HUD Model Documents for Housing Co-ops in Appendix 2 is reprinted from the *HUD Handbook* 4550.1, *Basic Cooperative Housing Insurance Handbook*, copyright © 1973 by the Bureau of National Affairs, Inc., Washington, D.C. 20037.

Copyright © 1983 by William Coughlan, Jr., and Monte Franke

Beacon Press books are published under the auspices of the Unitarian Universalist Association of Congregations in North America, 25 Beacon Street, Boston, Massachusetts 02108
Published simultaneously in Canada by
Fitzhenry & Whiteside Limited, Toronto

All rights reserved

Printed in the United States of America

(hardcover) 9 8 7 6 5 4 3 2 1
(paperback) 9 8 7 6 5 4 3 2 1

Library of Congress Cataloging in Publication Data
Coughlan, William, 1946–
  Going co-op.
  Includes index.
  1. Apartment houses, Cooperative. 2. Housing, Cooperative. I. Franke, Monte, 1954–   . II. Title.
HD7287.7.A3C68   1983   643′.2   82-72501
ISBN 0-8070-0868-0
ISBN 0-8070-0869-9 (pbk.)

*Dedicated to
all those who still rent*

Acknowledgments

It was seven years ago that Bill got the idea for this book. He had just finished *The Food Co-op Handbook,* and it occurred to him that a similar handbook on housing was needed. Four years later he met Monte. Since then, our time has been spent meeting and writing.

Over this span of seven years we have talked with innumerable people from Massachusetts to California. To list them all is impossible. Many of their names and organizations can be found in the text and the appendices. To all the rest, we say thank you. We thank OKM as well. We also have to admit to having a silent partner, one that organized us and didn't argue: our friend the TRS 80 Model II computer.

Our special thanks go to Patti for her understanding and support during all those lost evenings and weekends.

We hope this book will engender some debate in the co-op movement. It certainly did between us. Everything we have advocated in this book has been derived from our experiences. Bill has been active in the co-op movement since 1972, and this is his third book on organizing. Monte has been working for affordable housing since 1975, and it's his computer. This book is richer because two heads are better than one. It was a learning process for us, our writing got better, and we became friends as well. These are the rewards of a cooperative venture.

Our final thanks go to our editor, Joanne Wyckoff, for patience, persistence, and perceptive responses to our efforts.

Contents

ACKNOWLEDGMENTS vii

1. WELCOME TO THE CO-OP 1

2. THE CO-OP CHOICE 11
    Making the Decision
    The Basics of a Housing Co-op
    Size of Co-ops
    Types of Co-ops
    Who Joins a Co-op?

3. A BUYER'S GUIDE 27
    What Can You Afford?
    Searching for the Affordable Co-op Home
    Negotiations and Purchase
    Buyer Protections

4. STARTING YOUR OWN CO-OP 49
    Getting a Running Start
    Organizing Co-op Tasks

5. LEGAL MATTERS 63
    Incorporation

The Co-op Operators' Manual
Tax Requirements for Co-ops

6. FINDING AN AFFORDABLE BUILDING 75
    What Kind of Building Does Your Group Need?
    Selecting the Building or Property
    Inspecting the Building
    Rehabilitation
    Affordability Analysis
    Purchasing the Property

7. HOW TO FINANCE YOUR CO-OP 104
    Affordability Analysis Revisited
    Making the Square Peg Fit
    Putting Together a Loan Application Package
    Advice You Can Take to the Bank

8. REHABILITATION 127
    To Repair or Replace
    Planning for Rehabilitation
    Under Construction
    Sweat Equity

9. HOUSE POLICIES 149
    Carrying Charges and Collections
    Management
    Maintenance
    Capital Improvements
    Resale and Transfer Value
    Other House Policies

10. BOOKKEEPING 168
   Setting Up a Simple Accounting System
   The Co-op Accounting Cycle
   Other Money-Handling Matters

11. ROUNDING OUT THE CO-OP EXPERIENCE 187
    Building Participation
    Communication and Education

12. VISIONS 202
    The Grain of Salt: How to Take Our Advice

APPENDICES 1. Co-op Assistance Organizations 207
            2. HUD Legal Documents for Housing
               Co-ops 215
               Model Form of By-Laws 217
               Model Form of Certificate of Incorporation 230
               Model Form of Occupancy Agreement 233
               Model Form of Subscription Agreement 238

INDEX 241

1
WELCOME TO THE CO-OP

ONE OF OUR FRIENDS wrote us this letter recently:

Dear Bill,

I've got a problem with my landlord. He won't fix things in my apartment. I've got a leaky faucet that keeps me awake at night, and a window that won't lock so I don't dare sleep much anyway. Every time I ask him to fix things, he uses the excuse about how he would have to raise the rent in order to fix the place up to my liking. Then, the last time I spoke with him he said he was fed up with our complaining and he threatened to sell the building to a condo developer. He may have been bluffing, but I'm not sure. Several buildings in our neighborhood have gone condo recently, rents are going up, and I don't know where I could afford to live if this place were sold.

Last night I had dinner with my neighbors, Mark and Lisa, and they also have had problems with the landlord. Mark mentioned reading about tenants who bought their building and formed a co-op. Over a bottle of wine, it sounded like a great idea for us, but this morning we realized that we weren't so sure.

I promised to contact you. Do you think housing

2 / GOING CO-OP

co-ops are a good idea? Can we do one? How do we start? Write soon.

Kathy

This is just one of the several inquiries we have received from acquaintances over the last few years about co-ops. Although housing co-ops have existed in this country since the beginning of the century, it is only recently that they have been recognized as a potent consumer weapon against inflation and rising housing costs.

"Going co-op" has come to be thought of as a way of addressing a variety of housing problems. The key to the co-op is the opportunity to control one's own housing. Renters have become vulnerable to recent economic conditions that have forced housing prices and interest costs up. For most of the 1970s, housing prices increased at a rate greater than inflation. While this created a good deal for those who already owned property, it translated into higher rents and fewer affordable purchase opportunities for those still hoping to buy.

In large part, the recent rise in housing costs reflects a great expansion in the demand for housing. The post–World War II baby boom generation—80 million members strong—has just reached peak home-buying age. This group had caused the great suburban explosion of the 1950s, the tremendous expansion of public schools in the 1960s, and the growth of colleges in the 1970s. Today, this group is out in full force looking for better places to live, starting families, and buying homes.

It's one thing to let out your clothes because of a midriff bulge, but it's a totally different situation when you suddenly become forty pounds overweight. The large bulges cannot be hidden or ignored, and letting out the clothes no longer works. Although the great bulge in the need for housing had been forecast nearly two decades ago, our nation failed to "let out" the supply of housing to meet the needs and expectations of the young.

This baby boom generation of young Americans left high

school and college with good jobs and promising careers, and they expected to be able to buy homes at a much younger age than their parents did. But the abrupt arrival of so many new buyers on the market at the same time forced prices higher and higher, beyond the reach of first-time buyers. The lucky first few were able to buy before prices skyrocketed, but the rest have been left standing in line. At today's prices and financing costs, it is estimated that fewer than one-quarter of American families can afford to buy the average-priced new home.

"Our country has plenty of five-cent cigars, but the trouble is they charge fifteen cents for them." It seems as though this observation of Will Rogers can easily be adapted to today's housing prices. In these times of high prices and limited opportunities, what this country needs is a creative housing alternative akin to the "five-cent cigar."

We think that co-ops are the essential answer to this housing crisis. If you are a renter, co-ops may be your best alternative if:

- You want a chance to own your own home but cannot afford the current price for a single-family home or condominium or cannot qualify for a mortgage.
- You need a few years to save for the down payment of your dream home but want to have control over your own housing as soon as possible.
- You would like to own your own home but aren't willing to put all your savings into a single housing investment; you want to continue investing in a variety of things to better protect your savings and your future.
- You are elderly, and now that your children have left home you no longer need a large home but want security, fixed housing costs, and services.
- You want to live in a building where you know your neighbors and work together for a secure living environment.
- You do not want to continue to live with the risks of rent-

ing and the uncertainty of what your landlord may do in the future with the building.
- You face the possibility of losing your home to an investor who wants to buy the building and convert it into a condominium.
- You are dissatisfied that your landlord makes huge profits from your need for housing.
- Like our friend Kathy, you are tired of getting no response when you ask the building manager to repair the leaking faucet or fix the elevator, and you and your neighbors are convinced you can do a better job of managing the building.

A housing co-op is owned by the people who live in a particular building. The residents join together to purchase and manage their own housing, with the goal of providing themselves the best possible housing at the lowest possible cost. Housing co-ops are set up as business corporations, but they are unique businesses in two respects. First, they are operated exclusively for the benefit of their members. Second, they are democratic organizations, and all members participate in the activities of the co-op. The housing co-op is not just a business: it is a democratic way of doing business.

Co-ops provide their members with many benefits: the security and financial benefits of homeownership, the opportunity to participate in democratic management of the building, and the satisfaction of working within a community of people to achieve a safe and affordable living environment.

Co-ops are personal: they can be set up by you and your fellow co-op members to create any kind of living environment you want. You share in the control of the co-op — its rules, its finances, and the conditions of the building. Each co-op becomes a unique organization that reflects the will and the needs of its members. At the same time that control is shared by all members, your individual rights of ownership are protected. "Good fences make good neighbors," and a co-op corporation erects fences to protect all your rights of occupancy. You share in what needs to be shared but retain the privacy of your own home.

"I have lived in South Minneapolis for the past thirteen years... It seems like I have always been moving from one new rental place to another," Bonni, a 23-year-old Native American, described her life prior to The New Beginning.

With the help of Common Space, a Minneapolis organization that assists existing co-ops and promotes new co-ops, Bonni and three other women formed the New Beginning Cooperative and began renovating a dilapidated house. Two women dropped out, but replacement families were found. Over several months in 1980, the four women and their children learned how to rip down sheet rock, tear out lath and plaster, and do other demolition that reduced by more than $4,000 the cost of rehabilitating their co-op home.

This was only the beginning, however. As Common Space said in one of its publications, this project "combined no less than three sources of borrowed funds and six sources of subsidy... The numbers... simply cannot convey the ongoing effort of many which has been required to bring our projects along. Nor do they portray the critical human investments in time and labor contributed by the co-op members-to-be who have managed their building, made repairs, and simply held on through some frustrating times." Construction was completed, and the families occupied their two-bedroom homes in the spring of 1981.

Bonni reports, "For the first time I can say, 'This is mine,' and I have the advantage of sharing the building with people I know and trust... My family is very important to me. Besides my parents, I have five brothers and sisters. This is one way to make my family proud of me. It will give Becky [her three-year-old daughter] a sense of value, too... The greatest thing is that, for the first time ever, I will have room to invite my family for a visit... I know exactly what I want in home furnishings and such—it's been my dream since I was a teenager—it's going to be fun."

Co-ops are stable: in these times of rapid change, a co-op

offers the identity of belonging to a group, the integrity of owning some real estate, the security of knowing one's neighbors, and the stability of long-term membership.

"I had lived in my apartment building for seven years when I overheard my landlord making a sales pitch to two businessmen in the front hall," recalled one member of a Boston co-op. "I called another tenant, who called the landlord and asked for an emergency meeting. At the meeting we confronted the landlord about the possibility of a sale and convinced him to give us some time to buy him out first. Then several of us began knocking on the doors of other tenants in the building to talk about going co-op. Some of the tenants were strangers to us, even though there were only twelve units."

What the tenants proposed to their neighbors was a limited-equity co-op, which means that the cost of membership could not increase beyond certain limits. Some tenants balked: they did not want to buy into a co-op, did not agree with the limited-equity concept, or did not have money for the down payment. Still, eight of the twelve households agreed to join.

The landlord, tired after years of managing the building and also struggling with this active group of tenants, agreed to their offer "surprisingly fast," according to the organizers. The tenants convinced a local bank to finance the co-op at a reasonable rate as part of its program for the Community Reinvestment Act (federally sponsored legislation affecting all banks. Ask your bank about it). And the Roman Catholic Archdiocese of Boston agreed to help an elderly woman finance her down payment. With these pieces in place, the First Fenway Cooperative came into being.

"The whole thing was terribly exciting," one new homeowner explained. "We chose the name First Fenway because we want the Second, Third, Fourth, and Fifth Fenway Cooperatives to follow."

The excitement took on a new dimension just a few months after the tenants created the First Fenway Cooperative. A few blocks away, a developer purchased an entire block of buildings for a $26 million condominium conversion. One Fenway Cooperative member said, "Maybe we acted just in time to save our homes."

The democratic structure of a co-op allows members to determine the best housing and services that the group can realistically afford. Lowest possible cost can be achieved in several ways.

- Co-ops eliminate the profit line from housing costs, resulting in savings of 5, 10, or even 15 percent over what a landlord would charge for the same space.
- Co-op members often reduce construction and operating costs by doing some of the work themselves. This is known as "sweat equity," because members substitute their labor for their money. Co-ops that use sweat equity can cut construction costs by as much as 20 percent and operating costs by as much as 10 percent.
- Historically, co-ops have had lower turnover rates and more responsible members than other types of housing, which result in lower vacancy losses, lower collection losses, and lower maintenance costs. All that translates into lower monthly charges to members; many co-ops save 1 to 3 percent of their operating budgets this way.
- Because co-ops have a history of responsible and stable membership, they provide stable housing in the long run. The U.S. Department of Housing and Urban Development (HUD) reports that its co-op mortgage insurance program has the lowest default rate of any housing insured by its programs. Scuttlebutt in New York City is that no local co-op has ever defaulted.
- A co-op is assessed property taxes as a single building. In many cities this means co-ops pay lower taxes than condominiums, because condominium units are assessed individually.
- Co-op members may also be eligible for the personal income

tax deductions enjoyed by other homeowners. They are allowed to take their share of the deductions for the co-op's mortgage interest and property taxes. For many co-op members, this may mean a net reduction of 10 to 30 percent of their monthly housing costs.

What does all this mean for the bottom-line savings of going co-op? There is no simple answer because there are many types of co-ops. For some investment-oriented co-ops, the co-op will cost as much as any other type of housing, and the only savings to members are through tax deductions. In other co-ops members are able to fix their net housing costs at 20 to 40 percent below the rent an investor would probably charge.

Robert is a thirty-year-old single person working in Washington, D.C., for a professional housing organization. He lived in an apartment in a four-unit townhouse on Capitol Hill until he was displaced by a condominium conversion he could not afford. He moved to another apartment on Capitol Hill but soon concluded that he was "getting ripped off." Because he was in the housing business, he understood the dynamics of the Washington housing market and knew that he had to be careful about choosing another place to live. "The chances were pretty good that any place I found might later be converted to condominiums," he said. "I wanted to invest, but I had to find a place I could afford to either rent or own. I moved to Buckingham Village in Arlington, Virginia, expecting that a conversion was coming, but I had figured out beforehand that I could probably afford the prices I could expect to be charged."

Within two years the owners of Buckingham Village announced a conversion of 378 units, including Robert's apartment, to a co-operative. "I was caught off-guard only because they went co-op rather than condo. However, I sat down and figured it out and concluded that the price was reasonable and that it was still a good investment. By being an early buyer, I had my choice of units."

Robert bought the co-op membership for $47,000, which gave him occupancy of a one-bedroom unit. He put down $2,000, and the developer helped him to secure a mortgage for the rest. Combining his monthly mortgage payment and his maintenance fee, Robert found himself paying almost 50 percent more for housing than he had paid while renting, but with tax deductions and the growing value of his investment he estimates he comes pretty close to even, and "maybe a little bit more."

Robert is engaged to be married, so he knows that the small one-bedroom unit will not always be adequate to meet his housing needs. "Like almost everyone else, my long-term goal is a house with a yard. But this is a good first step, and I do think I will get a good return. It's a pretty good investment, and I've been making improvements to the unit with an eye toward getting the most out of it when I decide to sell."

Although we have focused on the value of the housing co-op to young, first-time buyers like Robert, co-ops have also proved to be immensely popular and successful in providing housing for the elderly. The difficulty of maintenance and the loneliness of the empty nest have caused many elderly individuals and couples to try housing co-ops. As mini retirement communities, such co-ops have provided a very active alternative.

Heddy is a resident of the 201-unit federally assisted Bishop Co-op for the elderly in Wyandotte, Michigan. "My husband is a handyman, even though he is seventy-nine. He does odd jobs for the people of the building, and he earns a dollar or two from that. He stores his tools in the hobby shop downstairs. I say 'his' tools—and they are—but they're also everybody's tools. They are for the co-op. After all, what are we going to do with them? We might as well lend them to the co-op.

"My husband has just gone to fix a piece of carpet. That's his contribution for today. Our contributions are appreciated. We have the sociability of all these other people our age, our monthly payments are very low, there is always something to do, we all look out for one another, and we are responsible for making the co-op work. That keeps us on our toes."

Henry Smith, president of Bishop Co-op, explains that "in a co-op, everyone is responsible for the building. If it is kept right, our monthly charges increase very little and everyone benefits. We have activities for the residents: cards, bingo, adult education classes, exercises, religious worship, and speakers like the fire chief, the chief of police, and the librarian. We have our own bus now, a little van that can take the residents shopping and even on daytime trips to places of interest. We also have a recreation room and an arts and crafts room, paneled by the men in the building. We've put in smoke alarms and insulated our hot water tank, and many other things.

"Of course, everyone cooperates. The custodian quit about six weeks ago, and all the men jumped in and helped keep this place clean for nothing—free."

The versatility of the co-op ownership idea makes it particularly valuable today to many different people: to the young person needing a price break on a first opportunity for ownership; to the middle-income family looking for a tax-sheltered investment; to the lower-income household needing a way of minimizing housing costs; and to the fixed-income elderly who need a home for which their costs are also fixed. For some, co-op membership is homeownership with the full price tag, but for many others going co-op is buying a piece of the American dream—at a discount.

2
THE CO-OP CHOICE

THIS CHAPTER concentrates on the personal choice of going co-op. We examine some of the factors that may be involved in your initial decision about buying into a co-op, then we explore different types of co-ops and co-op members.

Making the Decision

Perhaps too much emphasis has been placed on the financial incentives to buy a home, a condo, or a co-op in these inflationary times. The arguments for buying have focused on inflation and taxes. To many people, housing has become primarily a good investment as well as a tax-sheltered one. Put down a little, borrow a lot, take some tax breaks, and hope that when you want to sell it the house will be worth more than you paid for it. Home is where the investment portfolio is.

Let's step back from the financial argument for a moment and consider the many other aspects of homeownership. Ownership means control—the ability to control how you live. It means security—the safety of knowing that you will not be displaced or impoverished by another person who controls your home. It provides identity—the home is an extension and an expression of your personality.

At the same time, ownership carries with it a large set of responsibilities. There are many maintenance tasks you must do regularly yourself or pay someone else to do. There are

12 / GOING CO-OP

bills to be paid—and your costs are not limited to a rent payment. If you are part of a co-op or condo, you must attend regular meetings to make these decisions. You can no longer call the landlord and complain; now you are the landlord.

Ownership means a substantial investment from which you cannot just walk away. You have to find a buyer willing to pay the price. When recession hits or bad times fall on a particular housing market, you may be stuck or face a considerable loss if you need or want to sell. If your plans in the near future include moving, expanding your family, or shifting expenditures from housing to other costs, then buying may not be right for you at this time. Ask yourself if you will be willing and able to live in the same place for at least three years.

Ownership is not for everyone, although it is evident that the substantial majority of Americans want to own their own property.

You can't talk about co-ops today without comparing them to condominiums, and vice versa. They are the two most common forms of multifamily homeownership. Cooperatives have existed in the large urban areas of the United States for most of this century; condominiums are a more recent phenomenon, growing in popularity in resort areas during the 1960s.

Co-ops and condos have become popular because of their lower cost and convenience. They are less expensive than single-family homes because they are smaller. Many co-op and condo buyers can afford only smaller units and seem to prefer their convenience and reduced maintenance requirements. Demand for both condos and co-ops has grown, causing many rental buildings to be converted. In response to the number of the conversions and displacements, state and local governments have enacted laws limiting conversions and tenant evictions.

Both the co-op and the condo offer a legal means of common ownership. In a condominium, members legally own the air space of their unit as well as a share of any common spaces and land. A co-op member, in contrast, owns part of a corporation, which owns the building. The corporation in turn provides the member with lease rights to occupy a unit so long as the member household belongs to the co-op.

Too much can be made of the legal differences between these forms of ownership. The type of ownership most common in your community probably depends for the most part on the history of multifamily ownership in your area and the preference of lenders.

We feel that the case for condominium ownership has been overstated. Convinced that Americans need to own something tangible, developers extol "private ownership of air space" to promote the condo as the substitute for single-family ownership. Many lenders also have developed a preference for condos because the risk of the project is spread among many mortgages and several lenders. But the consumer—the critical participant as far as we are concerned—is not given any real advantage by the separate mortgage and the concept of owning air space. In fact, there are some significant disadvantages to the condominium owner. Condo buyers have to qualify for an individual mortgage, which can be an obstacle to the first-time borrower. Separate ownership of air space somehow creates the illusion for condo owners that their neighbors cannot affect them and that they can close the door and shut the others out. Nothing is further from the truth: condo owners need each other very much. They share walls; they share floors and ceilings; they share entrances and hallways; and, like it or not, they share lifestyles and rules for living. The argument about owning one's own air space is a dangerous marketing illusion that creates a mistaken, possessive attitude instead of fostering the cooperative attitude essential to peaceful shared living.

Co-ops, on the other hand, have one mortgage for the entire building. Individual members do not have to qualify for an individual mortgage. And, most important, co-ops do not create any illusions about members' ability to ignore their neighbors; rather, the co-op devotes considerable attention to creating and fostering a social democracy, the ideal basis for living in a shared environment.

The difference in the way a condominium and a cooperative make decisions is critically important to understanding the two concepts. In condos, voting rights reflect investment. If you own a larger and more expensive unit than someone else, your voting power is proportionately larger. Co-ops are democratic in decision making: each member household has one vote, regardless of size or investment. No single household is granted extra influence.

Co-ops have to limit absentee ownership to comply with IRS requirements; in doing so they usually foster a better living environment. Condos have no such legal restrictions. As a former or current renter, you know that a structure allowing absentee owners can create many problems for tenants.

The co-op member's right of occupancy is protected by a proprietary lease. A member must violate some term of the occupancy agreement to lose the right of occupancy, and a member can lose that right only after the situation has been reviewed by the co-op's democratic decision-making body. Since each member votes in the election of the body and helps set the rules, members' rights are doubly protected.

The Basics of a Housing Co-op

Housing co-ops are businesses. They are in the business of providing the best possible housing at the lowest possible cost. More important, co-ops are *a way of doing business*. Every co-op, regardless of its size or type, must exhibit certain characteristics to be called a housing cooperative. From the following basic characteristics, individual co-ops evolve.

SHARED OWNERSHIP

Co-op members own the housing in which they live. They typically own it through membership in a corporation specially created and limited to the cooperative ownership. The corporation owns the building(s), and the members own shares in the corporation. The number of shareholders equals the number of units.

Unlike condominium owners or single-family homeowners, co-op members do not own their living units individually. As a co-op shareholder, each member has purchased the right to occupy one of the units in the co-op, governed by the terms of a *proprietary lease*. The member retains the right of occupancy so long as his or her household meets the conditions of membership, abides by the rules of the co-op, and pays its share of the operating costs and fees.

Because the cooperative corporation, and not the individual members, owns the property, the corporation obtains the mortgage. Each member purchases shares of stock in the corporation to raise the money for the down payment on the property and then pays to the co-op a portion of the monthly mortgage and operating costs.

DEMOCRATIC DECISION MAKING

Co-ops are democratic enterprises, and decisions are made by the membership. The body of shareholders (members) holds the power to make most decisions and does so by voting in general meetings. Each member household has one vote.

For practical reasons, the shareholders assign most of the day-to-day decision making to a board of directors, elected from the general membership. The board conducts regular (usually monthly) open meetings which members can attend and participate in.

Meetings of the full membership may occur only once or several times a year for policy decisions. An annual meeting is required, and other meetings may be necessary to make certain decisions—including by-law changes and annual budgets—that must be voted on by the membership.

PARTICIPATION OF MEMBERS

A housing co-op is operated by and for its members. It is in the best interest of the co-op to have an educated membership, so that members can make informed decisions. Knowledge is power in co-ops, and participation expands knowledge.

Because a co-op depends on each member to meet both the financial and the participatory requirements of membership, it must carefully select new members and prepare them for membership. Orientation of members involves full disclosure of rights and responsibilities, acquaintance with other co-op members, and opportunities to participate in co-op activities. In addition, co-ops typically have ongoing programs of education and organized events at which members can interact.

FINANCIAL INTEREST

Although all member households possess one vote in decision making, they do not necessarily divide costs evenly. The share of responsibility for the costs of the co-op is divided among members based on the characteristics of the unit each member occupies. This share of the financial obligations is referred to as the member's financial interest (or, alternatively, beneficial interest). The units may be of different size or quality, and some may contain amenities that others do not. Some, but not all, units may have fireplaces and balconies, for example. In one co-op in Boston, some units have solar-assisted heating and others do not.

Co-ops may vary the price of membership according to the unit each member occupies. One co-op sells membership rights to a one-bedroom unit for $8,000 and two-bedroom units for $12,000. Other co-ops do not vary membership price. Instead, they vary the monthly carrying charges. A Washington, D.C., co-op has carrying charges of $210 for a one-bedroom unit and $260 for a two-bedroom unit.

LIMITED EQUITY

The original cooperative—started in Rochdale, England, in 1844—operated on the idea that the invested money of its members should receive a limited dividend. Through the years most co-ops have continued to adhere to this principle, protecting members' investments from losses as well as prohibiting excessive profit.

Unlike other types of co-ops, housing co-ops do not pay regular dividends because they provide housing at cost. The limited-equity and dividend principle instead applies to the value of the membership. Limited-equity co-ops limit the price of membership as well as the price members can obtain when they sell.

Not all of today's housing co-ops follow the limited-equity principle. As we explain later, some allow their members to buy and sell memberships at whatever price they can command.

Size of Co-ops

When E. F. Schumacher suggested that "small is beautiful," he noted that popular economic, scientific, and historical theories viewed evolution as a natural process of moving toward order on a larger scale. His thesis was that there must be a social balance of structures and organizations of different scale for people's different purposes. We take the argument one step further: people need structures of different scale for the *same* purpose.

Housing co-ops come in all sizes. There are two-family co-ops and there is New York's Co-op City, which houses more than 60,000 families. To suggest that there is some universally appropriate size within that range would be to ignore the many successful co-ops of different sizes and the individual lifestyle preferences and the varied kinds of housing available in different communities.

On the West Side of Manhattan, five families are operating their building as a small cooperative. Their building was owned by the City of New York, but the tenants purchased it under a city program to promote co-ops. According to the co-op's advisers from the Urban Homesteading Assistance Board, "This group had family ties, which meant they were close before they entered the program, but the co-op seemed to draw them even closer together. In fact, they appear to operate more as a family than as urban neighbors."

When they began managing their building, one of the members recalled, it seemed as though they were always meeting. The meetings weren't formal; they were held over dinner, snacks, or drinks in one of the apartments. The co-op members decided to do some interesting things. Maintenance tasks were assigned to the men, and the women painted the halls and decorated the entryway. A divorced mother was assigned the management and bookkeeping tasks, for which the co-op paid her a small fee to supplement her limited income. The members also decided to reduce the monthly charge to one elderly woman and credited her baby-sitting as part of her contribution to the co-op.

Most small co-ops—those up to fifteen units—operate in a similar fashion. Meetings do not resemble corporate board meetings: they are informal social gatherings, and business talk is squeezed in between conversation about children, vacation plans, and car repairs. Most management and maintenance activities are done by the members themselves. Members allocate the work by volunteering or by assigning tasks to those who have the skills and time.

In contrast to the small co-op, the Benning Heights Cooperative in Washington, D.C., is a 474-unit townhouse development spread out over 22 acres. A small group of tenants organized the co-op and bought the forty-year-old development in 1982 when the original owner decided to retire. Nearly three-quarters of the existing tenants decided to join the co-op.

The co-op has nine members on its board of directors. The directors take turns staffing the co-op office during evenings and weekends. They also have organized the townhouses into twenty-nine courts, each of which selects a court captain to represent members on a council. In addition, each building selects a building spokesperson. About sixty members take active roles in the co-op organization.

The co-op has committees for fund raising, membership, building rehabilitation, youth programs, and a monthly newsletter. The committees are responsible for about one co-op-wide activity per month. Recent activities include a Halloween disco, a trip to the racetrack, yard sales, and a May Day festival.

Large co-ops such as Benning Heights or New York's Co-op City may not be appropriate for everyone, but they do offer certain advantages. A large co-op can be thought of as a series of smaller, informal co-ops. This is especially obvious in Co-op City, where there are literally hundreds of social groups and special-interest groups that, as one member put it, tend to "honeycomb" the co-op and its members. Small-group identity within the larger co-op is important, perhaps even more than the singular identity of Co-op City. The informal communication networks rival formal lines of communication for mobilizing opinion. The co-op is really a full-service community.

Types of Co-ops

Size is one of the major determinants of the character of a co-op, but it is certainly not the only one. Each co-op is unique because of its members, the community in which the members live, and the co-op's rules of operation, among other factors. There are four major types of co-ops: the investment co-op and structured co-op among older models and the mutual housing association and full-service co-op, prevalent among co-ops that have appeared during the last ten years.

INVESTMENT CO-OPS

Many large apartment buildings on both the East and West Sides of Manhattan have been converted into cooperatives by and for the well-to-do. The co-ops, like nearly all real estate in Manhattan, are very expensive. Their acquisition cost and their monthly carrying charges are high. It is common for members to have to borrow the money to purchase membership, so they face monthly personal mortgage payments in addition to their co-op carrying charges.

Apartment ownership via the co-op corporation has existed in New York City since early in this century. The co-op idea was first brought from Europe by unions wanting to provide decent housing for workers as an alternative to city tenements and was later adapted to the high-rise apartment buildings of Manhattan. Developers recognized that in the tight housing market in Manhattan they could command a very high price for a building as a co-op. The value of parts of the building to many small investors became larger than the value of the whole to a single investor.

The demand for co-ops remains strong in New York because of rising property values and the attractive tax benefits of ownership. The rising value of co-op memberships is keeping pace with the value of other real estate investments. Many people purchase memberships purely as investments, often with the intention of subletting rather than occupying their unit. Tenants are also taking advantage of the opportunity to purchase their units at a discount with the intention of quickly selling the unit at market rates.

Because of the high cost of such co-ops and their legal control over who becomes a member, they have become very exclusive. Richard Nixon, Barbra Streisand, and other well-known people have been turned down by investment co-ops for nonfinancial reasons such as security and privacy.

Outside of New York, Chicago, Washington, D.C., and a few other cities, the investment co-op for middle- and upper-income families is less common and condominiums are more popular because of the preference of banks, developers, and other people in the real estate business.

STRUCTURED CO-OPS

Many older co-ops were started as a result of federal government support of the housing co-op idea. Grounded in the principles of stability and affordability, these co-ops took advantage of direct federal financing and insurance programs to establish homeownership opportunities for families. As of November 1982, HUD insurance was in force for 122,734 units in 1,009 housing co-ops across the country. Also as of that date only 25 insured co-ops (2 percent) had defaulted, with ownership assumed by HUD through foreclosure.

To ensure the success of co-ops and the security of its investments, the federal government requires that assisted co-ops be carefully structured. Standard bylaws, subscription agreements, occupancy agreements, and other forms have been developed by HUD for these co-ops. (Appendix 2 contains sample forms.) These documents provide for a very strong board of directors. The U.S. Department of Housing and Urban Development actively monitors the co-ops' financial operations and imposes strict requirements on record keeping and the maintenance of reserve funds.

Pine Grove Village in Lexington, Massachusetts, is a five-year-old mixed-income cooperative sponsored by the Roman Catholic Archdiocese of Boston. The announcement of available units brought applications from more than 600 families. Rents were very reasonable: in 1982 a three-bedroom unit rented for $394 per month, heat included. The co-op offers convenient access to metropolitan Boston for work and shopping and to one of the state's best school systems. Co-op members include whites, blacks, and Hispanics. There has been only one vacancy in the co-op's five years, and a waiting list of 140 still exists.

MUTUAL HOUSING ASSOCIATIONS

Some co-ops are set up primarily to spawn other co-ops. A nonprofit or philanthropic group sets up a central organization, usually called a mutual housing association, to generate capital and provide support to groups who wish to start a co-op. We are aware of mutual housing associations in Detroit, Minneapolis, Baltimore, and Boston, as well as one that is just starting in Walla Walla, Washington.

Growth-oriented co-ops are most common in Europe.

The best example may be the mother-daughter societies in Sweden. The mother co-op acts as developer of daughter co-ops. The daughter co-op, depending on the needs of its members, may contract with the mother organization for development services, management services, or technical assistance on a variety of co-op issues. When the daughter co-op is operating, it becomes a member of a federation of co-ops that supports future development activities of the mother co-op. The co-ops contribute membership fees and services to assist in the development of more co-ops. They also start savings accounts for children of member families so they can afford to join co-ops as adults.

Common Space, Inc. is a nonprofit development corporation established in 1977 by sixteen Minneapolis neighborhood groups to develop lower-income family co-op housing. It is controlled by a community-based board of directors whose members represent several inner-city neighborhood organizations, other nonprofit community developers, and the low-income housing co-ops sponsored by Common Space.

Common Space provides a variety of assistance services to groups that want to convert their current housing to co-ops. Its organizers work with tenants to explain the co-op structure and to organize the co-op corporation. Its staff helps new co-ops plan the finances for acquisition and rehabilitation and assists co-op members to take an active role in the rehabilitation. The staff also provides training in co-op management and bookkeeping. By October 1980, Common Space had been involved in the successful conversion of five cooperatives with a total of ninety-six family units.

Common Space activities are not limited to bricks and mortar. It also provides public information through a variety of media—publications, conferences, networks, lobbying, and special events. In 1981, it convinced the Minneapolis City Council to allocate nearly $4 million to a low- and moderate-income housing construction program. It provides housing management services and has set up a share loan fund for families that cannot afford memberships in assisted co-ops. And it provides ongoing assistance to all its co-ops.

FULL-SERVICE CO-OPS

A more recent type of housing co-op begins with housing services for its members and extends itself into other enterprises. Some housing co-ops have generated food co-ops, optical services co-ops, co-op pharmacies, co-op laundromats, cooperative health clinics, co-op recreational facilities, co-op day care, co-op cable TV stations, and credit unions.

The membership base for the co-op enterprises is the housing co-op's membership, although it is not limited to that membership. Such co-ops sometimes take additional members from the community, who then often want to get on the co-op's waiting list for occupancy.

Who Joins a Co-op?

You may be tempted to think that we assume all people are alike. We do not, but it is difficult to introduce all the subtle differences that income, education, cultural attitudes, type of neighborhood, and ethnic identity can bring to a co-op. A co-op that works for one group will not necessarily work for another. Many of the distinctions between co-ops are due to class-related characteristics of the members, and many co-ops are successful because they achieve a class identity among their members.

ELDERLY

No matter how severe inflation is, it affects some groups more severely than others. Rising prices take their greatest toll on those with fixed incomes, such as most elderly citizens. Consequently, senior citizens are prime candidates for co-op housing. Many co-ops are established for and by the elderly, and they can be enormously successful.

It is important for co-op groups whose members include

the elderly to keep in mind the special needs of the elderly. The elderly are not as mobile as younger people; their units should be convenient to exits and elevators. They also may need some assistance with certain activities and may greatly appreciate planned social activities that include them.

But even more important, co-op members should realize that skills acquired over a lifetime do not disappear with retirement. The elderly members of a co-op are potentially its greatest asset. They often have time to donate to many of the co-op's work tasks. Some have skills from years of business experience to help in the management of co-op affairs; others have had years of experience maintaining a home. The possible skills the elderly can bring to a co-op are numerous.

STUDENTS

Student communities often contain many idealistic people who have the spare time, energy, and commitment to work for nonmonetary rewards—all characteristics that make them ideal candidates for co-ops. Co-ops also make sense for students because they can be structured so that sweat can substitute for limited incomes. Strong student co-op movements exist in large campus communities such as Ann Arbor, Michigan; Berkeley, California; and Austin, Texas. Other smaller communities such as River City, Iowa, and Oberlin, Ohio, have also supported strong student co-ops.

A major problem for student co-ops is the transience of their members. Most students are in school and the co-op for a limited number of years and they frequently want to leave town during school breaks. Student co-ops thus have to structure themselves for turnover. One student co-op in Montreal solved the problem of turnover by turning itself into a hotel every summer—one of the least expensive in the city.

The North American Students of Cooperation (NASCO, 4312 Michigan Union Building, 530 S. State St., Ann Arbor, MI 48109) has substantial experience with student co-ops in all parts of the country, and has assembled an impressive library of publications for student and nonstudent co-ops.

UPPER AMERICANS

Eric F. Goldman, a Princeton historian, has defined as "upper Americans" college graduates now in their twenties, thirties, and early forties who grew up as part of the 1960s protest against middle-class American society. Though few are poor, the group is not characterized by income. It is defined by education and cultural choices. Goldman suggests that the group's members were educated in East Coast schools and in California and that they prefer wine and vodka to beer and bourbon. Whatever their choices, the group is now of substantial size and exerts considerable influence in society through both business and cultural organizations. Goldman estimates that they account for about 15 percent of the population.

A large portion of this group is now entering the housing market looking for ownership and investment opportunities. Being both trend setting and well educated, this group should be attracted to the co-op alternative. Brought up through the movements of the sixties, they learned that cooperative efforts require work. They recognize the tax incentive to own rather than rent, but they also want other investments. This group can make the housing co-op a well-known alternative.

MIDDLE CLASS AND WORKING CLASS

A middle-class community that includes lawyers, accountants, and business people does not lack managerial talent for co-ops. There is also a great likelihood of homogeneity. Working-class communities seem to have a higher tolerance for diversity and a greater mixture of people, including elderly, students, and young families. The availability of affordable housing draws all these groups together.

The middle and working classes can be expected to embrace more structure in their co-ops and in their relationships among members. Flexibility within the co-op will be more clearly preferred by upper Americans.

The main differences between a working-class and a middle-class co-op usually result from the different skills of their members. The middle-class co-op may be better run because members have business skills, but the working-class co-op may achieve important savings because of the electrical, plumbing, carpentry, and mechanical skills of its members.

MIXED-INCOME CO-OPS

Good inexpensive housing is a critical need for the working poor and for welfare families. Co-ops have demonstrated that they can fill this need. The successful mixed-income co-ops across the country have some common elements: involvement of the members from the start, careful training of members in management skills they have never had the opportunity to develop, and strong systems of accountability.

There are both successful and unsuccessful (that is, surviving but not thriving) mixed-income cooperatives. Mixed-income co-ops generally are sponsored by nonprofit groups which, while well-intentioned, often are inexperienced. New members often are unprepared for the differing lifestyles that the mixed-income families may introduce. Successful co-ops are able to use the democratic structure of the co-op to work out differences.

Mixed-income co-ops have learned that education and communication are critical. Many low-income members initially do not understand the difference between their co-op and previous rental situations. When they use "as much hot water as possible" in order to get their money's worth, they are still thinking like a renter. Training and early clarification of roles is critical to the success of such a co-op.

Having charted some general observations about co-ops and co-op members, we realize that we have not covered every type and every person. We've identified only those types with the most direct connections to co-ops. Each individual has to decide what type of co-op and co-op members suit his or her needs.

3
A BUYER'S GUIDE

SPENDING YOUR MONEY isn't really as easy as it sometimes seems. The wise consumer has to look at many features to decide which purchase is best. A housing consumer looks at price, location, appearance, layout, security, convenience, and a number of other factors in deciding what to buy. We can't anticipate your tastes and decisions on the finishing details of your apartment—the fireplaces, bathroom tile, kitchen decor, the view from the living room, or the bedroom furnishings. We leave those matters to you. But we can help you sort out the many considerations you face in choosing a co-op.

We have identified five central factors that lend some structure to a decision to buy into an existing co-op.

1. *The Cost.* Why try to ignore it? As much as we would like to diminish its importance, cost is still the number-one issue in whether to buy. Your decision may come down to two simple figures—down payment and monthly carrying charge. The next section of this chapter will help you figure out how much you can afford.

2. *The Co-op Corporation.* You are buying part ownership of a business. If the business fails, you may lose your home and all that you have invested in it, so the co-op corporation should be well financed and soundly managed. Existing co-ops have had time to establish a record of financial management; newer co-ops have not. In looking at both,

examine carefully the budgets and legal documents to ensure that reserves are adequate and that sound management procedures exist.

3. *Condition of the Building.* This is an important factor contributing to the long-term costs of the co-op. Some co-ops have failed because of physical problems they did not anticipate, such as seriously deteriorated plumbing and heating systems, structural damage, and other costly problems. Inspect the building carefully to avoid such pitfalls.

4. *The Members.* The other co-op members are going to be your business partners and neighbors. You will spend many evenings together deciding how to spend your money and maintain your building. Make sure that you meet as many members as possible and that your inspections include one or two co-op meetings.

5. *The Unit.* We deliberately put the apartment itself last. Many buyers fall in love with an apartment—its kitchen, its fireplace, its view, its address—and they are all too willing to overlook everything but price. We recommend that you carefully inspect the unit using the checklist in Figure 2 later in the chapter. Be fair and honest: list the bad features as well as the good.

What Can You Afford?

Until recently, lenders operated with a rule of thumb that a household should be able to pay for its housing with 25 percent of its income. This meant that monthly housing costs should equal about one week's pay. For a number of reasons, this rule no longer applies. Today's housing prices and interest rates force many families to pay more than 25 percent of their income. We have also come to recognize that net housing costs after taxes are a more useful figure than gross costs.

For most co-ops you will not need to borrow money to purchase the membership. In those cases, lenders' rules really don't matter. What matters instead is the portion of your income you feel comfortable spending on housing. We suggest that you begin determining that amount by answering the four questions on the Personal Finances Worksheet presented in Figure 1.

The worksheet in Figure 1 gives you some ballpark figures of what you can afford to spend and to borrow, based on the lending industry's notion of what people should pay for housing and loans. Of course, each household's financial picture is unique, and you should plan to talk with a lender about your personal situation if it looks as though you will need to borrow for the down payment. For now, focus on the optimal monthly housing cost from question 2 and confine your housing search to co-ops with carrying charges near that amount.

It is important to remember that as a co-op member you will qualify for certain federal tax deductions. These deductions are not taken into account by lenders, but they may affect how much you will be willing and able to pay for housing. All other things being equal, a co-op with a monthly charge that is the same as your current rent will be less expensive to you after taxes. This will ease the burden of buying somewhat.

Homeowners, including co-op members, are eligible to deduct the portion of their annual housing expenditures that goes toward interest on mortgages and toward property taxes. In a co-op, each member is allocated a share of the interest and taxes that the co-op pays. As you look at co-ops, ask what your share of tax deductions would be.

Searching for the Affordable Co-op Home

WHEN TO LOOK

The real estate market is busiest in the spring and early summer. There always seem to be plenty of buyers then, and sellers can afford to wait to get their asking price. If you can, wait until the end of the summer or even the fall to begin

Figure 1
Personal Finances Worksheet

1. **What are you currently paying for housing each month?**

Current monthly rent	$ _____
Plus: Utilities you pay for	+ _____
Plus: Housing insurance	+ _____
Plus: Other housing costs	+ _____
Total: Current monthly housing cost	$ _____
Divided by: Monthly household income ($_____)	=
Times: 100 percent	× 100
Equals: Current cost as percent of income	_____ %

2. **What can you afford as a total monthly housing cost?**

Monthly household income	$ _____
Times: 25 percent	× .25
Optimal monthly housing cost	$ _____

3. **What down payment can you afford from current funds?**

Savings and cash on hand	$ _____
Plus: Money market and other funds	+ _____
Plus: Insurance cash value	+ _____
Plus: Other sources	+ _____
Total funds on hand	$ _____

4. **What can you afford to borrow for the down payment?**

Monthly household income	$ _____
Times: 35 percent	× .35
Maximum housing and debt payment	_____

Current monthly housing cost (from question 1, line 5) $ _____
 Plus: Current debt, monthly payments
      Car loans   + _____
      Personal loans   + _____
      Credit cards   + _____
      Other   + _____
      Total current housing cost and debt payments $ _____
 If your total current housing cost and debt payments total less than 35 percent of your income (line 3 above), then you may qualify for an additional loan for the down payment.

looking for co-op housing. By then some of the sellers are getting nervous about selling and, faced with the prospect of retaining their homes through another winter, they may decide to accept a lower price. Of course, units that have been on the market for several months may be more than just overpriced: they may be lemons.

Make the market's ups and downs work for you. Like a good investor, buy when prices are temporarily down. Recessions have been occurring every few years, and housing prices usually drop during a recession. There are fewer people buying, and bargains are available.

WHERE TO LOOK

In most cities the number of existing co-ops—and consequently your choice—is limited. Unfortunately, there is no comprehensive listing of co-ops in most communities. We can suggest, however, some places you might start looking to assemble your own list.

Probably the most complete listing of co-ops in this country is available from the National Association of Housing Cooperatives (see Appendix 1). You can also check with your local government, the National Consumer Co-Operative Bank, and any local housing groups listed in Appendix 1.

Ask friends, neighbors, co-workers, and other acquaintances if they are familiar with any local co-ops. If there are any food co-ops in your community, stop in and ask the people there. When you have identified several co-ops, contact them and ask about opportunities for membership. If they have none at the time, ask to be put on a waiting list and also request that they refer you to other housing co-ops.

You could limit the search to realtors and their listings, but the unfortunate reality is that most of the best co-op units are never listed with realtors or advertised in newspapers. Many co-ops replace members with friends or maintain waiting lists. They don't have to come looking for buyers, so you will have to find them. Plan to begin knocking on doors. Never underestimate the value of legwork.

What you are able to pay determines where you can look or, more correctly, where you cannot look. No matter how attractive certain upscale neighborhoods may be, you have to recognize that it would waste time—for you, a realtor, and the co-ops—to look into units out of your price range. Co-op membership prices at first glance will look very attractive compared with condominiums because the mortgage is carried not in the purchase price but in the monthly carrying charges. When you call about advertised units, ask about membership purchase price *and* carrying charges.

KEEP NOTES

As you begin your search, you are going to be inundated with names, addresses, telephone numbers, apartment sizes, prices, and carrying charges. No one can remember it all. So start a notebook. One of our friends started a small spiral notebook—he titled it "Spiraling Opportunities"—and was surprised that he had twenty-five pages of detailed information before he purchased a co-op unit. Before you even consider inspecting a unit, obtain the following information over the phone for your notes:

A Buyer's Guide / 33

1. Address
2. Owner name and number
3. Owner history (how long has it been a co-op? how long has seller been there?)
4. Unit description (bedrooms? other rooms?)
5. Unit features
6. Membership price
7. Carrying charges
8. Annual tax deductions
9. Description of building and property (parking?)
10. Type of neighborhood
11. Reasons owner is moving

One of the most important pieces of information you can obtain is the reason for the sale. If the seller is selling because of a job change, family circumstance, financial problem, or other event forcing the sale, he or she may be willing to negotiate downward on the price. If the seller is leaving the co-op because of problems with other members, it may be a warning: check out the members very thoroughly.

If the member is leaving because of the unit itself, you may be able to uncover problems that otherwise would not be mentioned: noise, neighbors, lighting, security, plumbing problems, inadequate heat, rising costs, upcoming costly improvements, special assessments, and the like. In that case, the seller probably will not be willing to talk about problems openly. You may have to explore possible problems indirectly. If the seller will not give you an exact reason, exercise caution and inspect the building more carefully. Ask questions about neighbors, about the unit, about upcoming assessments. Explore until you discover the seller's reason.

After you have collected enough information by phone, schedule an appointment and prepare to conduct the inspection and interview as described in the following sections.

34 / *GOING CO-OP*

INSPECTING THE APARTMENT

Figure 2 is a detailed unit inspection form that you can follow while inspecting the unit. Most common problems and concerns are covered in this inspection, but you cannot expect this form to replace the trained eye of a housing inspector or construction contractor. It may be in your best interest to hire such a professional to inspect the unit with you. This person will be particularly helpful in examining the building structure and systems.

Inspectors are expensive, charging $50 to $150 per inspection, and the quality and quantity of their advice varies, so many people choose to avoid hiring one until purchase is likely. If you choose not to use a professional inspector, at least get a second opinion from a friend who is knowledgeable about construction.

As you inspect the unit, don't hesitate to ask anything of the seller. You will get some important information that you cannot gather by observing the unit, and you will serve notice that you are a shrewd buyer. If you have the opportunity, talk with neighbors as well.

It is unlikely that you will find the "perfect" apartment—the one that has everything you want within your price range. There are going to be positive and negative aspects of each unit you inspect, and your choice will be made by weighing price, size, quality, amenities, view, and other features. Use the checklist in Figure 2 to take systematic notes.

<u>Unit Description</u>. Begin by asking for a floor plan. If the co-op member does not have one, sketch one yourself. Bring a tape measure, and measure the main dimensions. Identify all major rooms. Mark the location of electrical outlets, plumbing fixtures, doors, and windows. The critical factors here are the total number of rooms, the number of bedrooms, and the sizes of the major rooms.

<u>Electrical system</u>. Hidden behind the walls is the electrical wiring system, one of the most important components of the

Figure 2
Co-op Inspection Checklist

1. Co-op address _____
   Number of units _____

2. Membership costs: Share price _____
                       Monthly carrying charge _____

3. Unit Description: Total sq. ft. _____
                       No. of bedrooms _____
                       No. of bathrooms _____
                       Other rooms _____
   _____

4. Unit conditions
   Electrical system _____
   Heating system _____
   Plumbing _____
   Floors _____
   Walls _____
   Windows and doors _____
   Kitchen _____
   Bathrooms _____
   Closet space _____
   Unit security _____

5. Building conditions and security
   _____
   _____
   _____
   _____

6. Co-op management
   _____
   _____

building. Safety is one issue; adequacy of service is another.

Old electrical systems may present safety problems. Since the wires are behind the walls, you cannot determine easily if the wiring is defective. Another problem with older systems is that they usually are inadequate for modern appliances. One way to determine the age and adequacy of the system is to look at the panel box, which is located where the electrical source enters the unit (near the electric meter). It contains the circuit breakers that automatically cut off the flow of electricity to any circuit that overloads or short-circuits. In old systems, fuses were used to break the circuit; in modern systems, the circuit breakers are switches.

While you are at the panel box, check the service. Add up the numbers on the fuses or switches—usually each circuit has 10 to 20 amperes (or amps). Most units should have total service between 100 and 200 amps. If the unit has an electric hot-water heater, electric range, electric washer and dryer, and air conditioning, at least 150 amps are needed, and each of these appliances should be on a separate circuit.

Locate the outlets on the floor plan. Are there enough to service your lamps, stereo, TV, hair dryer, home computer, and toaster-oven? Especially important are the outlets for kitchen appliances.

<u>Heating system.</u> There are several different kinds of heating systems you may encounter, each with advantages and disadvantages.

Gravity or forced hot air systems blow warm air from ducts in the floors, ceilings, and walls. Gravity systems rely on the property of hot air to rise, and movement of air is sometimes poor; therefore, some rooms may heat well while others heat poorly. Forced hot air systems use fans to move the hot air, and it is distributed better. The major complaint about all hot air systems is that the air is dry and has negative respiratory effects and can create problems with one's complexion. Humidifiers can be installed on the heating system or in rooms to offset the dryness.

Hot water systems are recognizable by the large radiators, usually placed in front of windows. Water movement through the pipes can be noisy. The hot water cools down as it moves through the pipes, so the farther a room is from the boiler, the less heat it will receive. Over time the pipes can rust, slowing the circulation. In addition, radiators often inhibit your arrangement of furniture.

Steam systems have smaller radiators, and the steam is pressurized to achieve better movement and heat distribution. The problems of the hot water system are reduced.

Radiant systems consist of pipes located in the walls, floors, or ceilings. The heat can be blocked by furniture and carpets. Service of these systems can be difficult.

Electric systems are common in newer buildings. Small baseboard radiators identify this system, which costs the least to install because there is no central boiler or heating plant; each baseboard creates its own heat. Even though each baseboard can be controlled individually, this is the most expensive heating system to operate because of the current cost of electricity.

Solar systems can be either active or passive. Active systems collect heat from the sun (usually on the roof) and move the heat to a storage area until the heat is needed. Passive systems usually incorporate features into the building design so that the building absorbs heat and stores it, releasing it slowly over time. Black masonry walls facing south, solar windows, special floor tiles, and rock beds under the floor are common passive-solar designs. Usually a solar heating system incorporates both active and passive features.

All but the electric heating system require a central heating plant of some sort: most likely it is a boiler fired by oil or gas. These two fuels are becoming similar in price, so the type of fuel should not be a primary concern. Rather, you should be concerned about the *maintenance and adequacy of the system.* If the heating plant is used for the entire building, include a visit to the heating room later and ask the maintenance person or manager about system maintenance. Ask the seller and neighbors about the adequacy of the system. If there is a single system for the building, you should be concerned about your ability to control the heat in your unit. Inspect the unit for heat controls.

Plumbing. The other system that hides behind the walls is the plumbing system. The critical factor is the condition of the pipes, but you can't easily inspect them. You should ask what type of pipes are in the unit and take a look at the pipes in the basement. There are four types of pipes.

Steel pipes are the oldest and are prone to rust. They are large and have a tinny sound when hit. Because they rust and break over time, they may affect the water pressure and the water could turn rusty. Steel pipes should be replaced.

Brass pipes are the most expensive. They are common in older buildings and are prone to corrosion only where the pipes are joined. They are thicker than steel or copper pipes and have a very solid sound. If properly maintained, brass pipes can last a long time.

Copper pipes are more common in recent construction. They are expensive, so they are often used only for hot water. Unlike brass pipes, which are screwed together, copper pipes are soldered, and consequently service costs more.

Plastic (PVC) pipes are a recent way of cutting construction costs. PVC pipes do not mask the sound of water as well as the others, and there has been some concern about unhealthy side effects. They should be used only for drain pipes.

Your major concern about pipes is to avoid older, rusted steel piping, but you also should avoid any leaking plumbing. Find out where the pipes run and inspect the walls carefully for leak marks. Check the water pressure in all faucets; if there is a problem with pressure or if the water looks rusty, you may face expensive replumbing in the near future.

Walls. Walls not only divide rooms, they also insulate from weather and noise. Drywall is a recent construction technique that provides minimal insulation. To compensate, insulation is usually installed behind the drywall. Drywall includes several types of sheet rock, gypsum board, paneling, and other wall material nailed into the studs and taped and painted.

Wetwall construction involves the use of plaster or other wet materials that are mixed on site, applied to the wall while wet, and left to dry into a hard barrier. Plaster, brick, and masonry walls are the main examples of wetwalls. Found in older buildings and well-constructed newer buildings, these walls provide better noise and weather insulation than drywall. They are less common in today's construction because they are expensive to install and also to repair.

Look beyond the paint job. You should be concerned that the walls don't have holes, gaps, or other defects that allow noise and weather to penetrate. Water marks on interior walls are telling signs of leaks from pipes; on exterior walls they indicate weather leaks. If the unit has drywall, inquire about insulation and noise. Kitchen and bath walls should have some type of water-resistant covering such as ceramic tile, vinyl tile, or greenboard (water-resistant drywall).

Windows and doors. The concern with windows and doors is that they be good weather barriers. Windows should operate freely but not rattle in the wind. There should be storm windows or the windows should have thermopane—double-layered—glass. Both doors and windows should be secured with adequate locks. You may want deadbolts or police locks on your doors as well.

Kitchen. Examine the age and condition of the appliances. Older appliances in good repair may be used for a long time. Is there a disposal and does the drain work well? Is there any sign of pests? Inspect the layout: Is the working space good? Are the countertops large and accessible? Are they in good repair and easy to clean? Are the cabinets and walls water-resistant? Is cabinet space adequate? If you like to cook and work in the kitchen, you probably have your own ideas about what makes a good kitchen.

40 / GOING CO-OP

Bathroom. The toilet should be in working order—flush several times to test it. Check the shower for water pressure and for proper drainage. Is the floor tiled? Is it in good repair? Are the walls water-resistant? If you see water marks ask about them. Is the bathroom properly vented? Is there adequate space for your toiletries?

Building conditions. Up to this point, the inspection has been confined within the walls of the unit. As we pointed out before, there are several critical factors about the building that should influence your decision about its condition.

If the heating and plumbing systems operate for the entire building, inspect the basement for the heating and hot-water boilers. While down there, look for serious structural problems in the foundation (see Chapter 6). Also check for rodent droppings and ask about extermination programs.

Check the building entryways. Are they secure? Are the lobbies and halls clean and attractive? Is there secure and accessible parking? What is the incidence of crime around the building? Is the outside attractively maintained?

Try to speak with some of the neighbors to get a sense of how friendly they are and whether they are satisfied living in the building and in the neighborhood.

Building management. What kind of building management and maintenance does the co-op have? Does it have professional management? Is management on site? Do management and members get along? Is the building well maintained? Some small co-ops manage and maintain their buildings themselves, and they do it very well. In other self-managed co-ops, the problems show. Your inquiries into the quality of management will reflect your concern for protecting your investment for the long term.

INSPECTING THE DOCUMENTS

When you have seen the unit and decided that you are seriously interested in the co-op, the next step is to inspect the corporate legal and financial documents. As we stated before, you are investing in a business, and the legal and financial stability of the corporation is of utmost concern. If the co-op is a newly created corporation, most states require that any potential investors be given a prospectus, or offering statement. Attached to this are the major legal documents of the corporation as well as budgets and projections of income. If you are buying membership in an existing co-op, there may be fewer disclosure requirements, and instead of being given a comprehensive document like a prospectus you may have to assemble your own set of documents. Important documents include the following:

- Certificate (or articles) of incorporation
- Bylaws
- Subscription agreement
- Proprietary lease
- Year-end financial statements (for existing co-ops)
- Mortgages
- Minutes of board of directors and membership meetings
- Prospectus (for new co-ops)

Certificate of incorporation. The certificate or articles are filed with the state to incorporate the co-op. They should be stamped "approved" by the state. The language of the certificate to pay attention to is the purposes of the corporation.

Bylaws. The bylaws are the rules governing the corporation. You should read these carefully. Important sections deal with the requirements for membership, regular meetings, election of the board of directors and officers, and limits on members' actions. The bylaws may include limits on your ability to resell the unit; examine such restrictions closely.

Subscription agreement. This is the paper that documents that you have purchased shares in the corporation. It includes a statement of the number of shares you have purchased and their value and the monthly carrying charges for which you assume responsibility (usually stated as a percentage of the total operating costs). It subjects you to the terms of the occupancy agreement. It states the priority of the co-op mortgage lien; in other words, the co-op mortgage is paid in the event of default before you or any of your creditors are paid. Finally, it states the rights of the corporation to cancel the agreement in the event of default by you.

Proprietary lease. Also known as the occupancy agreement, the lease states that you have the right to occupy a certain unit for a certain term—usually as long as the corporate mortgage runs—and that the lease automatically renews unless canceled by either party. The co-op may cancel the agreement only if you violate its terms. It is proprietary because the lease is inseparable from your ownership interest and you cannot lose the right of occupancy except for certain violations.

The proprietary lease includes a statement of your financial obligations to pay carrying charges, and it should make clear how those carrying charges are calculated. It also addresses the remedies in case of default by you or the corporation and contains specific language subordinating your rights as seller to the mortgage lien.

You should be concerned with the terms of the lease that limit your right to sublet or have other people occupy the unit and also the terms that restrict your ability to cancel the lease.

If you purchase membership when a unit is not finished or when it requires certain improvements prior to occupancy, add these improvements to the lease as conditions of occupancy.

Financial statements. In new co-op offerings, only projected budgets are included in the prospectus. Existing co-ops can provide the buyer with financial statements as well as budgets.

Actual operating statements, if you can obtain them, will give you a good indication of how much it costs the co-op to run the building. Budgets, no matter how carefully prepared, are at best only educated guesses. There are many examples of extreme underbudgeting of new co-ops, resulting in dramatic increases in carrying charges to unsuspecting members. For buyers of new co-ops, the only protection is careful review of the budget and questioning of cost assumptions.

For buyers of existing co-ops, the data on actual costs are available, and carrying charges are based on actual costs. Review the last several years' operating statements. Observe how costs have gone up and how reserves and carrying charges have changed. Patterns should emerge. Look at the new budget and determine if it is realistic compared to past years' costs. Your objective is to estimate how fast your carrying charges may rise in the future.

Watch for any indication that payments are being made to the developer. Some developers have leased the land to the co-op or still own the pool, parking garage, or recreation facility. Such long-term leases can have outrageous rent escalator clauses that add thousands of dollars to the co-op budget over the years.

Also look for abnormally low charges because of a developer's subsidies. The developer may be providing low-cost management, subsidized maintenance, or a subsidized mortgage for just a few years, after which costs will escalate.

Also ask to examine the mortgages. Some mortgages involve balloon payments—very large extra payments or even refinancing after a certain number of years. If your co-op must make a balloon payment, is money being set aside for it? If the co-op has to refinance, how much will mortgage payments, and therefore your carrying charges, increase?

<u>Minutes.</u> Minutes of meetings of the board of directors and of the membership can show you what problems the co-op has had to address and what problems still remain. The discussions at the meetings might give you some good hints that the co-op is in financial trouble, that big expenditures and special assessments are upcoming, or that something might happen in the near future to increase carrying charges. The

minutes also can give you an impression of how the members get along. If the board of directors has evolved into a complaint board, you might investigate members' relationships more.

Putting all this information together and analyzing it can be quite a challenge. The following are some hints about making effective use of the information you have gathered.

Avoid a co-op in which the developer remains active—as seller of the land, some of its facilities, or some of the unsold or rent-controlled units. If the developer can tie the co-op to a lease, escalating lease costs can become a problem. If the developer remains the seller of a large block of the membership, the co-op will probably encounter resistance to spending money. The developer's objective is to take profits out, not put money back in. Furthermore, the developer's financial interests could jeopardize the co-op's status with the IRS.

Take care when approaching any co-op building conversion with a large number of rent-controlled tenants. The co-op members may have to shoulder most of the burden of cost increases. Another caution flag should be raised when you approach a co-op conversion in which very few existing tenants have purchased memberships in the co-op. Existing tenants usually are offered substantial price discounts on conversions; if they fail to purchase at a discount, there may be some problems with the building that have deterred them.

Also approach very carefully a co-op conversion in which no new systems—electrical, heating, plumbing—have been installed. You may face very large replacement costs in the near future.

Finally, avoid buying from an existing co-op seller if the reasons for selling are somewhat suspect. The seller may be bailing out of a bad co-op or an undesirable unit. The unit may be noisy, unsafe, unsanitary, poorly designed, or it may have other problems.

Negotiations and Purchase

If your inspection of the co-op does not present any major problems and you would like to make an offer, first consider the following advice.

1. Set a firm price in your mind over which you cannot or will not go.
2. Investigate what the seller paid for the unit; most likely you will have to go to the Registry of Deeds to obtain this information. Add in the cost of any improvements the seller made and you know how much the seller has invested in the unit. Figure that this is the seller's bottom price and that the seller will be trying to get a reasonable return on his or her investment. If the asking price reflects a return of more than 10 percent per year, you probably can negotiate the seller down on the price.
3. Offer an amount that is less than the asking price and your maximum price. Most asking prices are set with the expectation that they will be negotiated downward 5 to 10 percent. If you offer less than was asked, state your reasons, which could be any of the flaws or problems you encountered during your evaluation.
4. If the seller disputes the offer or your claims, do not allow the negotiations to degenerate into an argument. Be businesslike. Ask for a counteroffer. Do not respond immediately or give in too easily.
5. If the seller will not come down in price, negotiate for improvements or extras. Most sellers will give in on non-cost items more easily than on the price. If you negotiate any extras, these should be placed in the purchase-and-sale agreement.

SALES CONTRACT

Also called a purchase-and-sale agreement, the sales contract is the legal document that binds both parties to the sale.

It states all the conditions of the sale and includes all the conditions that must be met by both parties prior to the closing, the actual transfer of the property title. The buyer places an agreed-upon amount of money in escrow with the seller as earnest money for the purchase.

All conditions should be placed in writing to protect the parties. Common conditions to the sale include the following:

1. Satisfactory physical and pest inspections
2. Buyer's ability to assume current financing or obtain new financing
3. Seller's making certain improvements
4. Designated fixtures, appliances, and furnishings remain
5. Date of transfer, occupancy, and other details of the transaction

Because you are placing a good portion of your down payment in escrow when you execute a sales contract, it is advisable that you have an attorney review the contract before you sign it. The attorney can help by including clauses that call for the return of your down payment if certain events beyond your control prevent the sale. If the co-op's board of directors rejects the buyer, for example, the seller has to return the down payment.

CLOSING

The closing is the actual point of transfer of the property. The papers certifying the legal transfer of the co-op stock are passed. Because the lease is proprietary and inseparable from the stock, the lease rights are conveyed as part of the same transaction.

Before the closing date, the buyer has to secure financing if needed to purchase the membership stock. If you must obtain financing, refer to the sections on lenders in Chapter 7. Also, during the period between the sales contract and the closing the buyer's attorney should investigate the title of the property held by the co-op. It is advisable to have an attorney handle the closing for you, since even the smallest error or detail can ruin the transaction.

If you have never used an attorney, ask friends for references. Do not hesitate to ask the attorney about his or her background, specifically previous experience in handling a co-op transaction. Because the co-op transaction characteristically lies somewhere between real estate and stock transactions, it is important that the attorney have experience in those areas. Ask the attorney to quote a fee structure for services. You might want to establish a set fee for the closing and an hourly rate for document review and advice prior to the closing.

At the closing, a series of small adjustments must be made to the final price: lawyers' expenses, outstanding bills on the unit, lien settlements, and other minor financial obligations that transfer with ownership.

Buyer Protections

It is very difficult to discuss buyer protections because they vary so widely from state to state and because the protections have been altered and increased within the last few years. Until the 1970s, most states treated the housing co-op purchase as an exclusively stock transaction, and many of the early home-buyer protections were not extended to co-ops. In recent years this interpretation has shifted, and more states now recognize the co-op purchase as a real estate transaction.

Throughout this chapter we have discussed disclosure requirements. Some state laws now cover the information that must be disclosed to a prospective buyer prior to purchase. The result has been a bulky prospectus, or offering statement, which is useful but at the same time overwhelming. If the required information is not disclosed, the sale can be voided in most states, and the seller may face punitive damages.

Because each state governs buyer protection, we cannot give specific information about laws that will apply to everyone. Instead, we will use an example of buyer and tenant protections in Florida state law. (Our information is based on a 1981 HUD report, *The Conversion of Rental Housing to Condominiums and Cooperatives.*) The Florida law requires that the prospectus include a property report. The report must contain information on the date and type of construction, prior use, recent termite report, and estimated useful life and architect's/engineer's structural analysis of the building and its systems. The prospectus must include an estimated operating budget and a schedule of expenses for each unit.

The Florida law does not provide for any warranties other than those expressed by the seller in the prospectus, although the co-op converter must establish a reserve or surety bond for capital expenditures on the plumbing and the roof if no warranties are provided.

In addition, Florida grants protections to tenants of a converted building. Tenants of six months or more are granted right of first refusal. They are given 270 days' notice of conversion and eviction, although counties may extend that another 90 days if the local vacancy rate is less than 3 percent. Relocation benefits may be paid in exchange for a reduction in the notice period. During occupancy under notice, tenants are guaranteed the right to quiet enjoyment, meaning that nonpurchasing tenants must be treated the same as those who purchase.

While these laws are in place to protect you as a buyer from deceptive practices on the part of developers and sellers, they do not protect you from all bad situations, nor do they always help you recover from a bad deal. Your best protection is your own ability to investigate the opportunities and judge them critically. Our best words of advice are to select a co-op that has an established history, a good developer, and/or a strong co-op organization behind it.

4
STARTING YOUR OWN CO-OP

IF NECESSITY IS THE mother of invention, then it might also be the father of the co-op. Historically and currently, housing co-ops have been created to meet consumer needs for affordable, decent housing. Since the turn of the century, when co-op housing was started by labor unions in New York City, many individuals and groups have started their own co-ops because they were dissatisfied with the costs and conditions of their housing. Today, inflation and speculative investment in housing have resulted in displacement of many people from their homes. Co-ops can help such people, but there aren't enough co-ops to go around. Not all people are able to join existing co-ops, nor do they want to. So people have to create new co-ops.

To start your own co-op, you may have to do many things you never did before. But the housing crisis is real, and chances are you want to persist in creating co-op housing. In doing this, you are going to become expert in many areas—organization, corporations, legal matters, finances, real estate. The point is not to know everything but to know what you need to know and to know it well.

You cannot do it all by yourself. Many hands are needed to build a new co-op, and you must recruit good people who will help build it. You must find reliable people with a strong commitment and a high level of energy that they can devote to the group. You must attract people who are open to learning or who are willing to share what they already know about housing or co-ops. Start to make a list of potential members. You are going to become an organizer. Don't worry. All of us have a bit of the organizer in us, from rearranging papers to rearranging furniture. Every member of the group is going to have to shoulder some of the burden for organizing, for working, and for becoming expert in new areas.

In starting your own co-op you need to balance two concerns: running the group well and getting the work done. In this chapter, we provide advice on how to get the group together, how to run those critical early meetings, and how to sustain members' commitment and energy over the long haul. We also borrowed a tool from the construction business to help you with planning and tracking the minutiae of the co-op organizing task. It's called the critical path method (CPM)—we've renamed it the co-op path method.

Getting a Running Start

The 474-unit Benning Heights apartment complex in Washington, D.C.'s Southeast section was developed at the end of World War II and had remained under the ownership of the original developer until 1980. Moderate rents—a two-bedroom apartment cost only $202 per month—and good landlord-tenant relations resulted in a stable base of tenants. Some of the tenants had been living in their apartments since they were first built, and several families had three generations living at Benning Heights. But in 1980, the owner decided to sell. Hoping to maintain his good relations with the tenants, the owner offered it to the tenants for approximately $2.5 million, a very attractive price.

As co-op member Robert Simon described it, "Some of us started talking about buying the property, but we had a long way to go. We called the city and found out that we

Starting Your Own Co-op / 51

had to first create a tenant association, which we did not have at that time. We also needed 51 percent of the tenants to sign a petition to initiate the purchase through the association. That's well over two hundred families, and I didn't even know my next-door neighbors."

With assistance from the city and a local technical assistance organization, Simon and a small group of neighbors began planning a co-op. They were not able to put it all together within the 120 days allowed by local law. It was rumored that the owner had begun talking to other potential buyers. Robert Simon said he "met with the owner and convinced him that he would not want four hundred families picketing his front door," and the tenant association bought a little more time to organize its co-op.

The co-op's biggest task lay in fund raising. The tenants had to raise about half a million dollars from memberships. At a membership price of $1,000, they were able to recruit just over half of the moderate-income tenants to buy into the co-op. The rest of the capital was raised through a seed-money loan from the city, some private loans, and a few fund-raising events run by the tenants. The co-op also had to borrow more than $2 million from the National Consumer Cooperative Bank. In May 1982, the formal conversion took place, and the 474-unit Benning Heights Cooperative was in operation.

Maybe your co-op ambitions are not quite as large as a 474-unit project and millions of dollars in capital, but we are convinced that any co-op conversion can be managed by a small group of previously inexperienced but dedicated people. The key is to recruit a core group of people who are willing to devote the necessary time and energy. To be practical, we think you need a TBC—or to be called—list. Our TBC list includes friends, neighbors, and acquaintances; groups of individuals; and nonprofit organizations and professionals. Of course, you can make up your own list.

After you have found some people who share your concern, talk with them about the co-op idea. Set up an informal meeting for those who are willing to discuss the idea further.

PREPARING FOR THE FIRST MEETING

Planning for the first meeting is especially crucial because that meeting sets the tone for the group and anticipates what future meetings will bring. The organizer has a chance to see how the members respond to and interact with one another. An agenda should be planned, including some mechanical but nevertheless important points:

- Discuss how much time each person could, should, and would put into work in the co-op.
- Set up a regular weekly meeting time of two to four hours.
- Sketch out a general program of activities for the group and ask for discussion. It is desirable to make the first organized project of the group a short-term one that has a high probability of success. This will give members a better chance to get to know each other and to filter out first impressions and can be used as a basis for attracting others to the group.
- Suggest to people in the group some specific assignments for the next meeting. For example, they might be asked to bring their current housing budgets. (See Chapter 3).
- Evaluate your own resources and the resources of the group. For example, how much time can people spend looking for buildings on weekends?
- At the first meeting, people should discuss their own expectations, politics, and goals.
- Try to set aside the first available weekend or an entire day for a conference to discuss co-op objectives. Schedule your conference beforehand, so as to avoid conflicts with other events. The participants at the conference should be prepared to talk about themselves and about the general assumptions under which the group will operate.

Remember, nothing kills a group faster than meetings that result in no progress but only more meetings.

GENERATING IDEAS AND MAKING DECISIONS

Early in the process of planning the co-op, the group should establish general principles and rules. You need ideas and opinions that flow from a lively discussion with a high level of participation from all members.

Brainstorming is an all-purpose technique for getting ten or ten thousand ideas, depending on the amount of time spent and the number of people involved. The basic theory behind brainstorming is that imagination and judgment are two distinct processes in the production of ideas and that imagination should be given free rein before judgment is used. When the goal is a solution, you want as many creative ideas as possible.

Brainstorming works especially well with groups of five to ten people, although it can work for smaller or larger groups. The leader of the group poses a problem in a way that stimulates thought and permits a wide range of responses. One person takes responsibility for jotting down all the ideas that are called out. The following are some guidelines for a brainstorming session:

- Criticism is out. Everyone should suspend judgment until evaluation time.
- Freewheeling is welcome. The wilder the ideas the better. Everyone should let his or her imagination soar. It is far easier to tame an idea down than to think of one.
- Hitchhiking is invited. Each person is encouraged to ride on, improve on, add to, divide from, or combine with everyone else's ideas.
- Quantity is desirable. The more ideas the better. Piling up ideas produces an atmosphere that encourages people to be spontaneous.

For best results, a time limit for each problem should be agreed upon in advance, ranging from five to fifteen minutes. When the brainstorming session is over, the list of ideas should be recopied in readable form and submitted for the group's analysis and judgment. The best ideas can then be selected and polished.

Once there is a list of ideas to be decided on, there are a number of ways to make decisions. We would like to offer two: consensus, and voting according to Robert's Rules of Order (available in your library). Consensual decision making involves discussing a matter until a position is reached that all group members agree on. This process has a cooperative aspect to it: it seeks to bring out solutions to a problem by an additive process rather than a win/lose situation.

While consensus may seem to be time-consuming, so is parliamentary procedure when the matter under discussion is highly controversial. Of course, in cases where consensus breaks down, some co-ops will revert to straight voting when there is no other way to resolve the question. This is done by agreement to suspend consensus rules in order to bring the matter to a vote. Bear in mind what Eugene Debs, the Socialist labor leader, observed: "Voting is the menu, not the meal."

In any type of group, division of opinion and debates are to be expected. It is important to realize the advantage of opposition and debate and not to attempt to squash them. Be prepared to understand opposing points of view. Listen to what other members have to say and how they say it. Attack the issue, not the person who supports it. Avoid making statements like "That's a rotten idea" and "You're crazy!" because that will only give opponents cause to attack you personally and divert the discussion from the real content. Try to identify the areas of both agreement and disagreement when there is opposition in the group. Finally, remember not to carry discussion too far. If your opponent is tired or in a bad mood, chances are that at some other time he or she will be more receptive to your ideas.

GETTING THE WORK DONE

Assignments should be discussed and divided among the whole group, with members reporting back to the group even if they reach a dead end or do not make much progress. One method for getting the work done is the TBD (to be done) list (this is different from the TBC—to be called—list we mentioned before). Write down everything that must be done and check each item off immediately upon finishing it. The list will remind you of the many things you may repress or forget. If this fails to get the work done, try bribing yourself or the group with some kind of reward.

Clearly, all the members of the co-op group are expected to contribute to the effort, but assigning tasks to individuals or small groups can be complicated. You can expect to have some people who are qualified or eager to do more tasks than other people, but the work cannot be concentrated in those few. The other people are also valuable and they can be made to feel important if the work includes them.

The exact method of assigning tasks depends on the composition of the group. Most co-ops operate to some degree on the principle of volunteerism. In some co-ops, an honor system binds individual members to volunteer for their share of the work. Other co-ops combine voluntary and assigned work: if no one volunteers, the group or its leader nominates someone.

Selection of an individual for a work task can be based on several factors: individual skills and energy; the time a person can offer; and a person's willingness to accept certain duties. The group should select a set of criteria for assigning individuals. Group members then know what to expect if assignments have to be made.

If there are more than a few days between meetings, it may be valuable to call people to see what is happening. A quick brainstorming session on the phone can keep everybody posted about what is going on, give new leads to people who have reached dead ends, and provide an idea of what the next meeting may focus on.

USING AN EXPERT

Some of the tasks on your list will require expert help. Housing, like any other field, has its share of experts. Usually, but not always, experts cost money. If you are a nonprofit tax-exempt organization, perhaps you can get expertise donated as a charitable contribution. Sometimes experts may volunteer to gain experience.

We have found that groups that look for experts without preparing adequately sometimes end up being run by the experts they hire. Prior to contacting and hiring an expert, the co-op group should decide what kind of expertise it seeks and discuss as thoroughly as possible the basic information and formulate the right questions to ask an expert. The expert's time—and the co-op's money—can be wasted on irrelevant questions. Members may bring up issues about which they are genuinely concerned but which are beyond the scope of an expert's services. The best solution is to reach agreement among members beforehand about exactly what issues are to be discussed with the expert and to require that all questions be put in terms of those issues. The expert should be asked to spend minimal time on immediate oral responses, and to provide written responses or a report prior to the next meeting. Ask that the report be written in plain English, not professional jargon.

Bear in mind that only half a million American households live in housing co-ops. The experts are few. In fact, your group members eventually will become experts in going co-op.

PULLING UP THE ROOTS

To keep a group together, try to balance the time between the pursuit of goals, the structure of the organization, and the needs of individual members. Making progress alone is insufficient. Members have to feel that they are part of the effort and that the effort will have positive results for them. This requires that everyone stop working once in a while and check on how both the group and its members are progressing. The question is, How often do we pull up the plant to see how the roots are doing? Pull it up too often, and you impede growth; too seldom, and the plant will outgrow the pot.

It is important also to monitor the vitality of group morale. Group anemia can occur at about the third or fourth meeting, as members begin to question the group's effectiveness or the commitment of individuals. Lateness, absence, and an inability to reach decisions are the earliest symptoms of group anemia. If the group members exhibit these symptoms, declare a "sick day." Stop the work and read the group's vital signs. Discuss the group's successes and failures. Ask all the members in turn to analyze whether the group is using their personal talents fully. Ask what they think the group will accomplish for them and what personal objectives they think it is failing to meet.

If the anemia is linked to the group's lack of progress, focus on tasks that are attainable and review progress made by the group on a regular basis. If the problem relates to lack of personal recognition, make more regular attempts to acknowledge member attendance and performance. If the group is failing to meet its goals, discuss how the group can respond, and take action.

Changing horses in midstream may be nearly impossible, but changing riders is not. People come and go in every group, especially groups with long-term projects. Do not view the loss of one person as somehow reducing the group's potential. Instead, the group must turn its attention toward bringing in a new member. Keep track of outsiders who express interest, so that candidates are ready when vacancies occur. Choose someone who can contribute effectively.

CO-OP CONVERSIONS

Organizing strategy should always include sharing information with other organizations when interests are compatible. If there is a tenants association in the building you want to convert to a co-op, organizing sense dictates that you sit down with the tenants to share what you know and what you intend to do. Share your information that the landlord is planning to sell; the tenants will understand your intentions better if you communicate directly. You can negotiate with them to gain their support and maybe derive a substantial portion of your membership from among them. (In some states, such as New York, the law requires a certain level of tenant support for conversion to a co-op.) While it is not always the case that tenants will support you, you won't know if you exclude them. If you allow the grapevine to spread the news about a prospective buyer, your good intentions may be misinterpreted and your efforts may encounter tenant resistance.

A different organizing strategy will be necessary if your building is for sale and there is no tenants organization to speak out for your interests. In this case, begin by organizing a tenants union. As tenants begin to bargain with the landlord over rents, maintenance and repair, pests, noise, and other issues, they may begin to realize that they can do a better job of managing the building and serving their own needs. The seeds of a co-op organization will be planted, and it is only a matter of time before the co-op idea will push itself aboveground.

Organizing Co-op Tasks

There are two ways to get into the water: you can stick your feet in first and slowly work the rest of the way in, or you can dive right in. Housing co-ops can be put together either way; it's a good idea to determine which method you and your group feel most comfortable with. The general set of tasks and procedures we describe for putting together a co-op occurs in either circumstance. Just the timing of the tasks changes.

When time is of the essence, many activities have to happen at the same time. Committee structure plays a pivotal role in the division and supervision of tasks. We suggest that the co-op group set up at least three committees, for the legal work, the building assessment, and the financial planning. Other committees can also be established if you have the people and the time.

Whether you use subcommittees or operate as a committee of the whole, we believe that *task management* is essential. Many separate efforts culminate in a new co-op. Somehow the group must keep the larger picture in mind. A schedule of tasks improves management of the effort by reducing the chances of omitting some tasks. It also creates interim steps and accomplishments to provide feedback on progress and to help maintain the group's awareness of its momentum.

For co-op task management we have borrowed a flow-chart method used in the construction industry to track large construction jobs, where many things must happen simultaneously. The construction industry's critical path method (or CPM) identifies and sequences all the jobs and tasks that are part of a project. It lays them out graphically, putting all tasks on a time line, connecting them with arrows to depict the order in which they must be completed and distinguishing the critical tasks that must be kept on strict schedule from other, more flexible activities.

We have renamed our version of CPM the co-op path method. CPM is simply a graphics tool to assist your co-op group in organizing your priorities and work tasks. Think about one of your recent Thanksgiving feasts. Early in November, you decided which friends and family to invite and contacted them. Sometime in the week before Thanksgiving, you began to plan the menu. You decided which dishes to make yourself and which to ask your guests to bring. You asked some to bring wine instead. By Tuesday, you completed your shopping. You spent Wednesday cleaning the house, thawing the turkey, and making pumpkin pies.

When Thanksgiving morning came you were up at 6:00 A.M. to stuff the 22-pound bird and put it in the oven. Then you began to prepare the vegetables and side dishes and finally set the table. By the time guests arrived, you were in the frantic stage: the cranberries were boiling; sweet potatoes were ready for the oven; the vegetables had to cook later; the bird came out of the oven; the rolls went in; and someone carved the turkey while you monitored the several dishes that were still cooking. You hoped the whole time that all the dishes would be ready at exactly the same time—that is, exactly when the turkey was carved and ready.

Remember how well our mothers and grandmothers used to plan and manage such major undertakings with uncanny timing? Now remember your first try to make everything come out of the oven at the same time. If you were successful your first time, it was probably due to a combination of good planning and a little luck. My first turkey was three hours late.

All the work for that feast could be laid out in a CPM (cooking poultry method?) chart. Each task could be placed in sequence and scheduled to occur at a certain time. You have to shop before you can cook. If you want to start cooking on Wednesday, you must complete shopping on Tuesday.

In co-op path method the fundamentals are the same as for the feast. Your objective is still to have everything ready on time, but your time line may be eighteen months long. More people are involved, and the work tasks are more diverse. These factors make it even more important that you sit down and try to schedule all the tasks and arrange them in sequence.

Each co-op has a slightly different path. Some co-op groups have a building, some a source of financing, and others ready-made bylaws that eliminate or change the relative importance of tasks. There is no single flow chart of activities that will represent the path for your co-op; but in Figure 3 we present a CPM chart to give you an idea of how one looks.

The tasks of organizing a co-op are explained in the next four chapters. To employ the co-op path method, you should first read those chapters and determine the activities your group will need to undertake.

When you're ready to begin using your own CPM, list all the activities that will be relevant to your co-op. Jot down your ideas about the time and resources the group will need to complete each activity. Use a three-by-five-inch file card for each activity, and clear the kitchen table. (Plan to eat at

Starting Your Own Co-op/61

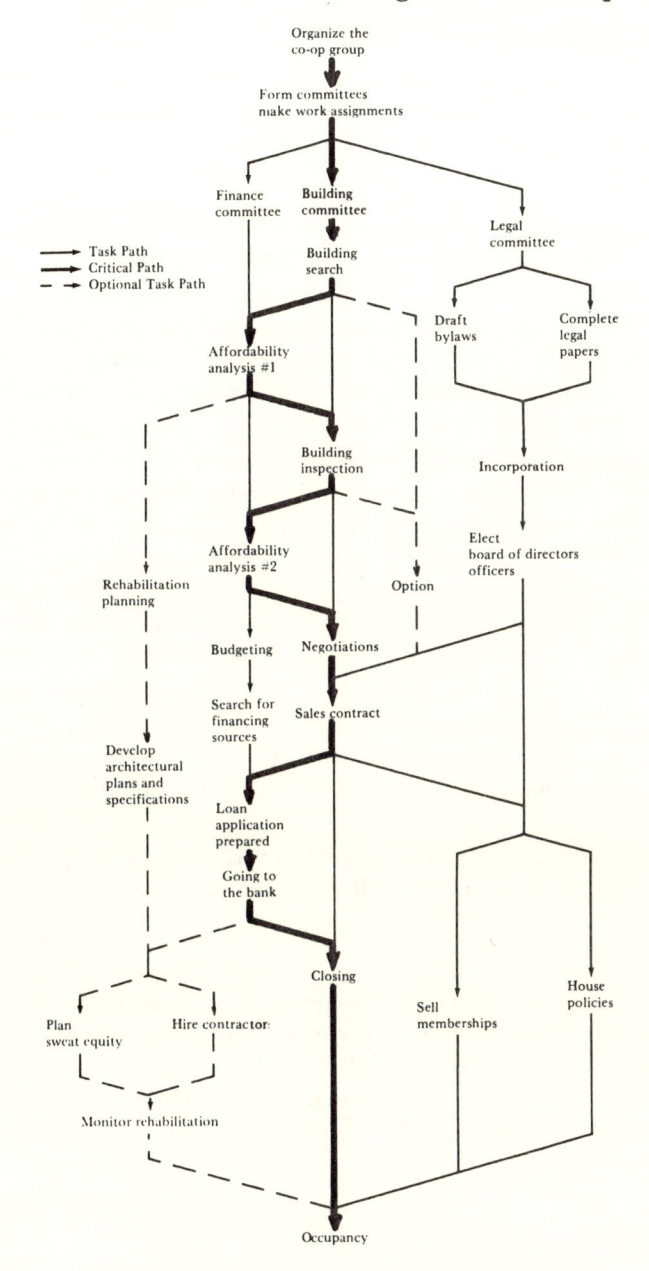

Figure 3 The Co-op Path Method

the counter for the next few days.) You are going to arrange and rearrange these cards into the CPM for your co-op. Everything will not fit at first, but it will all fit together in the end. Here's how to go about shaping those cards into a CPM flow chart.

1. Convene your co-op group around the table. Assemble the file cards you created as you read Chapters 5–8.
2. Place the cards on the table in an estimated sequence from left to right. Events that must occur at the same time should be stacked in the same vertical row, one above the other. Use paper arrows to show all connections between the cards.
3. Set a deadline for having the co-op building ready to live in. Work your way backward to figure out how much time you have to complete each task. Don't worry about being arbitrary; in the beginning you have to be.
4. Note: Certain activities are going to dominate, not because of their size or complexity, but because other activities cannot proceed until they are completed. Those dominant activities are the critical ones, the select few you must continually focus on to keep the co-op organization on schedule. The activities that can be flexible about completion are noncritical activities and do not require constant attention.
5. Assign people or committees to each task, making sure that the work is evenly divided and the assignments reflect what each person or committee can be expected to accomplish on time.

Over the course of the project, use and review the flow chart to determine your progress. Push activities that lag behind schedule, if it is possible to do so without antagonizing the members who are working on them. Offer help and more people, and revise the schedule if necessary.

5
LEGAL MATTERS

YOU'VE LOADED THE core group of people onto the co-op bandwagon, and now you are ready to start your journey. But as you look at your CPM road map, you see there are two routes to take. One route should be selected by the co-op groups who are under a time deadline. They most likely have an immediate opportunity to purchase a particular building —often the one in which they live—and they must buy it before the opportunity goes to someone else. These co-op groups need to have several committees active simultaneously.

The legal committee follows this chapter to complete the task of incorporation, while other committees work on inspecting the building, calculating costs, negotiating the price, and obtaining financing (Chapters 6–8). All committees need to finish their work at nearly the same time—the time of purchase.

The other route can be taken by groups not constrained by a deadline. They have the time to devote to their own internal organization before they head out to find and acquire their new co-op home. For these groups, counting time is not as important as making time count. We recommend that they start with the task of incorporation as outlined in this chapter. The luxury of the extra time can be spent wisely on deciding the operating rules of the co-op as part of the bylaws.

Your state government has laws applicable to the housing co-op business. Regardless of your path, you have to comply with those laws in order to borrow money and protect your co-op members from individual liability. The first requirement is that you create a legal vehicle for conducting your business—a co-op corporation. This must be done prior to any business transactions by the group.

A disclaimer: We are not lawyers; if we were, we would be selling this information for legal fees rather than for book prices. We try to avoid courts, judges, and lawyers as much as the next person, but we also recognize that co-ops are businesses that need to protect their members. Read this section before you consult a lawyer. Remember, most lawyers charge by the hour.

Incorporation

WHY CO-OPS ARE CORPORATIONS

Cooperatives are businesses. They are organized to purchase, own, and manage real property for the purpose of providing housing to their members. As an entity that owns property, collects income, and incurs expenses, the co-op must be a formal organization, it must operate in conformance with standard business practices, and it must maintain records according to generally accepted accounting procedures. The structure and procedures are intended to make the co-op accountable to its members and to the rest of society through government agencies.

Although they are not required to be, nearly all housing cooperatives are corporations, mainly for the protection of the members. Corporations are governed by formal rules of internal decision making that cannot be changed easily or arbitrarily. Most decisions are made by a board of directors, which has been democratically elected by the general membership; no individual member can make decisions for the corporation without prior consent of the board.

Incorporation also protects members from personal liability for the debts and obligations of the corporation. In other words, creditors cannot collect from a member personally for what the co-op owes. Creditors are limited to the assets of the corporation, which include the money you have invested in the co-op but not any of your personal assets.

HOW TO INCORPORATE

Each state has slightly different procedures for incorporating a housing co-op. We encourage you to contact a lawyer about the procedures in your state. If you intend to do the legal work involved in incorporation yourself, contact the secretary of state in your state government.

The incorporation tasks could be handled by a committee or by a committee of the whole. The argument in favor of a committee of the whole is that the bylaws are critical rules for running the co-op and they should be debated as broadly as possible among the members. The drawback to a committee of the whole is that it takes some time, but if you have a few weeks to devote to this task, set the time aside for several meetings at which you can debate the bylaws. In the meantime, a lawyer can draft the certificate of incorporation.

The process of incorporation usually involves a meeting of incorporation, at which the group adopts the certificate of incorporation and the bylaws and then elects the board of directors. The incorporation documents are filed with the secretary of state (usually with the office of corporations).

Certificate or articles of incorporation. The certificate of incorporation, known as the articles of incorporation in some states, formally announces the creation of a new business entity, the date and place at which it begins to operate as a corporation, and the purposes for its creation.

Bylaws. The bylaws are the formal rules by which the corporation operates, holds meetings, and makes decisions. Spend some time working on them, but remember that bylaws ought to be few enough to avoid confusion yet plentiful to cover the subject. Major sections of the bylaws address the following points. (Appendix 2 contains the standard bylaws that

HUD provides to its insured co-ops, to give you a concrete example.)

- *Membership.* Eligibility, selection, voting privileges, other rights and powers, and procedures for terminating membership.
- *Meetings.* Required meetings, notice of meetings, and rules that govern meetings.
- *Board of directors.* Powers, procedures for election, notice and other requirements of board meetings, rules that govern meetings, and committees of the board.
- *Officers.* Offices and procedures for election and removal.

The bylaws are the formal rules of operation. How you operate meetings internally may differ from the bylaws without violating them. For example, your co-op may decide to have a rotating chairperson for meetings; in that case, members take turns chairing meetings. When dealing with the outside world, however, officers and directors are the spokespersons for the corporation, and major decisions must be recorded in the minutes as formal votes.

The Co-op Operators' Manual

Once you have created the co-op corporation, it replaces your co-op organizing group as the decision-making body of the co-op. At the meeting of incorporation, the board of directors is elected. The board then holds its first meeting to elect officers and to take over operations. We encourage the new board to create committees immediately in order to maintain momentum and continuity. The transition from group to corporation should happen easily and quickly.

We call this section an Operators' Manual, although to be fair the remainder of the book deserves that name. Here, we provide you only with the information to get started. In particular, we review the activities and powers of each set of actors in the co-op corporation.

ORGANIZATION CHART

The bylaws establish formal lines of decision making and authority within the co-op, usually as follows:

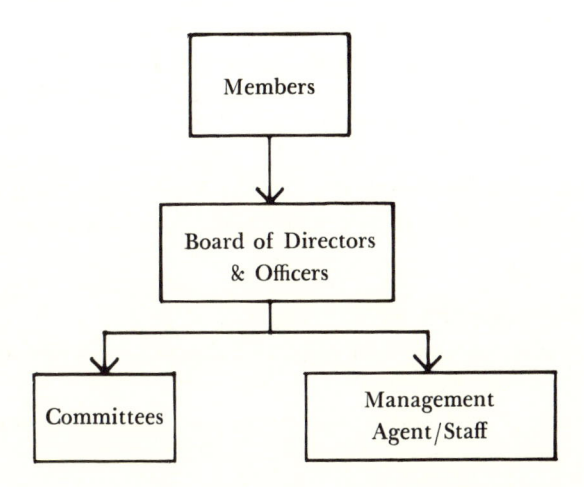

```
          ┌─────────────┐
          │   Members   │
          └──────┬──────┘
                 ▼
       ┌───────────────────┐
       │ Board of Directors│
       │    & Officers     │
       └─────────┬─────────┘
         ┌──────┴──────┐
         ▼             ▼
    ┌─────────┐  ┌─────────────┐
    │Committees│  │ Management  │
    │         │  │Agent/Staff  │
    └─────────┘  └─────────────┘
```

The co-op stockholders are the ultimate decision makers of the corporation. To facilitate decision making and day-to-day administration, the members elect from their own group a small number of directors in whom much of the decision-making authority of the corporation is vested. The board of directors can in turn create committees of members to advise it. The board also hires and supervises the management agent or staff.

While this organization chart may appear to be indistinguishable from that of any type of business corporation, the relationships within a co-op between the members, the board, and the management are more complicated than those in a business. Co-op members are much more directly involved in the affairs of their corporation. The members serve as unpaid directors and officers, and members volunteer their time for committees and co-op activities.

BOARD OF DIRECTORS AND OFFICERS

The board of directors is the democratically elected decision-making body of the co-op corporation. We have found co-op boards ranging in size from three to thirty-seven members, although most fall between six and nine. In the board is vested direct responsibility for every phase of the co-op operation. The general membership retains authority to approve or reject board decisions and to vote to replace members of the board. But the day-to-day responsibility for decision making and operations rests with the board. The co-op board of directors is typically expected to act in the following areas:

Membership

- Select or approve all new members.
- Oversee development of recreational, social, and educational programs for members.
- Provide proper notice to members of meetings, votes, and decisions.
- Appoint members to committees to advise the board.

Building management

- Adopt and change co-op operating policies.
- Develop, publicize, and enforce house rules.
- Develop and enforce architectural standards.
- Employ, direct, and monitor the management agent and/or employees.
- Provide for effective physical maintenance.
- Provide adequate insurance.

Financial Management

- Establish sound financial policies and maintain accurate records.
- Develop and announce budgets and charges to members.
- Approve all major expenditures.
- Take appropriate legal action against delinquent members.

The bylaws usually obligate the board of directors to meet regularly (typically monthly), to notify all members well in advance of the meetings, and to conduct an open meeting at which co-op members can attend and be heard. The bylaws also require that minutes be kept and distributed to all members.

The bylaws also designate the officers of the corporation. Officers are elected from the board of directors, usually to the following positions and responsibilities:

President. The elected head of the co-op. The president calls and chairs meetings of the board and of the general membership (although the co-op can designate someone else to act as the chair); acts as official representative of and spokesperson for the co-op; and personally reviews financial activities of the co-op. It is common for the president to be cosigner of checks and documents.

Vice-president. Serves in the absence of the president and assists the president in completion of duties.

Secretary/clerk. Is responsible for maintaining written records —minutes, leases, deeds, mortgages, corporate papers, and contracts—and for handling all official communications. Included in these duties are taking and distributing the minutes for all meetings.

Treasurer. Maintains or supervises the financial records of the co-op; is typically the cosigner of checks and other legal documents.

Officers carry the day-to-day management responsibilities for the co-op. They are empowered to take certain actions on behalf of the board between board meetings. It is important to note this distinction between an officer and a director: An officer has certain powers to act outside of the board meetings, while a director may exercise his or her authority only during board meetings.

The bylaws empower the board to establish committees, and some co-op bylaws list the specific committees. As noted above, the initial board should act quickly to continue the working committees established by the organizing group prior to incorporation. We suggest a number of different standing (permanent) and temporary committees in Chapter 11.

MEMBERSHIP

Co-op members are in a unique and sometimes difficult position within the co-op. Members play dual roles: they are owners of the co-op, with the rights of stockholders; and they are also customers, or tenants, of the corporation, occupying co-op units under the terms of a proprietary lease. Each role has a separate set of rights and responsibilities, which are guaranteed in separate legal documents of the co-op.

Subscription agreement. The subscription agreement records the purchase of co-op membership shares by individuals. The number of shares purchased is determined by the size and value of the unit.

As an example, let's consider a co-op that has ten units, five one-bedroom and five two-bedroom. The co-op needs to raise $100,000 for the down payment (the rest of the money will be borrowed from a bank). The co-op decides to sell one-bedroom units for a membership price of $8,000 and two-bedroom units for $12,000. To do this, it issues one hundred shares of co-op stock, each with a value of $1,000. A buyer who wishes to occupy a one-bedroom unit buys eight shares of co-op stock for $8,000.

All financial obligations and benefits (tax deductions) are allocated to members on the basis of the number of shares of stock they own. The member with a one-bedroom unit owns 8 percent of the total stock. Therefore, this member is responsible for paying 8 percent of the operating costs of the co-op and gets 8 percent of the tax deductions. This percentage is known as the member's *financial interest* in the co-op.

Voting rights, however, are not based on financial interest. Each co-op member (meaning the household that occupies a co-op unit) has one vote in decisions and elections of the corporation, regardless of the amount of stock that member may own.

This vote may be exercised at the annual meeting and at any additional meetings of the stockholders (members). Each member may vote in elections of co-op directors and may run for the board. Proxies (assigning one's right to vote to another person) are generally prohibited. But certain decisions cannot be made by the board alone. The stockholders must vote on matters such as amendments to the certificate of incorporation or bylaws, purchase or sale of major corporate assets (such as buildings), and changes to the co-op through dissolution or merger.

Occupancy agreement. Members of the co-op occupy units under the terms of an occupancy agreement or proprietary lease. Typical proprietary leases run for fifteen to fifty years. Such a lease automatically renews so long as the co-op continues to operate and the member abides by the rules stated in the lease. HUD-sponsored or -insured co-ops may have shorter lease terms—three to five years—because HUD wants to make it easier for its co-ops to evict bad tenants.

The occupancy agreement contains very specific clauses about the following matters:

- *Carrying charges.* What expenses they cover, what they currently are, and how they may be increased.
- *Subleasing.* In most cases subject to the co-op's approval.
- *Improvements to the unit.* The member must obtain prior approval of the co-op.
- *Repairs to the unit.* Some repairs may be the member's responsibility rather than the co-op's.
- *Compliance with co-op regulations.* The member agrees to abide by all rules of the co-op for membership and occupancy.
- *Default.* Defines the terms under which a membership can be canceled.

- *Late charges.* Members who make their payments late may be assessed extra charges.
- *Inspection and right of access.* Describes the conditions under which members must allow the co-op or its agents access to the unit.

<u>Carrying charge assessments.</u> Co-ops have used many different methods and criteria for deciding the financial interest associated with each unit. Financial interest is expressed as a fraction or percentage of the whole. It can be based on any or all of the following:

1. *Unit value:* the financial interest of a single unit is determined by dividing the originally assessed value of that unit by the total value of all co-op units.
2. *Market price of unit:* the financial interest of a single unit is determined by dividing the price of membership rights to occupy that unit by the total price of all units.
3. *Unit size:* the financial interest of a single unit is determined by dividing the square footage of the unit by the total square footage of all co-op units.
4. *Number of units:* the financial interest of all individual units is equal and is obtained by dividing one by the total number of units.

We have also encountered some mixed-income cooperatives sponsored by nonprofit development groups in which the financial interests of a certain percentage of the units are arbitrarily reduced to make the units affordable to low- and moderate-income families. This method is called *internal subsidy.*

Tax Requirements for Co-ops

CO-OPS AND THE IRS

The IRS generally offers co-op members the same tax treatment as it offers other homeowners. In particular, co-op

Legal Matters / 73

members may deduct their share of the co-op corporation's deductible interest and taxes, if the corporation meets the following conditions:

1. The corporation must have only one class or type of stock outstanding. This means all stockholders must have the same rights and voting privileges.
2. Because of ownership of the stock, each stockholder has the right to live in a house or an apartment owned or leased by the corporation.
3. No stockholder may receive any distribution out of the capital assets of the co-op, except on a partial or complete liquidation of the corporation.
4. The tenant-stockholders must pay at least 80 percent of the corporation's gross income for the tax year. For this purpose, gross income means all income received during the entire tax year, including any received before the corporation changed to cooperative ownership. (From IRS Publication 588, revised November 1981.)

Tenant-stockholders are defined by the IRS as individuals only; corporations and other business entities, while allowed to be members and to occupy units, cannot be included to meet the 80 percent rule. Shares of stock owned by or units leased by a government agency are not considered in determining whether a corporation qualifies as a housing co-op. This criterion protects government-assisted or -insured co-ops from losing eligibility in cases where the government is required to own a second class of stock (nonvoting stock). Bank acquisition of shares via foreclosure of loans to individual members also does not cause the co-op to automatically lose its eligibility.

Construction interest and taxes are considered part of the original equity investment and are not deductible. Points paid by the co-op for permanent financing are deductible.

Co-op members may take the residential energy tax credit for their share of eligible improvements, and they may take allowable deductions for use of the co-op unit in their business. The co-op owner is required to keep track of the cost, or basis, of the co-op membership and of all permanent improvements so that the owner can pay the capital gains tax upon sale of the unit or defer the tax by purchasing another home in compliance with IRS rules.

Tax returns must be filed annually for the co-op corporation, as required of all businesses. The tax deductions for interest and taxes, which are passed to the members, may not be included as expenses for the co-op. But the co-op is unlikely to face any tax liability because the corporation provides its housing services at cost and therefore generates little or no profit on which tax must be paid. If any "profits"—actually, unrefunded overassessments—are generated, the depreciation expenses associated with ownership of the co-op building are usually sufficient to offset these profits.

A co-op that directly employs management or maintenance staff must comply with IRS regulations for employers. State tax returns also are required.

STATE TAX REQUIREMENTS

Corporations are legal entities created under state law. Each state requires corporations to make annual filings declaring the corporate officers and other information. Check with the secretary of state in your state for these requirements.

6
FINDING AN AFFORDABLE BUILDING

IT'S TIME TO TALK OF "bricks and mortar." Up to this point, we have talked about building the social and business structures that make the co-op organization. Now your organization is ready to find its home.

We leave no brick unturned as we go into details of the physical and financial aspects of residential buildings. This information is critical: your co-op group is going into the housing business, and you must make a sound investment now so that the group can live safely and economically in future years. With the help and information in this chapter, we hope your group can avoid being the butt of the joke: "How many co-op members does it take to change a light bulb?"

Review the co-op CPM chart in Chapter 4 (Figure 3). Note that the search for housing can branch off into rehabilitation planning, but that the connecting lines indicate that rehabilitation is an optional activity. Your co-op building may not require rehabilitation, or your members may have decided that the group cannot afford rehabilitation at the time of purchase. If you decide to rehabilitate the building at the time of purchase, read Chapter 8.

What Kind of Building Does Your Group Need?

Before you go looking for a building, know what it is you are looking for. We suggest that you determine answers at least to the following questions prior to your search:

1. How many and what size units does your group need?
2. What kind of building(s) do you prefer? (Single building, clustered buildings, scattered buildings? High-rise, mid-rise, low-rise? New, old?)
3. What other facilities do you want—public spaces, community rooms, laundry and other service facilities, parking, terraced or landscaped yard, recreation facilities, security provisions?
4. In what areas of the community are you willing to live?
5. What monthly costs can your members afford? What down payment can you afford?

One way to answer these questions is to pass around a questionnaire in your early group meetings. Compile and discuss the results in the group or in the housing committee. The composite answers to these questions and any other instructions become the group's specifications for its housing search.

Selecting the Building or Property

Finding the right building, or property on which to build, is the next important step for the co-op group. For some groups, the choice is an obvious one: the building in which you live is available, and you want a secure future in a co-op for yourself and your neighbors. You thus may decide to consider only that building. Current residences may not be available or desirable to other co-op groups. Their search for a co-op building must go beyond the front doorstep.

This chapter helps you recognize an *affordable* building, considering all the costs of acquisition, development, and op-

Finding an Affordable Building / 77

eration, whether it is the building you are living in or a building you want to purchase. We call the process getting the total cost picture.

GETTING THE TOTAL COST PICTURE

Buildings and developable properties vary considerably in cost, and we don't mean just the cost of purchase. Total cost includes the purchase price *plus* construction or rehabilitation costs that may be necessary to make the property livable. Also figured into the total cost picture are the annual operating costs. Consider these three eight-unit buildings:

- Building 1 is for sale for $200,000 and needs no rehabilitation. Annual operating costs (exclusive of debt service) are $30,000.
- Building 2 is available for $150,000 and requires $30,000 in emergency repairs. Its annual operating costs after repairs would be $35,000.
- Building 3 is offered at $160,000 and could use $10,000 in cosmetic improvements. Its annual operating costs are $38,000.

Which one do you choose? And how do you make your choice?

All other things being equal, you would probably base a decision on which one is the most affordable, considering all costs. For the co-op, affordability means membership prices and monthly carrying charges that members can reasonably be expected to pay. So the overall building costs must be converted to individual monthly costs for you to make a decision.

The choice cannot be made without a fast pencil or calculator because the figures that make up the total cost are computed and paid for on different terms. The purchase price and rehabilitation costs are capital costs; that is, they are usually borrowed funds, and payment is spread out over the period of the loan. The operating costs are current costs that the co-op must pay at the time the cost is incurred. You're dealing with "apples and oranges" unless you convert all the costs into similar units for comparison.

The simplest approach is to convert the capital costs—costs of acquisition and rehabilitation—into operating costs, or expenses, by calculating the annual expenditure for debt service (loan payments). Once you have calculated total annual expenditures by adding the annual loan payments and the annual operating costs, you can estimate monthly carrying charges to individual members. Assuming 15 percent, 25-year financing for Buildings 1, 2, and 3, the annual costs would be as follows:

	Building 1	Building 2	Building 3
Total loan (purchase price plus rehabilitation, if any)	$200,000	$180,000	$170,000
Annual debt service	$ 30,360	$ 27,324	$ 25,806
Annual operating costs	$ 30,000	$ 35,000	$ 38,000
Total annual expenses	$ 60,360	$ 62,324	$ 63,806
Monthly carrying charge per unit	$ 629	$ 649	$ 664

These calculations point to Building 1 as the most affordable. While this example may oversimplify the affordability decision, it does demonstrate how to evaluate opportunities.

The next few sections of this chapter will guide you through all the steps involved in getting the total cost picture, from finding a building to negotiating a price to estimating all the necessary rehabilitation and operating expenses. When you have completed those steps, you will be ready to perform an affordability analysis, which involves calculating the initial membership price and the members' monthly carrying charges and determining whether prospective members can afford those costs.

WHERE TO LOOK

Co-op groups that need or want to consider buildings other than the one they are living in must conduct a search for a building that is available at a reasonable price and that fills the needs of the co-op members.

Location is the single most important word to many people in the real estate business. In large part it determines the value of a given property. To understand the impact of location on value, put an imaginary building—a building that you envision will be perfect for your co-op—on wheels and move it around to different parts of your community. Try to estimate the value of the building in each place you "park" it. What patterns do you see?

The property's value probably increases the closer the building is to the key activity centers of your community: downtown, work districts, shopping centers, and bodies of water or other natural amenities. The property's value is also affected by the properties surrounding it. If neighboring buildings have been converted, upgraded, or sold recently, then the price of your building probably will reflect improving market conditions. In neighborhoods that have not had recent upgrading activity, the market value of the building may be lower.

Private investors try to buy properties with rising values because the appreciation in value will increase their profits. They choose as "hot" investment locations those areas where rising prices suggest future appreciation. Co-op groups don't need to take that approach to their investment. Co-ops go into business to provide affordable housing to members. As a member, you should be more concerned about minimizing monthly housing costs than maximizing future investment return. Part of your return will come every month in the form of lower housing costs.

80 / GOING CO-OP

"Hot" areas tend to be overpriced, but your co-op group can choose areas that are not so "hot." Be a leader, not a follower of the market.

Of course, no amount of planning replaces luck. A member of the group may overhear a conversation at lunch about a building, or you may get a tip from a friend at a party. Your group may stumble across a building that is ideally suited for a co-op. On the other hand, you may be faced with what looks like a great deal financially, but the building does not fit your specifications exactly. It may be twice as large as the group wanted, or the unit sizes may be wrong. In that case the group must decide whether to take the building and possibly change the group's makeup or its plans or to keep looking in the hope of stumbling upon an equally good building that meets the group's specifications.

USING REALTORS

Realtors have information about many of the buildings that are on the market, and they know what price ranges are reasonable for buildings. A realtor can help your group determine the type of building that will suit the group's needs, direct you to available buildings, conduct negotiations for you, and help you arrange the legal details of the sale. These are very valuable services, and you are likely to pay realty fees in the range of 5 to 7 percent of the purchase price. Often these fees are paid by the seller, but in that case the seller asks a higher price to reflect the fee.

We recommend that you use a realtor who has prior experience with co-ops, if you can find one. Few realtors are experienced in co-op transactions. Realtors may be reluctant to try to put together a co-op deal for your group because they don't know how to do it or they fear that local lenders will not loan to co-ops. Today's realty industry is characterized by a glut of realtors scrambling for a limited number of sales, however, so you should be able to find some realtor who will make the extra effort required to make your special deal.

Some communities are fortunate to have realtors who specialize in packaging limited-equity conversions. An example is the Alternative Realty Center (ARC) in Oakland, California. ARC acts as the developer of co-ops and provides consulting and management services in addition to its realty services, which it offers at 4 percent (rather than the standard industry fee of 6 percent). ARC reports that currently it is assisting two San Francisco nonprofit groups to package 400 co-op units in five buildings. It is also organizing two other buildings, one in Berkeley and one in San Francisco.

FINDING A BARGAIN

Everyone searches for the bargain buy—that rare property that can be purchased at a price well below its market value. Usually, those bargain buys happen through personal connections. How do you find a bargain?

At a co-op group meeting, ask every member to make a list of friends and relatives in the immediate area. Call those people to see if they know any landlords or are aware of any buildings for sale. Ask them to keep their ears open. Opportunities often come from unlikely sources.

If the price is right, some property owners are always willing to sell. Other owners may be eager to sell because of special conditions, such as illness, financial problems, or retirement, and the need to sell quickly may cause them to sell at a low price. Ask around: your timing may be just right.

Your local government is one of the most likely sources for finding a bargain building. Governments can take title to properties for a variety of reasons—one of the most common is the owner's failure to pay property taxes—and few cities care to act as long-term landlords. New York City is an exception. The city is quick to take title of tax-delinquent properties and has developed an exemplary alternative management program for many of the 80,000 units it owns. Most other cities avoid taking title to properties unless they have a buyer waiting, or they put the property on the auction block immediately upon acquisition.

The Department of Housing and Urban Development (HUD) is another potential source. HUD is the largest landlord in the country, with a large inventory of available single-family and multifamily housing acquired through foreclosure of loans.

Investigate in your local government agencies. Find out which local agencies are responsible for holding and disposing of properties. If you don't know where to start, call the local government information number. You may be referred to the assessor, the real property department, the sheriff's (or police commissioner's) office, the housing authority, the planning department, or the community development department. While you are asking about city-owned properties, also inquire about HUD-owned properties in your area and local programs to help residents buy housing or set up co-ops, such as a local homesteading program.

CONTACTING THE OWNER

Contact the owner as soon as you identify a building you are interested in. This contact will establish (1) whether the owner is interested in selling, (2) whether any other parties are interested in buying the building (against whom you must bid), and (3) the initial asking price. (The local registry of deeds or the assessor's office can tell you who owns a particular property if you do not know.)

Designate one person to contact the owner, even if your group has a building committee. It reduces confusion within the group and it prevents the owner from thinking there may be more than one interested buyer (which can drive up the asking price). For the benefit of the other committee members, the designated spokesperson should take careful notes during telephone conversations. If you meet the owner in person, no more than two people should accompany your spokesperson.

If the owner indicates that the building is available at what appears to be a reasonable price (see the section on affordability later in the chapter), prepare to do a little homework before making an offer. The owner should grant you access to the building during reasonable hours so that you can inspect it. He should also provide you with information on the physical condition of the building and with the most recent figures on operating costs.

Your strategy for contacting the owner may be different if your group is trying to buy the building in which you live. In this case, the group members have an ongoing relationship with the owner. If the relationship is good, discussions may be able to proceed informally and candidly. However, if your relationship is bad, you may need to proceed cautiously. Should you approach the owner at the earliest stages or wait until you are sure you have enough interest among tenants? Should you have one of the tenant leaders meet with the owner and try to use the leverage of rent strikes and other tenant negotiating strategies to get the owner to accept your position? Or do you keep tenant leaders out of the picture and have someone who gets along with the owner make the first inquiries? Regardless of your choice of strategy, make sure that you carry into the negotiations a sound understanding of finance and building operations so that you can negotiate shrewdly. The tenants at 149 Massachusetts Avenue in Boston were activists, and they used their leverage as activists to make the owner listen to them, but they were able to close the deal and start the First Fenway Cooperative because they presented a sound proposal to the owner and the banks.

The following advice applies both to newly formed groups looking for a building and to tenants planning a conversion of their own building. The best approach is to assume you know nothing about the building—you may be surprised to find out how little you do know even about the building you live in.

Inspecting the Building

Before entering final negotiations with the owner, you must develop a fairly detailed understanding of building conditions. You need to determine precisely what you are purchasing with your money and to estimate the additional money you must invest in rehabilitation to make the building suitable for occupancy.

As you estimate the rehabilitation needs of an existing building, bear in mind that improvements may be either necessary or optional. You may not be able to afford immediately every improvement you would like to make, but you have to recognize improvements that must be done right away. Also remember that every improvement can be made at several levels of quality and cost. You may be able to get an improvement done by a less expensive method, but there is a good chance the improvement won't last as long.

WHO SHOULD DO THE INSPECTION?

Few people outside the construction business are qualified to conduct reliable inspections of properties. Given the hundreds of thousands of dollars your group will be risking on a building, it is safe to suggest a professional inspection. On the other hand, professional inspections are costly, and few include a guarantee that the professional will detect all problems. A professional inspection may leave you feeling as though you paid a lot to learn very little that you would not have surmised yourself. If you use a professional inspector, make sure you check references.

A real estate broker or financial consultant usually can help you assess general building conditions. If you have any friends in the real estate construction business—people you can trust—ask them to walk through the building with you. (Note that we recommend that a professional friend walk through the building *with you*. You too must become familiar with building conditions.)

If your co-op group chooses to do its own inspection, the building committee should review the following sections dealing with building conditions. These sections will not qualify you to conduct a professional inspection, but they will draw your attention to the telltale signs of the most serious build-

Finding an Affordable Building / 85

ing problems. Conduct the inspection by committee: several sets of eyes increase the likelihood that you will detect problems.

STRUCTURAL CONDITIONS

The first and most obvious place to begin your inspection is the structure of the building—the foundation, walls, roof, and other parts of the building "envelope." Several visible signs of structural problems may rule out your further interest in the building or reduce the price you will offer. Some of the problems may not be visible to an untrained eye, but look for the following signs:

- *Cracks in the exterior walls and foundation walls.* Diagonal cracks in the exterior walls indicate the possibility of settling in parts of the foundation.
- *Leaning, bulging, or sagging exterior or interior bearing walls.* Such walls may have been standing intact for many years, but they may collapse when you begin rehabilitation. You can spot severely leaning and bulging walls by standing near one edge of the wall and sighting up and down it. A sag in the parapet wall (on the roof) may indicate problems below.
- *Missing or cracked exterior lintels.* A lintel is the horizontal beam or masonry directly over a door or window opening that extends beyond the opening and supports the weight of the wall above. This is important in masonry (brick or concrete) buildings where the weight of the structure needs to be distributed. If lintels are cracked or missing, the walls may be weakened or there may be other structural problems. The masonry above the lintels will show cracks or sagging if there is a problem.
- *Sloping floors.* Sloping must be expected over time in wood-frame buildings because of the natural sagging of aging wooden floor joists (the wall-to-wall beams below the flooring), but it may indicate more serious problems. Poorly engineered buildings sag over time, and sometimes the sag

occurs because bearing walls were mistakenly removed during a prior rehabilitation job. If you see a problem, ask the owner about the building's history: when it was constructed and when, if ever, it was rehabilitated. Your local building department or public library may have the original plans and all building permits on file. Use these to reexamine the problem. Look for structural walls and beams (they are usually marked with a solid line on the blueprint). Check whether all original structural supports are still present in the basement.

- *Termites.* You might notice termites or carpenter ants around the outside of the building where the frame meets the foundation or in the basement of wood-frame buildings. Termites may weaken some of the wooden members of the structure. Find out about past termite inspections. Have your own pest inspection done before you purchase. Pest inspection companies, like all businesses, can be good or bad. Be sure to select a reputable firm and check references.

- *Water or fire damage.* Such damage, visible in the basement, floor joists, or attic, weakens the structure. Investigate the history of fires in the building; the local building department and fire department can provide records if the owner cannot or will not.

- *Faulty roof.* Much of the structural damage to a roof occurs from leakage of water, and a faulty roof can cause considerable damage to the building over a period of several years. A roof that is not tightly sealed also will increase heat loss.

- *Missing bricks and crumbling mortar.* While possibly only a superficial flaw, problems with bricks and mortar may be symptoms of a crumbling structure. Examine the masonry closely. If the building has been recently pointed (that is, the exterior mortar patched), ask the owner about the pointing work: when it was done, why, and by whom. Pointing may have been done to improve the appearance of the building for sale, but it also may hide some serious defects.

Finding an Affordable Building / 87

While these structural faults can be corrected, such repairs can be very costly. And undetected structural faults can cripple the co-op financially or endanger lives during or after construction. The clues are subtle, but they can be detected by a qualified inspector.

CONDITION OF THE BUILDING'S SYSTEMS

The systems of a residential building are the *mechanical* systems of heating, ventilation, and air conditioning, often called HVAC; the *electrical* system; and the *plumbing*. Repair or replacement of these items usually eats up most of your rehabilitation dollars. If your building is old, it is likely that some or all of the systems will need to be replaced. Those systems that are in good operating condition may be repaired or upgraded at a cost lower than replacement cost, but you should consider the trade-offs. Your co-op has the choice of a large replacement expense now that can be financed over a ten-to-thirty-year mortgage term versus a small repair expense now and the risk of higher operating costs and a possible large replacement cost in the future.

GENERAL BUILDING CONDITIONS

While the structural and systems work constitutes the major portion of *essential* rehabilitation, many other cosmetic improvements can dramatically increase the total cost of rehabilitation. You should give priority to improvements related to energy conservation. New windows and storm windows, insulation, and other improvements are cost-effective because their costs can be recovered through utility cost savings in the future.

Other improvements may not be essential to the safe and sanitary occupation of the building but nonetheless may be important to the co-op because they are "selling" features. Prospective co-op members may be attracted by new kitchens or bathrooms. Such improvements are costly, however, and may be deferred if the members think costs are too high.

Co-op members will want to include painting, masonry

pointing, facade and entrance upgrading, and landscaping in the rehabilitation. The members want to live in an attractive building, and the exterior improvements become additional sources of pride in their co-op. While these improvements are desirable and important if you need to recruit more members on the open market, they must be considered lowest-priority expenditures until all other costs are considered. If you cannot afford these improvements now, be sure to include some reserves in your operating budget for a few years from now, or save money by having members do painting and landscaping. (See Chapter 8 on sweat equity.)

Still another set of general improvements is for building security. One co-op in Boston had tremendous security problems. When rehabilitation was completed, the buildings stuck out as the best buildings on a street of otherwise run-down buildings. The co-op buildings became marked as an easy hit. Doors were easy to jimmy, security bars had not been installed, and the twenty-two member households were still too unfamiliar with each other to recognize who should be coming and going, and when.

Some households installed security bars on windows, only to find that burglars could also break in through their apartment doors. They installed police locks on their apartment doors, but burglars broke in by punching through walls. Better exterior locks were installed, but some residents buzzed in criminals because they failed to check who was ringing the doorbell. Door release buzzers were disconnected, but people started to leave the doors unlocked for friends. The buildings remained marked. Finally, the residents realized that the problem could not be eliminated with hardware alone. After several meetings, memos, and informal conversations, people began watching the building more closely, and soon a burglar was spotted by a neighbor and arrested.

The moral of the story is not that security expenditures are useless; rather, security hardware can help only those tenants who also watch out for each other. Because co-ops require that members interact, they are ideal organizations for promoting security watches or informal cooperation in watching each other's unit.

Rehabilitation

Rehabilitation is the process of returning a property, through repair or alteration, to a condition that makes possible efficient contemporary use. Old buildings require different degrees of rehabilitation. There is a great difference in cost and amount of work required in an occupied building that needs only minor repairs and in an abandoned, vandalized building that needs to be substantially rebuilt. How much rehabilitation you must do depends on several factors: the age of the building; the quality of original construction; the quality of maintenance through the years of occupancy; the changes in layout and use included in the plans; and, most important, what you can afford. Rehabilitation work can involve intensive repair, moderate rehabilitation, or substantial rehabilitation, or it can mean historic preservation.

INTENSIVE REPAIR

Very often, buildings that are occupied but suffering somewhat from age or neglect can be rehabilitated through a concentrated fix-up program, often called intensive repair. Repairs are made to the building systems, and limited cosmetic improvements are made to interiors and the exterior, with as little inconvenience as possible to the residents. Hallways are repainted, storm windows installed, the heating plant repaired, and some plaster work done on the cracks in the ceiling. By patching and fixing what already exists, co-ops with limited financial resources can rehabilitate a building one repair at a time.

Intensive repair work is usually done over a long time, often several years. Costs per unit usually do not exceed $5,000 and can be paid out of replacement reserves from monthly carrying charges, special membership assessments, or additional loans. (See Chapter 7 for a discussion of replacement reserves.)

MODERATE REHABILITATION

With age and use, some building systems require replacement, and often even some of the finishing work (painting, tiling, wood refinishing) must be done over. Bathrooms need new fixtures or tile; the heating plant should be replaced with a more efficient system; new windows are needed; the flooring needs to be repaired and replaced in spots; and all walls need to be patched, sanded, and painted. This combination of repair and replacement constitutes moderate rehabilitation.

Moderate rehabilitation can be done in occupied structures if the work is properly staged, but it is preferable that the work be done while the units are vacant, because often utilities must be turned off temporarily. Moderate rehabilitation usually costs between $5,000 and $15,000 per unit.

SUBSTANTIAL REHABILITATION

Substantial rehabilitation is warranted when it is too costly or difficult to save anything but the basic structure. It is often called "gut rehabilitation" because you gut or demolish the interior of the building down to the bare beams, structural walls, and subfloor before you begin to reconstruct completely new apartments within the existing frame. Substantial rehabilitation must be completed prior to occupancy. Its costs are only slightly lower than the costs of new construction: plan to spend $20,000 to $45,000 per unit for substantial rehabilitation.

HISTORIC PRESERVATION

Historic preservation is a special category. Preservation means rehabilitation to return a structure to a condition that makes possible efficient contemporary use while preserving features of the property that are significant to its historic, architectural, and cultural value. It is a combination of repair and replacement, and certain features are restored without regard to cost.

The Economic Recovery Tax Act of 1981 introduced dramatic changes in the federal tax treatment of investments in real estate, particularly those involving historic preservation. Certified rehabilitation projects approved by the U.S. Department of the Interior or the National Park Service are afforded the most favorable investment tax credit and depreciation status of any real property. An investment tax credit of 25 percent of the rehabilitation cost is permitted, and the owner is also permitted to depreciate the full amount of rehabilitation costs over fifteen years without reducing the depreciable basis by the amount of the tax credit. (This provision may be changed by Congress.)

If you feel that your building is eligible to be certified a historic property, carefully examine the legal requirements, the potential tax benefits, and the extra costs. Bear in mind that you should apply for certification before you begin any rehabilitation.

ESTIMATING THE COST OF REHABILITATION

Once you have inspected the building and determined its rehabilitation needs, you can estimate the costs of rehabilitation. The costs of rehabilitation affect the price your group should be willing to pay for the building. As a general rule, the more rehabilitation required, the lower the purchase price. Remember, your objective in estimating the cost of rehabilitation is to arrive at a total development cost, rehabilitation included, that your members can afford.

Estimating gross rehabilitation costs is quite simple. Two methods can be used. One method is to estimate approximate cost per unit, such as we noted above for the different levels of rehabilitation. A second and more accurate method involves the following steps:

1. Obtain the approximate square footage of the building from the owner, or figure it out yourself by measuring the outside dimensions of the building and multiplying that number by the total number of floors (including the basement).
2. Establish the average cost per square foot for rehabilitation in your community. Your inspection has established the level of rehabilitation the building requires as well as a list of the specific work that needs to be done. Ask a local contractor to give you a ballpark figure for construction costs per square foot for the level of construction you are planning.
3. Multiply the two figures: square footage of the building times construction costs per square foot. The answer is the approximate cost of construction.

Some incidental costs that your co-op must pay in addition to the construction costs include architect fees, legal fees, and interest on construction loans paid prior to occupancy. These are costs that you must pay before you are able to generate revenue from the building, and it is common for co-op groups to borrow this money. Add about 20 percent to the cost of construction for these indirect costs. The total is a rough estimate of the total cost of rehabilitation.

Let's consider a simple example: A six-story, six-unit brick rowhouse is available for $70,000; its approximate dimensions are 22 feet by 36 feet; it requires substantial rehabilitation at a cost of about $45 per square foot. The calculations look like this:

Gross square footage (22 ft. by 36 ft. by 6 stories)	4,752
Times: Construction cost per sq. ft.	$45
Construction cost	$213,840
Plus: Indirect costs (20% of construction cost)	42,768
Total cost for rehabilitation	$256,608

Keep this building in mind. We will follow this example through the rest of the chapter and into Chapter 7.

Affordability Analysis

Affordability analysis refers to the calculations that a co-op group or any other real estate developer makes to determine whether a development project can be completed at a cost that makes the units affordable. For co-op groups, affordability analysis requires two steps. First, the group must estimate the initial membership price and the members' monthly carrying charges. Second, the group must compare the incomes of group members with the estimated charges to determine whether prospective members can afford to join. If they can't, a third step may need to be taken to explore ways to reduce the costs and make the co-op affordable.

Your building committee should have assembled enough numbers to begin the process of determining whether you can afford to convert a particular building into a co-op. Your first-run cost calculations are popularly referred to as a "back of the envelope" affordability analysis because you can do the analysis just by jotting down a few numbers on the back of an envelope. Later you will go through the same steps in full detail and with specific cost estimates, but for now work with gross estimates.

An affordability analysis worksheet is presented in Figure 4. Follow this worksheet as we discuss one co-op example and then use the worksheet to do your own affordability analyses.

The first affordability calculations should be done by the building committee before it is ready to enter purchase negotiations for a building. In later stages, the detailed affordability analyses should be done by the finance committee.

The total development costs (line 2.3) are a one-time capital expense incurred at the purchase of the building, but much of the cost is borowed and paid in monthly installments over the life of the loan. We will look for the best financing deals in the next chapter, but here you need to estimate a

Figure 4

Affordability Analysis Worksheet

1. CONSTRUCTION COSTS
    1.1 Gross square footage of building _____
    1.2 Times: Construction costs per sq. ft. × _____
    1.3 Construction costs $ _____
    1.4 Plus: Indirect construction costs + _____
    1.5 Total construction costs $ _____

2. TOTAL DEVELOPMENT COSTS
    2.1 Total construction costs $ _____
    2.2 Plus: Purchase price + _____
    2.3 Total development costs $ _____

3. MONTHLY CARRYING CHARGES
    3.1 Maximum mortgage amount $ _____
    3.2 Monthly mortgage payment (debt service) $ _____
    3.3 Plus: Monthly operating costs + _____
    3.4 Total monthly operating costs $ _____
    3.5 Divided by: Number of units ÷ _____
    3.6 Monthly carrying charges per unit $ _____
    3.7 Percentage of member average income _____ %

4. NET MONTHLY CARRYING CHARGES
    4.1 Annual interest costs $ _____
    4.2 Plus: Annual property taxes + _____
    4.3 Total co-op deductions $ _____
    4.4 Divided by: Number of units ÷ _____
    4.5 Annual deductions per unit $ _____
    4.6 Times: Individual tax bracket × _____
    4.7 Annual tax savings $ _____
    4.8 Divided by: 12 months ÷ 12
    4.9 Monthly tax savings $ _____
    4.10 Net monthly carrying charges (3.6 − 4.9) $ _____
    4.11 Percentage of member average income _____ %

5. **AVERAGE SHARE PRICE**

5.1	Nonmortgageable development costs	$ _____
5.2	Plus: Co-op working capital	+ _____
5.3	Total co-op capital requirements	$ _____
5.4	Divided by: Number of units	÷ _____
5.5	Average share price	$ _____

ballpark figure for financing costs. Mortgages are typically granted in the range of 70 to 80 percent of the total development cost. In past years, fixed-payment corporate mortgages for about 80 percent of the total development cost were common, and it was a simple operation to calculate the monthly mortgage payment using amortization tables (you can find such tables in the real estate finance books in the library). Today, the conventional fixed-payment mortgage is less common. Ask a local banker (maybe at the bank that holds your checking account) to disclose the approximate terms of a co-op mortgage. (Remember that co-op loans are treated as corporate loans and that they are likely to be given at a different rate from the home mortgage rate.) Calculate the approximate monthly debt service, that is, the monthly interest and principal payment on the loan (line 3.2).

Estimate monthly operating costs. Add a factor for inflation to the annual operating costs the owner has given you. Calculate one-twelfth of the resulting figure and enter it on line 3.3. If the owner will not provide this information, assume that operating costs exclusive of debt service will run roughly $175 per unit per month. (This is a 1982 rule of thumb for large cities. Ask property managers locally for rules that apply to your area.) Add monthly operating costs to monthly mortgage payment to obtain the total monthly operating costs (line 3.4). Divide the total monthly operating costs by the number of units. This is your "back of the envelope" estimate of the monthly carrying charge per member (line 3.6).

Consider that figure. Can you afford to pay it each month

instead of your current rent? If it is close to what you and other members can afford, continue pursuing your plans to purchase and rehabilitate the building.

Let's calculate sections 2 and 3 of the worksheet for our six-unit co-op example. Assume that the co-op can obtain a conventional 80 percent mortgage at 16.5 percent interest for 20 years.

2. TOTAL DEVELOPMENT COSTS
    2.1 Total construction costs $ 256,608
    2.2 Plus: Purchase price   +   70,000
    2.3 Total development costs $ 326,608

3. MONTHLY CARRYING CHARGES
    3.1 Maximum mortgage amount $ 261,286
    3.2 Monthly mortgage payment $ 3,683
    3.3 Plus: Monthly operating costs   +   1,050
    3.4 Total monthly operating costs $ 4,733
    3.5 Divided by: Number of units   ÷   6
    3.6 Monthly carrying charges per unit $ 789
    3.7 Percentage of member average income   34%

Line 3.7 assumes a married couple earning $28,000 annually. The monthly carrying charges represent 34 percent of their monthly income of $2,333, which may or may not be more than they will want to spend on housing. Before they reach any conclusions, they should figure the tax deductions available to them and then determine their net monthly carrying charges (section 4 of the worksheet).

If the co-op mortgage is new, interest costs in the first year will be about 95 percent of the mortgage payments. (If the co-op is assuming a previous owner's older mortgage, the interest portion of the payment will be much lower. In that case the owner or the lender should divide the mortgage payment into interest and principal.) On your own worksheet add property taxes to the annual interest charges and divide by the

Finding an Affordable Building / 97

number of units. The result is the average annual deductions allocated to each member (line 4.5).

Multiply annual deductions per unit by your personal tax bracket and divide by 12. This is approximately your monthly tax deduction. Subtract it from the monthly carrying charge for a net monthly carrying charge after taxes (line 4.10). Does it look more affordable now?

Let's continue the calculations for the married couple with combined taxable income of $28,000 and a 1982 tax rate of 29 percent.

4. **NET MONTHLY CARRYING CHARGES**

4.1	Annual interest costs (95% of $44,196)	$	41,986
4.2	Plus: Annual property taxes	+	8,000
4.3	Total co-op deductions	$	49,986
4.4	Divided by: Number of units	÷	6
4.5	Annual deductions per unit	$	8,331
4.6	Times: Individual tax bracket	×	.29
4.7	Annual tax savings per unit	$	2,416
4.8	Divided by: 12 months	÷	12
4.9	Monthly tax savings	$	201
4.10	Net monthly carrying charge ($789 − $201)	$	588
4.11	Percentage of member average income		25%

This couple will be paying about 25 percent of their income for housing after tax deductions are included, most likely an affordable housing cost.

There is one remaining issue involved in determining affordability: the cost of joining the co-op. The initial price of membership is based on the up-front capital and working capital needs of the co-op. The co-op corporation needs cash up front to meet expenses before the mortgage money is available and to create a positive cash flow. For the present calculations, assume two months' worth of operating costs are necessary.

For the six-unit co-op example, add the two capital amounts in section 5. The total is the amount of capital the co-op must raise through the sale of shares to members (line 5.3). Dividing this by the number of units results in the average share price (although share prices may vary according to individual unit sizes and amenities).

5. AVERAGE SHARE PRICE
    5.1 Nonmortgageable development costs $ 65,322
    5.2 Plus: Co-op working capital (2 × $4,733) + 9,466
    5.3 Total co-op capital requirements $ 74,788
    5.4 Divided by: Number of units   ÷   6
    5.5 Average share price $ 12,464

Calculate the share price for your co-op. If it is "just a bit too expensive," several things you can do to make the project slightly more affordable are presented in Chapter 7. Right now, the purpose of the affordability analysis is to determine if you are "in the ballpark." If monthly costs are $50 too high, or the share price is $1,000 or $2,000 too high, you may be able to bring the costs down. If you are off by $200 per month, maybe you should look elsewhere.

Purchasing the Property

The inspection and affordability analysis have provided your co-op group with the information it needs to decide whether to attempt to purchase the building. Now is the time to make a move toward the owner.

Before you do, however, meet with the entire co-op group. Discuss what you have found. Discuss the costs that members can expect to incur. Talk about group and personal financial limitations. Entertain suggestions on how to negotiate and come to agreement on a few parameters for the negotiation: initial offering price, conditions of purchase, maximum price, necessary concessions by the owner, and other matters that are important to the members.

The group should decide exactly how negotiations will

proceed. One or more people have already had contacts with the owner; these people should continue to make the contacts, although the member of the group who is best or most experienced in negotiations should become the lead negotiator. You might also consider asking the group's lawyer to conduct the negotiations.

NEGOTIATING THE PURCHASE

Negotiating strategy depends on the results of your inspection and affordability analysis. If the project appears to be affordable, then your strategy should be to try to negotiate with the owner to arrive at a lower price than the initial asking price. Bear in mind that most owners expect to compromise on the price. Make a reasonable offer. Offers should be made in writing, with all conditions of the sale listed. Legal advice is important: consider the amount of money that your group has at stake.

If the affordability analysis indicates that the project is too expensive, take a slightly more aggressive approach. Tell the owner of the problems you found in the inspection and the type of rehabilitation costs you expect to incur. Build the argument that you will spend so much in putting the building into acceptable condition that you must offer a much lower price than the asking price. Offer a price that the affordability analysis indicates you can comfortably afford. Still, be reasonable and leave room for the owner to respond with a counteroffer. Don't use a take-it-or-leave-it approach yet.

Ask the owner if there is any current financing on the buildings that you can assume. "Assuming a mortgage" means that the buyer takes over the responsibility for an existing mortgage rather than obtaining a new one. If the owner has held the building for several years, it is possible that the mortgage has very attractive financing terms and is assumable. Also ask if the owner is willing to finance any part of the sale price, such as through a "takeback" second mortgage. If you partially finance at below market rates, this will change what you can afford. Recalculate debt service and all subsequent figures on your affordability worksheet to reflect any special financing.

Remember the strategy "I'll have to talk with my partners." In negotiations, silent partners in the background can be an asset. The owner doesn't know what those other people are thinking. Some well-timed interruptions in the negotiations can unnerve the owner. Use this tactic wisely. Your co-op group members are not just straw people for a negotiating tactic, however. Your group has a right to know what is happening, and they may be able to suggest some additional points for negotiation. Talk with them frequently.

OPTIONS

If the negotiated price seems right, and you are seriously interested, you may wish to reserve your right to purchase the building for the period of time you need to conduct the affordability analysis. This right is purchased through an *option,* which enables you to purchase the building at the stated price during a specified time period, usually several months to a year. The price of the option is negotiable; generally, the longer the option, the more it will cost.

By the end of the option period, you should have determined whether the project is feasible for your group. If it does not appear to be affordable at the asking price, try to use this negative information to negotiate the owner's asking price down to a level that would work for your co-op. If negotiations fail, you may be able to sell the option to someone else; otherwise you lose the money.

If the negotiations appear to be moving toward a successful conclusion, the finance committee should start the financial work outlined in Chapter 7. They also should begin discussions with a lender (or more than one lender) about financing.

THE SALES CONTRACT

The next step is to negotiate a purchase-and-sale agreement, or sales contract. The agreement is a legal document

Finding an Affordable Building / 101

that sets all the terms of the sale in writing. It includes a full description of the property to be transferred, the sale price, the deadline for transfer to occur, and the conditions under which the agreement may be canceled.

The building committee may wish to continue to conduct the negotiations, although it is advisable to have a lawyer negotiate or at least review the contract for you. The sales contract will be secured by a down payment, so your dollars are now on the table.

Certain terms of the contract are critical to the buyer. They delineate the only circumstances under which the buyer may withdraw from the purchase and have the down payment returned. If the transaction fails for reasons other than stated in the conditions, the money may be lost. Certain common conditions in purchase-and-sale agreements state that the buyer is bound to purchase only if the following occur:

- The seller delivers the title to the property free and clear of any liens or other encumbrances, except those stated in the sales contract.
- The property satisfactorily passes both a physical inspection and a pest inspection, and the building conditions match those represented by the owner during negotiations.
- The buyer is able to obtain financing within a specified period of time, and/or the buyer is able to assume the current mortgage(s) if assumption is permitted.
- The seller delivers the property in an agreed-upon physical condition and occupancy status, that is, with or without current tenants.

These are the most common, but by no means the only, conditions. As buyer, you want to qualify your purchase by as many conditions as the seller will accept so that you may retrieve your down payment if things don't work out. Anticipate all problems that may prevent your co-op from buying, and negotiate the sales contract to protect your interests.

We would be remiss if we did not underscore the matter

of current residential tenants. Displacement is a big problem in building conversions to occupant ownership. If the building has tenants, your group has several options. Clearly, the preferred option is for the tenants to join your co-op. The Benning Heights Cooperative in Washington, D.C., was converted by tenants after the owner indicated he wanted to sell. Nearly three-quarters of the tenants in the 474-unit complex signed up to join the co-op; the remaining units are occupied by tenants who rent from the co-op.

Some states have protections for tenants against displacement or other hardship in co-op conversions. A New York state law, for example, requires 35 percent of the tenants to approve the conversion. However, as we noted above, some portion of the tenants may not want to join the co-op, and others may not be able to afford it. For these tenants, your group has a moral responsibility to address the relocation problems or rent increases that your conversion will impose.

In the states of Florida, New York, and California, you will have a legal responsibility to give a certain amount of notice or relocation benefits. The state of Florida requires that all tenants receive 180 days' notice of a co-op conversion; a tenant of six months or more must receive 270 days' notice. In Florida tenants can trade part of their notice period for relocation benefits. Counties with less than a 3 percent rental vacancy rate are empowered to extend notice provisions an additional 90 days. The tenants are also granted right of first refusal on their units.

THE FINAL DAYS

Between the time of the sales contract and that of the transfer of title, you must do several things. You should subject the building to a rigorous professional inspection to ensure that actual physical conditions match those represented by the owner and assumed by your group for the feasibility analysis. The focus of this inspection is on the structural conditions and the systems. You are looking for things that you hadn't already planned to repair or replace.

Ask your lawyer to conduct a title search of the property, which will determine if there are any liens, easements, or other encumbrances that are financial obligations of the owner or that would limit your use of the property. You may purchase title insurance from a private insurer; some lenders require it. This insures you (and the lender) against financial loss in case the title is not cleared.

During this time you also must secure a final commitment from your lender on the mortgage. Financing is discussed in Chapter 7. If immediate rehabilitation is intended, it may be in your group's best interest to secure rehabilitation financing at the same time as the mortgage. If you decide to do this, look ahead to Chapter 8 so that you can complete your rehabilitation plans prior to the loan.

THE CLOSING

The closing—actually the beginning—is the legal event that transfers title to the property. It's a day when the lawyers pass a series of papers relating to title transfer, final settlements, down payments, mortgages, and municipal filings. A good lawyer will explain thoroughly every document the co-op will sign prior to the closing. The co-op officers (whomever the board designates) sit by with pen in hand, signing documents in rapid-fire succession. Somewhere in the shuffle your co-op becomes the owner of the property.

Congratulations. Sit back and savor the moment. Have a party for the group members and let testimonials flow. Publicly thank every person who has contributed to the effort. Then enjoy a restful night's sleep; we'll talk about the next steps tomorrow.

7
HOW TO FINANCE YOUR CO-OP

IN THE PREVIOUS CHAPTER we left out one detail in the steps leading toward your acquiring a building: financing. It's a big enough topic that it deserves its own chapter, and it's a big enough task that the co-op group should assign a separate committee to do the "numbers crunching" that is involved. Buy the committee a financial analyst's calculator; it's one of the best investments you will make.

This chapter is written primarily for co-ops that must borrow money. Following from the work begun by your group in the previous chapter, we detail the final stages of affordability analysis, suggest ways you can make the project more affordable, and provide some advice your group can take to the bank. Even if your co-op does not need to borrow—and we hope you'll tell us how you've avoided it—or has already arranged financing, we suggest that your finance committee and board of directors give some attention to our analysis of the components of a co-op operating budget.

Affordability Analysis Revisited

In Chapter 6 we introduced affordability analysis as a way of determining whether the co-op group can afford to turn a particular building into a co-op. Your group will go through the same set of procedures several times before it will purchase a building, and each time you will add a little more precision to the numbers until the estimates become acceptable evidence for prospective members and lenders.

The first time you did an affordability analysis, your numbers were gross estimates of construction costs and operating costs. Now it is time to add precision to your other numbers, particularly the operating costs.

If your group is under a time deadline, detailed estimates of the operating costs can be made by the co-op's finance committee while the building committee works on the acquisition and construction costs. The finance committee should also assume responsibility for putting all the numbers together in the end.

Many of us have tried—and probably failed—to put ourselves on a budget. To attempt it, we first figured our monthly living expenses, such as rent, utilities, insurance, and food. Then we added allowances for irregular expenditures such as clothing, gifts, and vacations. Subtracting these from our monthly income, we calculated the amount we could put aside as savings. A co-op must go through the same exercise, but in a more detailed fashion and probably with a few extra zeros behind the numbers contained in personal budgets.

If your co-op plans to have professional management, you may wish to select the manager quickly, so that he or she can assist you in estimating the budget. Remember, however, that the members, not the manager, dictate the budget. The limit of the manager's input is to indicate what the co-op can buy for the budget it considers. In particular, the manager should caution the members against unrealistically low estimates for budget items.

ESTIMATING THE CO-OP OPERATING BUDGET

For the "back of the envelope" affordability analysis, you might use a gross operating expense figure based on the number of rooms, the number of units, or the percentage of debt service. Before you carry your proposal to a lender, you must go into significant detail about your budget, distributing realistic portions of it among the major expense categories. For this level of detail, each line item should be separately estimated based on the experiences of similar buildings. Consequently, you are no longer working on an envelope; it's more like an accounting pad.

The following is an example of a typical annual operating budget for a 22-unit co-op building.

Revenue	
Member carrying charges	$87,767
Minus: Allowance for vacancies	2,000
Plus: Parking	2,200
Plus: Interest	400
Total revenue	$88,367
Expenses	
Debt service	$40,991
Taxes	16,584
Insurance	8,029
Utilities	
Heating	0
Domestic hot water	3,500
Electricity	3,750
Water and sewer	2,000
Administrative costs	200
Management fee	4,800
Maintenance and repair	
Supplies	500
Salaries	1,500
Services	1,500
Security	0
Replacement reserve	4,500
Operating reserve	513
Total operating expenses	$88,367

To do your own budget, first estimate the necessary expenses and then calculate the revenue your co-op needs in order to carry those expenses. Below we suggest how to estimate expenses and determine revenue needs. If your estimates of revenue run too high, we include several suggestions on how to reduce costs.

ESTIMATING OPERATING EXPENSES

<u>Debt service.</u> Some or most of the money your co-op needs to purchase, construct, and/or rehabilitate your building will be borrowed. Most loans cover 70 or 80 percent of the total development costs, although some federally insured co-ops can be financed up to 100 percent. The money may be borrowed from a private lender or a public agency, or it may come from a private loan with public insurance. These options are discussed later in the chapter.

The money that you borrow will be paid back to the lender monthly. The monthly payment—the debt service—is usually the single largest item in your co-op operating budget. The amount of debt service depends on the principal borrowed, the loan term, and the interest rate. For most mortgages, the debt service is fixed, that is, it stays the same for every month of the loan term. However, some other types of mortgages have payments that change regularly.

You have estimated your co-op's monthly debt service as part of the total development cost calculations in Chapter 6. Use this estimated figure in calculating your operating budget until you can obtain a more exact figure from your lender. Remember to list monthly debt service amounts for each mortgage if you are going to carry more than one.

<u>Real estate taxes.</u> Your co-op will pay real estate taxes just as any other property owner does. The amount of taxes you will pay is based on two pieces of information: the local property tax rate (usually per thousand dollars of assessed value) and the assessed value of the property. Each local jurisdiction has a different tax rate and a different way of assessing the value of property. It is best to consult with the local tax assessor to determine your real estate taxes.

For purposes of budget estimates, it may be sufficient to use the current tax bill of the property you are considering. If you don't want to ask the owner, you can look it up in the tax rolls maintained by the assessing department in your town. While you are looking up the tax bill, find out when the property was last assessed and when it is scheduled for another assessment. You don't want to base your financial planning on a tax bill that is artificially low.

Some local governments have a policy of reassessing properties whenever they are sold, and they base their assessment on the sale price. Find out if this is the policy in your community. If it is, calculate a new assessment based on your purchase price. Ask the tax assessor to help you calculate the new tax bill. Tell the assessor that you are considering purchasing a property for a certain amount of money and that you need to estimate the taxes before you decide whether to buy.

You may be reluctant to ask the tax people anything for fear of drawing attention to your property. But bear in mind that all information about taxes is public information. You can request it without identifying the property. Private developers conduct this kind of research all the time and manage to protect the confidentiality of their development plans; so can you.

All property owners believe that their tax bill is too high. To deal with complaints, most communities have tax abatement policies, which allow individual property owners to request and receive a reduction in their annual tax bill. Find out what the abatement policy is in your community and determine if your co-op might qualify under any of the conditions.

<u>Insurance.</u> There are two kinds of insurance you must carry for the property: fire insurance (also known as hazard insurance) and public liability insurance. They are usually covered with separate insurance policies.

Fire or hazard insurance protects the co-op against losses

How to Finance Your Co-op / 109

if the property is damaged by fire, storms, vandalism, or other hazards. The amount of coverage is usually determined by your insurance company, based on its calculation of the value of the property and the amount of claims for property loss in the event everything is destroyed. Private insurers have been reluctant to insure in certain central-city neighborhoods, so the federal government requires every state to establish a Fair Access to Insurance Rates (FAIR) Plan. The FAIR Plan rates are usually higher than private insurance because the pool of insureds covers properties in high-risk areas; consider it insurance of last resort. If the first agent you approach cannot find a private insurer, ask another agent to search for you. Also ask the property owners near your building who their insurers are.

Public liability insurance protects you in case someone is injured on your property. Insurance agents can provide you with cost estimates and can recommend how much coverage you should have.

The insurance business is highly competitive, and you can find bargain insurance rates if you are willing to do some shopping. Your job is to find a good insurance agent; the agent does the shopping for you. Some agents sell insurance only for certain insurance companies, while others are independent. The one who can get you the best deal is usually the one who shops the most. If you do not have an agent already, you might want to ask more than one agent for estimates.

An insurance company that is financially unsound or is slow to pay out claims is not desirable. Your agent should examine the financial soundness of the company, or you can do it by checking the report on the company in *Best's Insurance Reports* (in the business reference section of your local library). Also ask how quickly and efficiently the company handles claims. Your agent should be able to tell you of other local customers who have been serviced by a particular company.

In some states, companies located within the state are

required to add sales or excise tax, while companies located outside the state (but still licensed to sell insurance within the state) are not required to do so. This is a potential source of savings for your co-op, but carefully investigate how out-of-state companies handle claims. They should have a local insurance adjuster to whom they can assign the claim on the same day the claim is reported.

Finally, we must offer a plug for cooperative insurance companies. There are many mutual and fraternal insurance companies that are themselves co-ops. Your board may wish to set a principle of doing business with other co-ops. We maintain that generally it is good business practice.

<u>Utilities</u>. Rising energy costs have bankrupted many landlords of older buildings and forced them to sell. When you are considering the purchase of an existing building, carefully examine utility costs. There are four typical utility costs for a co-op: heating, domestic hot water, electricity, and water and sewer. If you are in the Northeast or Midwest, heating costs are the most important utility cost. In the South and Southwest, electricity costs for cooling may be the highest. In other areas, the domestic hot water costs may be the greatest single expense for utilities.

Some building systems are designed so that each unit is metered separately. If this is the case in your building, utility costs may not be an important part of the co-op budget, but they will be very important to the budgets of individual members.

To estimate the utility budget, begin with the current utility costs as represented by the present owner. Then adjust the figure upward for expected increases in fuel costs over the coming years. Annual increases at about the rate of inflation can be used. Also adjust your estimates downward to account for utilities savings related to any weatherproofing or systems replacement you plan to include in your rehabilitation. (See the notes on energy conservation in Chapter 8.)

How to Finance Your Co-op / 111

<u>Administrative costs.</u> This is actually a catchall category for a variety of necessary management expenses. For a typical co-op building, administrative costs include office and bookkeeping supplies, accounting services, legal services, mailing costs, and advertising. For most small co-ops, administrative costs (other than legal and accounting fees) amount to only a few hundred dollars annually. Accounting fees typically are for an annual audit and tax filings, which for a small co-op will run to only a few hundred dollars.

Legal fees, on the other hand, are difficult to estimate. Some co-ops don't have to consult their lawyer during an average year except for a few minor corporate matters. Other co-ops face thousands of dollars of legal expenses from membership sales, evictions of tenants, disputes with suppliers and neighbors, and other aggravating incidents. You can expect first-year legal costs to be high because of turnover of occupancy. The legal costs associated with the property purchase, financing, and initial membership sales are usually capitalized (that is, included in the total development costs and paid from the loan money rather than the operating budget). Any lingering legal costs will be carried in the operating budget.

<u>Management fees.</u> If you plan to hire professional management, carry a management fee expense item of 2 to 6 percent of the total co-op revenue. This is the range of standard industry fees charged by professional management firms to cover their costs of collections, bookkeeping, communications with co-op members, and other administrative matters. It also includes their profit for services. (See Chapter 9.)

<u>Supplies.</u> Supplies refer to materials used to maintain the co-op property, including such items as light bulbs, keys and locks, fertilizer, cleaning aids, and trash bags. Plan that your first-year supplies budget will be double your expected annual supplies budget, since you will be creating from scratch a supplies inventory.

Maintenance and repairs. If you have any regular custodial staff, the salary costs should be carried in the operating budget as a line item separate from other maintenance and repair costs. The co-op has legal obligations to pay certain benefits for personnel, including Social Security contributions, unemployment insurance, and workers' compensation insurance. If you are going to have salaried employees, talk with your accountant about these obligations and include the fringe expenses in your line item for salaries. Failure to meet these obligations can result in stiff penalties from the government.

Plumbing, electrical, and other kinds of repairs often require the skills of professionals. Carry a budget line item for maintenance and repair services not provided by your staff. If your own members will do the repairs, at least include some money for purchasing materials.

Security. It may be necessary to budget some money for security, depending on where your co-op is located. Some co-ops find it necessary, or at least desirable for peace of mind, to have full-time or part-time security services. Others find it helpful to have a line item for locks, bars, jimmy-proof doors, and other security improvements. Don't throw only money at a security problem. Burglars can break into any apartment, if they have time and privacy. A building watch or neighborhood watch may be part of your solution.

Replacement reserves. All parts of your building are going to deteriorate or break down eventually. Replacement can be very expensive, and you cannot always borrow more money to cover those costs. You must plan ahead for these expenses and set aside some money every year to cover unexpected or expected replacement costs. Even if your building is new, start setting aside some money. The replacement reserve should be calculated at 2 to 6 percent of the co-op's annual operating budget.

Operating reserve. Co-ops need to set aside funds for emergency expenditures that are not related to replacement. The higher fuel bills of a very cold winter are an example. Emergency needs are paid from an operating reserve fund, usually 1 to 3 percent of the operating budget.

ESTIMATING REVENUE NEEDS

You now have a detailed estimate of what the co-op is going to spend both for debt service and for operating costs. You have to raise at least that much money through your various sources of revenue: member carrying charges, parking fees, charges for laundry facilities, rental fees for space in the building other than the residential unit, and interest on savings and checking accounts. Revenues must be divided into those that are collected from members for housing and those that are collected from members and nonmembers for nonhousing services. The reason for this division is that the IRS requires that the co-op collect at least 80 percent of its income from members for housing and housing-related services.

First, estimate the revenue from the other sources (laundry, parking, and interest), and subtract this from the total revenue target. The remaining revenue must be raised through member carrying charges. Allow for a 3 to 5 percent vacancy rate, or more if you do not expect to achieve full occupancy early in the first operating year. (Older, more stable co-ops do not have vacancies of this magnitude, but new co-ops have to establish themselves before this real estate rule of thumb can be adjusted.) Divide the total revenue figure by the number of units, or by the financial interest of each unit, to determine the monthly carrying charges. Can the group members afford this?

Also estimate the share price for your co-op. If it is "just a bit too expensive," we can offer several ideas you might try to make the co-op slightly more affordable.

Making the Square Peg Fit

It certainly won't surprise us—and we hope it won't discourage you—if in your first affordability analysis you reach a bottom-line price that is too expensive. Don't give up. If you drive some distance to visit a friend, you don't walk away from the door after one knock goes unanswered. You knock several times and then maybe look in the windows or try another door. You have come too far to give in so easily.

If you have reached this stage in planning your project, you have already invested quite a bit of time and hope. Don't let the numbers discourage you. Most of the housing development projects around you probably appeared to be financially impossible in the first analysis. The numbers are based on quite a few assumptions, so there are likely to be errors and room for adjustment. But remember that you can't change your numbers without good reason.

MAKE MORE MONEY

If carrying charges are too high and you want to reduce them, you may want to explore other ways of making money. The IRS allows co-ops to raise up to 20 percent of their income from sources other than member charges. Some other income sources may include the following:

- *Leasing commercial space.* Many multifamily buildings have first-floor commercial space or are zoned for commercial use. Check the rents on commercial spaces in the neighborhood around your building. You may be able to raise the rents for current commercial tenants or find new tenants. A local store may need nearby storage space and may be willing to lease your underutilized basement.
- *Leasing parking spaces.* Most buildings have some parking, and co-ops in congested neighborhoods can raise money by renting these spots. Co-ops usually make the parking spots available to members first and then to outsiders at a higher rate.

- *Charging for other member services.* Some co-ops provide storage space for rent; others provide a laundry room in the building to raise some revenue. Still others provide domestic cleaning services and cooperative buying clubs for food and household supplies. Cooperative buying reinforces the notion of working together to control costs of living.

Remember the 20 percent IRS rule. If you violate this rule, your members may lose their right to deduct mortgage interest and property taxes from their federal income tax—a costly penalty.

CUT REHABILITATION COSTS

If you are planning to buy and rehabilitate a building all in one fell swoop, read Chapter 8 to plan the rehabilitation part of your project. If you are anything like us, your eyes are larger than your pocketbook. You may be inclined to plan more rehabilitation than you can afford. If so, there are many things you might do to reduce your rehabilitation costs. Go back to your first estimates and review your numbers with the following notes in mind.

Reduce the scope of the rehabilitation. With the help of the building committee, reexamine the scope of the rehabilitation you have planned. How much of it is necessary and how much can you call optional at this time? Can you go without certain improvements that should be considered luxuries? Are there some items that could be repaired rather than replaced? Can other improvements be put off a few years to a time when they may be more affordable? Be careful, however, to consider the effects on your budget of deferring rehabilitation. Keeping the old boiler probably means higher fuel costs, for example. If necessary, ask the building committee to go back and try to reduce rehabilitation costs by a certain amount.

Be your own general contractor. Typically, a general contractor is hired to complete a construction job. The contractor is responsible for hiring and supervising all laborers and subcontractors necessary to do the work. In return for these services, the general contractor includes in the construction price a fee of 10 to 20 percent on top of all construction costs. If your construction job is relatively small, consider acting as general contractor yourself to reduce your direct costs by approximately 10 percent.

Understand, however, that construction contracting is a difficult business with a high failure rate. The general contractor's role is demanding and time-consuming. If your building requires substantial rehab, you must hire and coordinate a large number of subcontractors. It is a role the co-op should not assume if no one in the group has ever been involved in construction before.

If you do act as general contractor, hire a professional to do your planning, scheduling, hiring, supervising, and firing. This person, called your construction manager, is your employee and will act in your best interest to complete the job on time and within budget.

Reduce the costs of materials. This is a difficult area in which to reduce costs. You can cut some corners off the budget by recycling materials from your building, but note that any savings on recycled materials may be offset by the time it takes to salvage them. If members are doing demolition themselves, the extra labor does not require a cash outlay.

Reduce labor costs. It may be possible to reduce the labor costs of rehabilitation by substituting sweat equity—your own labor—for paid labor.

REDUCE YOUR OPERATING COSTS

Try energy conservation. Certain rehabilitation expenditures can conserve energy and reduce utility costs. Inexpensive weatherproofing, insulation, and storm windows can reduce annual fuel bills enough so that in just a few years you will have saved as much in fuel costs as you spent for the improvements. All future savings are then a bonus.

Choose different sources of financing. As we write this book, financing costs for real estate are hovering at all-time highs, and new construction has hit a thirty-year low. Every developer is searching for cheap sources of money and innovative ways of structuring the financing to keep costs down. We know of no magic words that will open the door to inexpensive financing for your co-op; it's the biggest challenge you have to making your co-op work. Review the advice offered below and conduct a thorough investigation into local sources of money that may reduce your financing costs.

Try self-management. Look back at your operating budget. You may have included a fee of 2 to 6 percent for a management agent for the services of maintaining the building, collecting the revenue, paying the bills, and keeping proper records. Can co-op members do these things themselves? If your co-op is fairly small, the simple financial management system we present in Chapter 10 may be handled by a member or committee of members. One word of caution: the lender may insist on professional management to ensure proper financial controls. Expect the lender to at least question you on that matter.

Try self-maintenance. In addition to the management fee, you are carrying a budget item for the management agent's employees for general cleaning, maintenance, and repairs. Can't your members do some of these things and save your co-op a little money? See Chapter 9.

Apply for a tax abatement. Many local jurisdictions have policies for granting reductions in tax bills to owners who can establish that their taxes are excessive. Visit your local tax assessor and compare your tax bill with those of buildings similar to yours. Some local governments also grant abatements to housing that is reserved for low- and moderate-income people. A limited-equity co-op may qualify for an abatement. Some cities are willing to grant abatements in the form of a promise not to raise the assessed value of your property when you rehabilitate it. In New York state, this program is called J-51. A similar tax agreement in Massachusetts is called 121A. Talk with your lawyer about applying for an abatement.

<u>Reduce your reserves.</u> It is common to try to cut operating costs by reducing or eliminating regular contributions to reserve accounts. In a word: *don't*. If money is so tight that you cannot afford operating reserves and replacement reserves, then you will certainly not be able to afford those unpredictable and extraordinary expenses that are bound to happen a few years down the road. Do not put effort into a co-op that can be pushed into default by one failed boiler, one leaking roof, or a similar emergency.

TRY A DIFFERENT TYPE OF CO-OP

If you have tried all these ways of reducing costs and still cannot afford the costs, try one of the following options.

<u>The limited partnership.</u> The limited partnership may be a useful legal tool for low- and moderate-income co-ops to purchase properties yet keep membership prices low. The ownership entity has two types of partners: general partners (the co-op members) who both own and manage the housing, and limited partners (private investors) who own but do not control the operations of the housing. The limited partners buy a share of the project from the general partners to gain the tax shelter generated by depreciation of the building. The tax benefits are of greater value to investors—who are usually in the highest tax bracket—than to members, and the cash generated from the limited partners can be used to reduce member subscription prices. The co-op retains the responsibility for all day-to-day management and decision making.

How to Finance Your Co-op / 119

The leasing co-op. It may be possible for your co-op group to negotiate with the owner a lease arrangement with an option to purchase. Leasing the building from the owner rather than buying it enables the co-op to occupy the building while the members attempt to find financing that makes the purchase affordable.

The co-op members may also find that leasing the building is less expensive than buying in the short run. Because the co-op corporation does not have to raise money for the down payment on a purchase, member subscription prices can be substantially lower than if the building were purchased. Carrying charges also may drop. If the owner is carrying an old mortgage with favorable financing terms and he or she retains the tax benefits of ownership, then the lease costs should be lower than new mortgage financing. By leasing the co-op also avoids property tax reassessment. These savings can give the co-op members their start on setting aside money for future purchase.

To the members and most of the outside world, the leasing co-op appears and operates as an ownership co-op. The owner of the property cannot interfere in the affairs of the co-op or its day-to-day operations. Like an ownership co-op, the members and their elected board of directors make all the decisions, and members occupy their units under a long-term proprietary lease.

Remember that tax deductions are not available to co-op members if the co-op building is leased. Because of this, the leasing co-op arrangement is most attractive to low- and moderate-income people as a long-term housing solution, but it is only an interim arrangement for co-ops with higher-income members.

A little creativity and a lot of nerve may be necessary to make your co-op work financially. Although this solution may not be for those who prefer to avoid taking risks, one co-op bought *more* property than the members could afford and resold pieces for net profits that are used to subsidize the co-op. The 1210 Massachusetts Avenue Cooperative in Washington, D.C., was started in 1981 by nine families who wanted to buy their building before it was sold to a developer but who in the process bought three buildings. The owner wanted to sell all three buildings—two of which were vacant—and insisted that the co-op group buy all or none. The tenants scrambled and found a buyer for one of the three buildings, which enabled them to buy just two.

The co-op obtained a one-year loan from the National Consumer Cooperative Bank, a loan that was intended to give the co-op time to find permanent financing. Since the purchase, the co-op members have been trying to keep the wolf from the door. They have been working on ways to obtain long-term financing for their co-op without raising their monthly costs. One strategy is to sell the other vacant building. The members hope that rising property values will translate into a large profit on the resale, reducing the amount they must refinance. A second strategy is to refinance the occupied building for a much larger amount—also taking advantage of the rising values—and use the extra borrowed funds to set up a fund to help pay their higher mortgage costs, keeping the monthly payments close to their current levels.

Putting Together a Loan Application Package

The finance committee really has to sharpen its pencils and get down to work when the time comes to apply for a loan. The numbers are no longer just a financial exercise; they are now the foundation of a loan proposal to one or more lenders. With financing, your co-op proceeds; without it, the co-op will never be. The finance committee needs the support of the entire co-op group in this effort, but the committee members must take primary responsibility for preparing a loan proposal that is complete and attractive. There can be no addition errors and no typos.

There is no single preferred approach or method of organizing the information in a loan application. Each lender

How to Finance Your Co-op / 121

wants to see things in a slightly different format or prefers an additional piece of information that other lenders do not request. Although we provide some general information on loan application packages, we recommend that you contact several lenders before you try to assemble your application. The lenders, if they are interested in receiving a proposal, will inform you of the kinds of information to include.

Take your banker to lunch. We say this to urge the finance committee members or co-op officers to begin talking to lenders early in the process. Anonymity is no asset in applying for a loan; quite the contrary, it is a liability. You are asking a lender to finance a new business for you, so he or she needs to know you. Convince the lender of your intentions, your diligence, your sincerity, and your desire to establish a business on sound financial principles. More important at this early stage, try to educate the lender about co-ops.

WHAT'S IN THE PROPOSAL?

Borrowing money is not just a sales job. There must be a solid business plan as the foundation of the proposal. A business plan includes accurate projections of income and expenses over the first several years of the business, taking into account the financial impacts of the proposed loan. These financial statements can be generated as part of your budgeting work for the affordability analysis.

The business plan also includes a detailed explanation of the co-op's management. Co-op management has two components: physical management of the building and property, which are the assets that secure the loan; and fiscal management, which includes a sound policy of revenue collections, accounts management, and fiscal overview. We discuss the management options in Chapter 9. Remember that the lender's paramount concern is to maintain the value of the property, since the property is the security for the loan.

An important financial aspect in the new co-op's business plan is the amount of working capital. In common business usage, working capital is the net amount of money readily available to your co-op, taking into account all current bills. Working capital is important to the newly created co-op because bills must be paid before the co-op begins to collect revenues. In Chapter 6, we suggested that the amount of working capital should be equal to at least two months' expenses.

The new co-op also needs to demonstrate to the lender that it has a sound marketing strategy for the sale of co-op memberships. Co-op carrying charges are calculated assuming full occupancy, with a small allowance (usually 3 to 5 percent) for vacancies. In the first year, slow sales can put the co-op in desperate financial straits.

SOURCES OF FINANCING

It seems as though we hear of a new financing scheme nearly every day. Recession and high interest rates have dried up housing funds and, while it may be hard to predict the longer-run impacts of the current financial market problems, we see that new co-ops will have to become a little more creative in finding financing.

The standard 30-year, fixed-payment mortgage is unlikely to be available to co-ops, and bank loans will have shorter terms and interest rates that float with market conditions. The co-op may still have a bank loan as the primary mortgage, but it may have additional loans from other sources. Because of the complexities of today's financing, we cannot tell you what financing is available or what financing is best for your co-op. What we can do is help you to start your search.

Banks are an obvious place to start, but before you go walking into any bank, we suggest a little research. Find out which lender has provided financing for the current owner. Find out which lenders have provided financing to other co-ops in your area. Check with friends, relatives, and friends of friends who may live in co-ops. If you are in a rural area, find out which lenders finance local farmer cooperatives. Find out which banks have lent to the nonprofit development corporations in your community. Lenders with a history of lending to these types of ventures are more likely to be receptive to your co-op proposal.

Then take a banker to lunch. We said it before, but it is worth repeating. A luncheon or other informal meeting is a good way to get to know the lender and to introduce the co-op idea to him or her. Do not expect the banker to know everything about co-ops. Take along this book, and let the banker borrow it.

While some of your members explore the financing question with private lenders, other members can start researching public sources. The National Consumer Cooperative Bank (NCCB) has been set up expressly to lend to co-ops. There are ten regional offices of the bank (check Appendix 1 for the one closest to you). The NCCB is limited by Congress to lending only 35 percent of its funds to housing co-ops. It has already filled that quota, but recently the Federal Home Loan Mortgage Corporation ("Freddie Mac") has agreed to buy co-op loans from the NCCB and other sources under strict underwriting guidelines. This may help the NCCB and other banks to become active co-op housing lenders again.

HUD has also promoted co-ops through a variety of programs. One of the most important programs in the past has been HUD's Section 234 insurance program, although co-op loans from private lenders can be insured under almost any FHA insurance program. Authorizations for most housing programs have been curtailed in recent years, but all the insurance programs appear to have carryover funds to continue insuring co-op loans for several years. Contact the chief of the Multifamily Housing Program Branch of the HUD field office in your state (your local housing agency can provide the address) about insurance program underwriting standards and the application process. You should also find a banker willing to process the insured loan.

State and local governments also have a variety of housing programs, some of which may be able to assist your co-op members. We suggest that you call your local housing agency and that you contact the state housing finance agency.

A word of advice: bureaucracies exist at all levels of government, so find a friend at one level who can help you make contacts with all the others.

Advice You Can Take to the Bank

Many people are intimidated by lenders and are reluctant to approach them. This is a mistaken attitude and could jeopardize your ability to obtain financing. A good lender can be one of your co-op's most valuable advisers as well as your source of financing. The demands that a lender places upon you for information are only part of the role that the lender must play as a potential investor in your co-op project.

Your co-op is a business. You are approaching the lender for a loan to operate your new business, and you will pay back that loan over an extended period of time out of the income received from your activities. Although the lender will conduct his or her own feasibility analysis of your project, it is your responsibility to convince the lender that your co-op will be carefully managed and financially strong.

The Community Reinvestment Act (CRA) of 1977 encourages lenders to be responsive to the credit needs of their community. Federally regulated lenders (commercial banks, savings and loan institutions, and other federally chartered or insured lenders) must be able to demonstrate that they are lending within their own immediate community if they want federal approval of their requests for mergers or changes in bank branches. With the recent increase in bank mergers, your co-op group may have an opportunity to use the leverage provided by the CRA. Ask any lender you approach to provide its CRA statement.

Your co-op has to decide how to approach the lender. The financial committee may know the numbers best, yet it is important that the officers of the co-op get to know the lender since they will be binding the co-op to a mortgage.

Also, it is important that your representatives have a little bit of the salesperson in them—that they be able to maintain composure under questioning and articulate the co-op's positive aspects while sitting at the loan officer's desk. One approach is to send the president and the finance committee chairperson. As we noted earlier, only one person should take the lead as spokesperson.

WHAT THE LENDER LOOKS FOR

Lending is not an exact science; neither is it a mystical art. Lenders recognize that each loan request is unique, so they apply broad financial evaluation criteria that give them some flexibility in making the lending decision. Each lender invests in a number of different opportunities, only some of which are loans for housing. The total package of loans and investments is called the lender's portfolio.

The lender tries to maximize profits by seeking high-return lending opportunities and spreading investments around to a variety of opportunities so that no crash of a single market or type of investment can seriously damage the portfolio. It's called diversification. The lender's willingness to lend may be based in part on the current condition of the institution's portfolio, whether too much is invested in long-term loans, whether too much is invested in housing or in your neighborhood. These are concerns of the lender that do not relate to your application but that nonetheless may cause your loan to be approved or disapproved.

Aside from the lender's portfolio needs there are several things about your business proposal that will affect a lender's decision. If you are aware of some of the lender's interests, you will be able to highlight the advantages and to respond to weaknesses the lender will detect in your proposal.

The lender looks at the soundness of the business plan and then at you—at your willingness and ability to pay the costs. Because the borrowing entity is a new corporation without a prior history of borrowing and repaying money, the lender must look at the officers and members of the corporation. The lender usually wants to be assured that individual members have a sufficient amount of money invested in the co-op so they will not be tempted to walk away in default.

These two components—your co-op's business plan and your members—figure into the lender's calculation of the risks of your project. Lenders must minimize the risk of default. As in any business, risk is highest in the first two years of a co-op. To counter these risks, banks may require security that is evidence of less risk or that reduces the likelihood that members of the co-op will be willing to default. The requirements of the lender may be that the co-op be near full occupancy. The lender may be willing to give a loan for 70 percent of the total cost rather than the usual 80 percent, thus raising the amount of money the individual members will contribute and reducing their likelihood of default. Or the lender may want to see working capital sufficient to cover several months of mortgage payments. Or the lender may want all these things.

If the lender decides to provide a loan, get the exact terms of the loan and rerun your affordability analysis with the exact figures for debt service. If it is affordable, congratulations. Go back to Chapter 6 and complete the acquisition of the building. Your co-op is about to own a new home.

8
REHABILITATION

EARLY ONE MORNING YOU are awakened by a drip... drip... drip. You stumble to the bathroom sink and turn the faucet tighter. The drip stops, but the sound does not. You head for the kitchen sink, only to discover that the drip is coming from the roof. You tiptoe through a puddle of water and reach for the phone to call the landlord, but realize that you are the owner. As you slump by the kitchen table and gaze at your reflection in the puddle, you recall discussions you and your neighbors had about whether or not to replace the roof when you purchased the building.

Buildings age more rapidly than humans, but they can be rebuilt to nearly new condition. The average residential building lasts about thirty years before it needs to be substantially rehabilitated, and there are all kinds of things that need to be replaced in between—roofs, heating systems, hot-water heaters, plumbing, electrical systems, bathroom tiles and fixtures, ceilings, floors, windows, and doors. Repair problems always seem to come at the worst time—but is there a good time?

Those unexpected outlays of precious dollars can really hurt. As we noted in Chapter 7, the co-op should build a replacement reserve for such emergencies, but the funds can be exhausted by several repairs in succession. The only other options for repair funds are special assessments or loans. Either way, the members end up digging deeper into their pockets to come up with additional money for the co-op.

The co-op faces some critical decisions—at the time it purchases an existing building, and at several times in future years—about whether to rehabilitate the building and its systems or to wait and take chances that major repairs or replacement will not be needed for many years. The decision is not simply one of the co-op members' willingness to take financial risks. Other things such as the co-op's ability to borrow more money, the building's appearance, the members' desire for higher living standards, member health and safety, and future peace of mind affect the co-op decision.

In this chapter, we address the issues surrounding the decision to rehabilitate. Because every co-op sooner or later will face a major rehabilitation job, we also provide suggestions about how to plan for the rehabilitation, how to hire and supervise architects and contractors, and even how to take advantage of members' labor to reduce rehabilitation costs.

Some co-ops do substantial rehabilitation immediately upon purchase and prior to occupancy. They do so because rehabilitation is essential for occupancy, and they can afford it or they are borrowing additional funds for rehabilitation as part of their purchase mortgage. Other co-ops address rehabilitation after several years of occupancy, when members' incomes have increased, a replacement reserve has been generated, and rehabilitation is needed. The contents of this chapter apply to either case. A permanent building committee should be charged with regularly assessing building conditions and making recommendations for rehabilitation, replacement, and repairs.

To Repair or Replace

The decision to repair or replace is really the critical issue for the co-op facing rehabilitation. While a co-op typically will be making the decision to rehabilitate on the basis of many building conditions, the analysis is the same for one repair item or several.

Consider this example. A co-op has just been created, and

it has purchased an existing twelve-unit building. Among other repair needs, the boiler for the central heating system in the building is very old. The co-op's options are to

1. Pay $2,000 now for a thorough cleaning and repair (including replacement of the circulating pump); incur repair bills of approximately $1,000 per year; and replace the boiler within five years at a cost of $15,000.
2. Replace the boiler and pump now at a cost of $13,000 and buy a maintenance contract for the new system for $600 per year.

How does the co-op make a decision?

The repair option defers the bulk of the expenditures into the fifth year. Throughout those five years the co-op will lay out $21,000 ($2,000 + four years' repairs at $1,000 + $15,000). The replacement alternative creates costs of only $15,400 over the five years ($13,000 + four years' maintenance at $600). Depending on how the co-op factored in inflation—that is, figured that it would be paying for a new boiler five years from now with cheaper dollars—there may be less difference in cost between the two options.

But there are several factors we haven't yet figured into the calculations:

- The financial risks associated with waiting to replace the boiler, including possible higher repair costs and necessary early replacement.
- The health and safety risks of an old boiler, such as failure during the winter.
- The additional utility costs of an inefficient boiler.
- The additional member charges to build a replacement reserve for future replacement of the boiler.
- The possibility of financing the boiler replacement now as part of the purchase mortgage or a second mortgage for rehabilitation.

It's hard to quantify the first two items, but they are real concerns. We may sound like disciples of Murphy's law. We're not, but everything has a certain probability of happening, and co-op members must recognize that costs may be greater than they had expected somewhere down the road.

We can look at some numbers related to the last three items: utility costs, replacement reserves, and financing costs. Assume that annual heating bills total $4,000 with the old system. The new boiler because of higher efficiency will require only 85 percent of the fuel, or $3,400 per year. That adds a $600 per year "cost" to the decision of keeping the current boiler, $3,000 dollars over the five years (or more if you assume rising fuel prices).

The replacement reserve must be expanded to accommodate the $15,000 expense at the end of five years. Assuming a reserve savings account of 5.5 percent interest, the co-op must set aside $218 per month, or $2,616 annually, to accumulate the needed capital.

By tying the boiler replacement into general rehabilitation financing, costs are spread over several years and the co-op avoids the big one-time expense. Assuming a 16.5 percent, 12-year rehabilitation loan, the new boiler expense of $13,000 is replaced by monthly payments of $205, or $2,460 annually.

Let's take a look at how this affects the co-op boiler alternatives. Replacement means annual loan payments of $2,460 and a maintenance contract of $600, or $3,060 per year. The repair-and-wait scenario presents the co-op with annual costs of $5,216 in the first year and $4,216 in the following four years ($2,000 in repairs now, $1,000 in subsequent years for repairs, $600 per year for extra fuel, and $2,616 per year for additional replacement reserves.).

Given these facts, the costs clearly point to replacement now. It is the "pay now or pay more later" decision. Your co-op may decide that it cannot afford to pay for replacement now, but we ask: If you cannot afford something now, can you afford it a few years from now?

In Washington, D.C., the Benning Heights Cooperative has tried to protect long-term elderly and lower-income tenants, but at some expense to their rehabilitation plans. The co-op members had made a commitment early in the conversion to try to minimize rent increases and to avoid displacement. Rents were very reasonable—$202 per month for a two-bedroom unit—and the co-op wanted to comply with rent control laws in the district.

Although conversion plans—including rehabilitation—began in 1980, co-op ownership was not finalized until May 1982. Interest rates were near their peak, and the co-op faced higher than expected interest costs. Not all residents chose to join the co-op, and since the co-op refuses to displace tenants, nearly a quarter of the units are still occupied by renters.

With higher costs and an undersubsidized membership, the co-op has found that its plans for rehabilitation cannot be implemented. The building committee, which had been planning for moderate rehabilitation of the units, has begun planning and implementing a step-by-step repair and improvement plan to use the limited funds available. It has begun with windows and other energy conservation items. As membership continues to expand in the future, the co-op hopes to do more of the improvements it has planned. As the co-op president put it, "We *are* making progress, and that's important."

Planning for Rehabilitation

The methods we have presented of estimating costs have been very rough. You have only guessed at rehabilitation costs to figure out the level of rehabilitation your co-op can afford. Significantly more detail is necessary before you proceed with rehabilitation. Lenders require more financial details, contractors require more physical details, and your members require both.

The next step is for your co-op group to complete preliminary plans and specifications from which detailed construction cost estimates can be made. Preliminary plans for moderate or substantial rehabilitation projects are typically drawn by licensed architects; local and state building codes may require it. You may choose to render the preliminary drawings yourself if you know something about construction and you are planning only intensive repairs that do not need building department approval. Remember, however, that design errors can be costly.

We cannot give you prices for construction or rehabilitation. If we include the current costs in Boston at the time this is written, the information would mislead readers in the rest of the country. And by the time the book goes to press, our figures may not be reliable even in Boston. Instead, we urge you to consult local construction people for average costs in your area, or refer to the *Dodge Reports* in the real estate or business section of your local library. Other sources of information may be the local housing rehabilitation program or local nonprofit housing development corporations.

HIRING AN ARCHITECT

Finding a good architect is critical. It may be hard to find one that you feel has the experience of working with groups, the ability to design within your cost constraints, and an attractive fee structure. Have the co-op building committee begin the search. Ask members to suggest architects they know. Then ask friends, neighbors, and professional acquaintances about reliable architects. Talk to local government agencies and local nonprofit development groups.

If you do not have funds to pay an architect until you obtain financing, perhaps an architect will agree to render the preliminary drawings "on spec"—that is, on the understanding that the architect will be hired to do the full set of drawings if the project is financed. Also, you might be able to locate free architectural services through a local architecture school or community design center.

It is best to interview several architects and to check their references on past design work very carefully. Looking at glossy photographs of past designs is not enough; you should visit the sites and ask owners and residents some questions. Did the architect follow instructions from the owner? Did the architect design a project that fit the owner's budget? Were there any design-related problems with the development? Is the architect's design livable? Would the owner use the architect again?

Negotiating a contract with the chosen architect should be fairly straightforward. The American Institute of Architects (AIA) has developed standardized architectural agreements that protect the rights of both the architect and the owner. Ask your architect for a copy of the standard AIA agreement—there's a short form and a long form. If you make only minor changes to the standard agreement, you can avoid legal fees.

WORKING WITH THE ARCHITECT

The reviews of architects working with groups are mixed. There are many successes but also some failures. The critical element in many cases appears to be communication. Bad experiences resulted from a group's failure to provide a clear set of directions to the architect and the architect's failure to persist until clear instructions were given. In these conditions, the results have tended to be overdesigned and too-expensive projects.

A group of five single professionals, for example, wanted to form a co-op in a large house in the Haight area of San Francisco. The group selected an architect who was a friend of one of the members. The architect met with the group, agreed to do a set of schematic designs on spec, and then went about the work of turning the large house into five units. She talked with her friend about the design, although she did not meet with the group again until she came back six weeks later with a design and a cost estimate of $140,000. The group was shocked. With a purchase price of $185,000, they could not afford the total development cost. They dropped the co-op idea when the architect refused to do another set of designs unless she received payment.

When the architect was asked later about the situation, she suggested that her friend had seemed to like the design and had never indicated a problem with costs. If the group had made their financial limitations clear to her, she said, she could have designed five bedroom/bathroom suites around common living facilities at less than half the cost. She refused to do additional work because she was not sure that any design would please both the group members and their pocketbooks. In her opinion, their perception of what rehabilitation dollars can buy was "way off base."

The burden lies with you and your group to make sure that all instructions are clear. Before you meet with the architect, you must determine within the group exactly what you want and what you can afford. Run through a rehabilitation feasibility analysis as described in Chapter 6. If you have a finance committee, it can do the calculations, and then let every group member have an opportunity to discuss his or her bottom line. You may wish to have the architect attend one meeting of the whole group to hear everyone's opinions.

Start your instructions to the architect with your estimate of the dollar value you can afford for rehabilitation; understate the amount by 10 percent to leave some room for added design features later. Ask the architect to help you choose the improvements to be included now. Always ask these two questions about every improvement: "Can we forgo the improvement at this time?" and "Is there a less expensive alternative?"

Specify your group's housing needs: number and size of units, number of bedrooms and bathrooms, and special amenities or safety features. Also specify the special design features you will want to consider for any tenants with special needs, such as the elderly, handicapped, or families with small children.

FINAL PLANS AND SPECIFICATIONS

A final set of architectural drawings and specifications is necessary when moderate or substantial rehabilitation is planned. Both the local building department and your lender will require that they be completed by a licensed architect. The lender may make a preliminary commitment of funds conditional upon approval of plans by the building department.

Most established architects will charge about 6 percent of the total construction cost for full design services, although some smaller architectural firms with low overhead costs can do the designs for as little as half that standard fee.

The full set of architectural drawings may include any or all of the following, depending on what is included in the scope of construction:

- Plot plan
- Foundation and pilings plan
- Front and rear elevations
- Floor plans (one for each floor, although identical floors may be represented by a "typical floor plan")
- Roof plan
- Mechanical (HVAC) drawings
- Electrical drawings
- Landscaping plan

These plans are usually accompanied by a book of specifications, which contains the written details of each item of work and the materials to be used. Some materials, such as flooring and windows, may be specified on the drawings rather than in the book of specifications.

The drawings are not as difficult to understand as they may appear at first. Don't be afraid to ask questions. Your architect is obligated to explain them to you. These drawings will become the legal documents to which the contractor must conform during construction. Your ignorance can be costly in terms of both construction dollars and potential dissatisfaction with the results.

We think that a formal review session by the group is warranted. Ask the architect to make a full presentation of the design, and open the discussion for questions from members. Ask all members to attend. You should have no problem gaining good attendance at this meeting; after all, it's the first "tour" of the members' future homes.

Under Construction

The final plans and specifications will serve as the scope of work on which contractors will bid. This is an important step: you are putting a lot of *your* money into someone else's hands.

The responsibilities in this phase can be shared by the board of directors and the building committee. One alternative we prefer is for the building committee to review bids and provide recommendations to the board. The board selects the contractor(s) and negotiates the contract(s).

HIRING A CONTRACTOR

Construction is big business. One out of every eight dollars of the gross national product (GNP) comes from the construction industry. Construction is also a volatile business. Layoffs and bankruptcies are common, even among the larger and seemingly more stable companies in the industry. Construction is beset by its share of disreputable business people who will cut corners on labor and materials wherever they have a chance. Hiring a contractor presents you with a lot of choices and a lot of risks.

The construction industry can be thought of as a pool of professional trades, each of which plays a small part in any construction job. The owner of a property to be developed hires a *general contractor* to plan, schedule, and monitor the various tasks of construction. In turn, the general contractor hires *subcontractors* to complete the different tasks.

Seeking bids. The purpose of putting your proposal out for bids is to obtain the best price for the construction work. You and your architect have estimated the approximate cost of construction, and bids can be expected to come close to that amount if the estimates are correct. Prices will vary from contractor to contractor because each contractor has some "tricks" for providing a very competitive cost—careful management, low-cost or highly productive labor crews, inexpensive subcontractors, discount suppliers, economies of scale related to other jobs in the immediate area, or some other means of legitimately cutting costs.

The rule of thumb for the number of bids to seek is three; that way, two reasonable bids are likely to bring attention to a bid that is unreasonably high or low. Your architect probably knows of several reputable contractors from which you can solicit bids directly, or you may decide to go out to public bid. (When public funds are involved in the construction, public bidding may be required. Check with the agency providing the financing.) In the latter case, notices are placed in the major local newspapers and construction industry publications. You may ask contractors to pay for the reproduction costs of the specifications and plans or to place a deposit (usually about $50) that is refundable if the contractor places a bid. This cuts down on wide distribution of expensive plans to contractors who are unlikely to bid.

Some contractors will underbid deliberately. They need the work to keep their people busy, to build their reputation, or to branch into a new type of construction. In order to win the job, they may cut their profit or overhead to get a price edge on the other bidders. Caution is advised: the lowest price is not always the best offer. Low bids are sometimes questionable. A contractor who has been careless in making a bid may also be a careless manager. A contractor caught unexpectedly in a low bid may attempt to reduce losses by cutting corners on the quality of construction and materials. A low price also may reflect desperation on the part of a contractor about to go out of business or near bankruptcy. The construction funds you lay out may go to pay old debts for a time until the contractor does go out of business and saddles you with construction liens against your property. If you want to consider the low bid, be diligent in checking the contractor's references on *current* construction jobs.

Bonding the contractor is one way of ensuring your choice of contractors. There are two kinds of bonding: performance bonding, which is third-party insurance that the contractor will complete the work as specified; and payment bonding, which ensures that the contractor will pay subcontractors and suppliers. Bonds cost the contractor 1 to 5 percent of the insured amount of construction, depending upon the track record and current financial condition of the contractor. Considering the money at risk, bonding might be a wise insurance policy for the co-op.

Bidders should provide several references for recently completed construction projects; they also should provide a listing of *all* current projects. (References more than two years old should not be accepted.) Contact the references. Did the contractor complete the work thoroughly, on time? Did the contractor stay within the budget? Were the overruns attributed to the contractor's performance? Did all the subcontractors perform satisfactorily? Were there problems or delays related to the contractor's performance? Have any construction deficiencies become apparent since completion? Did the contractor correct warrantied defects? Would the person hire the contractor again?

If you have read the contractor advertisements by public agencies in your local paper, you have probably seen a version of the clause "We reserve the right to select the *lowest and best* offer." These are important words of advice to the co-op. Select the contractor offering the best combination of lowest price and best reputation.

Negotiations. Once you have identified the contractor with the most advantageous offer, enter one-on-one negotiations to prepare a construction contract. From the standpoint of financial risk, this contract is probably the single most important document your co-op will sign. Have your lawyer review it.

There is a little fat in any bid. Contractors add a little extra when they are unsure of the conditions or specifications. Try to find that fat. Tell the contractor that you would like to hire the firm, but that the bid exceeds the funds available. Ask the contractor to go through the scope of work and suggest where the scope could be reduced without jeopardizing the quality of construction. Many architects tend to overspecify rehabilitation, and contractors often know some less expensive ways to accomplish the job.

Cutting specifications need not seriously reduce the quality of construction. You might, for example, be able to retain some existing doors that had been specified for replacement, do less finishing work in basement or utility rooms, or substitute a newer, less expensive material than specified. Since it doesn't really cut into their profit, contractors are often willing to offer some of these cost-cutting ideas to make sure they get the job.

Once the price and scope of work are firmly established, you and the contractor negotiate the other terms of the construction contract. Important contract clauses include the following:

- Completion date or period of performance (if start date is unspecified)
- Penalties for late performance or nonperformance
- Compliance with all state and local codes, including inspections and certification for occupancy
- Subcontractor and supplier payment clauses, which require the contractor to provide proof of payment and which hold the co-op harmless in the event the contractor does not pay (note that this is the legal grounds for suit against the contractor, but it does not prevent a lien being placed on the property by an unpaid subcontractor)

- Procedures for submitting change orders for approval by the co-op
- Utilities provided by each party
- Requirements that the contractor protect the property, secure it, and regularly clean the premises during the construction period
- Rights of the co-op to inspect the property and review the accounting books kept by the contractor on the job
- Warranties for quality of work and materials
- Provisions for payment and retention of partial payments by the co-op as security, pending substantial completion of the job

Upon agreement, the contract is executed, and the contractor is issued a proceed to work order, which designates the starting date of the contract period and requires the contractor to start work within a specified time.

MONITORING CONSTRUCTION

Architects usually have a clause in their contract providing for supervision of construction, but their duties are primarily to ensure that the plans are being followed. The co-op needs someone to make sure that all materials are delivered and installed according to the specifications and that invoices reflect actual work accomplished. Things happen quickly in construction. Yesterday's work may be covered over by today's, so it is important that the co-op have a method of watching construction progress on an almost daily basis.

One way to protect the co-op's interests is to hire a clerk of the works, an experienced construction supervisor who inspects the site on a daily basis and keeps a written record of work, materials, and labor. The clerk is under contract to the co-op and reports regularly to the co-op, attends all construction meetings, and reviews and approves all invoices.

<u>Construction schedules.</u> The clerk of the works needs a schedule of the contractor's activities with which to monitor prog-

ress and calculate progress payments. Contractors use a variety of scheduling methods to plan the purchase of materials and the hiring of subcontractors and labor crews in advance. In Chapter 4, we introduced the critical path method as a technique contractors use to plan and monitor construction. If the contractor uses this method, insist upon receiving a copy.

Construction meetings. Even the construction business is overrun by meetings. During the busy periods of construction—usually the middle third of the construction period when several work crews are on the site every day—it is considered wise to have construction meetings between the co-op and the contractor once a week. During less busy periods, a meeting every two weeks can suffice.

The purpose of the meetings is for the co-op to review progress, to approve invoices for progress payment, to select fixtures and other materials subject to the co-op's approval, and to resolve any construction problems. The meetings save quite a few telephone calls and get things decided on the spot. The meetings are usually held at the construction site so that any construction problems can be observed directly. It is not accidental that the most productive workdays tend to occur immediately before and during the construction meetings.

The clerk or co-op representative should keep careful notes of such meetings. If critical decisions are made, a letter should be sent to the contractor confirming the meeting and any decisions reached.

Acme Construction Co.

Dear Tom:

This is to confirm several decisions made at our construction meeting yesterday.

First, we have no interest in an indoor pool. You will repair the water leak that has flooded the basement.

Second, the architect's failure to specify the types of doors for the second-floor units does not mean you can omit the doors. You will install doors to match the specifications of the third floor.

Finally, the neighborhood kids should not be climbing your scaffolding in the front of the building. We assume no responsibility for this and insist that you stop allowing it.

Sincerely,

Bill Coughlan
Co-op President

<u>Change orders.</u> Very few projects are able to be constructed exactly as the architect designed them. Something always comes up: Some previously unseen part of the structure has deteriorated and must be replaced rather than reused; a specified material is not available; or someone breaks into the building and steals the fireplace mantelpieces. To accommodate extra work or materials, a contractor requests a change order, and the owner approves or disapproves. This must be done in writing, and the written change order must specify the changes in labor and materials and the costs of those changes.

Not all change orders cost extra money. Sometimes change orders end up providing "deducts." The contractor, for example, may decide that certain existing doors, windows, or drainpipes can be saved. Don't expect to have a lot of deducts unless your clerk of the works is looking for ways to save money.

When construction disputes end up in court, change orders invariably play a very big role. Often the contractor claims to have been authorized to incur some extra costs and the owner denies authorizing the changes. If a contractor requests a change order, insist that the request and your answer be in writing.

<u>Progress payments.</u> Progress payments are common when construction lasts for more than a month. The contractor needs

partial payments to pay laborers and to pay for materials on delivery. The co-op, on the other hand, does not want to pay more than reasonable costs to date, and it wants to withhold enough money to make sure the contractor continues to perform.

To serve the interests of both parties, a schedule of progress payments should be developed that ties payments to completion of tasks and delivery of materials. This schedule enables the owner to anticipate the contractor's requests for progress payments and to draw funds from the construction loan account just before they are needed. A retainer—5 to 10 percent of the payment—is held by the owner from each progress payment until the work is substantially completed. The purpose of the retainer is to give the owner some financial leverage to cause the contractor to complete the work.

Sweat Equity

Many co-ops have found that they can reduce their rehabilitation costs through sweat equity. Members contribute their time and labor to rehabilitation or repair tasks, reducing the amount of money the co-op must raise from members to pay contractors. In effect, the members have substituted their labor (sweat) for their money (equity).

Self-help housing construction or rehabilitation is certainly nothing new. Many of the housing units in this country —particularly in rural areas—were built by laypeople rather than professionals. Sweat equity is a more recent phenomenon in multifamily buildings. HUD conducted a national multifamily sweat equity homesteading demonstration in six cities. The demonstration proved that sweat equity can work for moderate-income co-op groups that want to limit their initial cash investment, but it also indicated that sweat equity must be carefully managed to be successful.

All the sweat equity co-ops in the demonstration were sponsored by city agencies or nonprofit community development corporations. Sponsors contributed seed money, initial planning, borrowing capacity, organizational skills, and supervision. While sponsorship is not essential, it is certainly helpful. Talk with local community development corporations and other nonprofit agencies to determine if any would like to sponsor your project. Even if they cannot subsidize your group, some free technical advice will help you avoid many costly mistakes.

SELECTING SWEAT EQUITY CO-OP MEMBERS

We cannot make generalities about the kinds of people who are most successful in joining sweat equity co-op ventures. The characteristics that make one willing and able to contribute labor are purely personal and cannot be said to exist in certain income groups or types of people. One observation made in the HUD demonstration is that sweat equity projects have been more successful with families than with one-person households. Since many of the improvements are made to the individual apartments by each member household working on its own, a single person may not have the time to meet the work requirements or may be frustrated by the difficulty or amount of work. Couples or larger households that can share in the work seem generally to be more successful.

Sweat equity co-ops should select all their members as early as possible. Some of the sweat equity tasks happen early (demolition, for example) and it is important that all members share in all tasks. Members who are selected after the sweat equity work is completed in part or in whole cannot possibly understand the blood, sweat, and tears that the other members have already put into the co-op.

We hasten to add, however, that sweat equity projects are not limited to the hale and hardy. Not all sweat equity work involves strenuous exercise. The work must be divided so that all members—even the elderly, the handicapped, and the young—can contribute. While physically capable members of the co-op may hang sheet rock or sand floors, less physically able members can make telephone calls to order supplies, do bookkeeping, decorate finished spaces, and even cook meals for the workers in the timeless fashion of the barn raising. A little group planning will help every member find a way to contribute.

THE SCOPE OF SWEAT EQUITY

Many co-ops may be drawn to sweat equity by the appeal of cost saving, but it is dangerous to overestimate the amount of work members can realistically be expected to contribute. The work your members can handle depends on their willingness, their abilities, and their commitment. Each co-op group must choose a set of sweat equity construction activities that fits.

In New York City—where the multifamily homesteading concept had its start—sweat equity is commonplace. With a local network of experienced people and support groups, the scope of sweat equity in many projects is extensive. The members do demolition, and then contractors install or repair systems. When the contractors are finished, the homesteaders do the finishing work, including finishing walls (insulation, drywall, taping, patching, painting), putting in subflooring and/or carpeting or refinishing floors, installing bathroom and kitchen fixtures, decorating, and landscaping.

Not all groups can undertake this amount of sweat equity work. In Cleveland, an eight-family co-op planned to do all finishing tasks listed above, as well as boarding up, insulating, and refinishing as walls approximately one-third of the windows for energy conservation. Inadequately trained and supervised, the members soon fell behind schedule. Four of the eight families dropped out, and the contractor's work was delayed until new members were found. The co-op sponsor re-evaluated the sweat equity plans and reduced the scope to the finishing tasks of painting, floor finishing, and decorating so that the contractor would not be held up by the members' work. The extra rehabilitation work required additional financing, but the group was able to secure foundation and city grants to meet costs. Under the new plan, sweat equity participation by all families was more successful, and the eight families were finally able to occupy their new co-op homes.

Because the city of Cleveland was involved in the project, a financial bailout was possible when problems occurred. However, your co-op probably won't have this insurance. We recommend the following to protect your co-op against such problems.

- Make the scope of work realistic to the abilities and time availability of the members.
- Find a good sweat equity supervisor who can train the members and work with them on their tasks.
- Do not plan sweat equity tasks that can interrupt or impede the contractor's work; schedule tasks that can take place before or after the contractor's work.

BUDGETING SWEAT EQUITY WORK

Just because you are doing certain construction work yourselves does not mean you will avoid all costs. Sweat equity eliminates only direct labor costs. Your co-op still must purchase all the materials needed for sweat equity tasks, and it should pay a qualified person to serve as sweat equity supervisor. Be sure to include these costs in your estimates, but separate them from the rehabilitation costs estimated for contractor work.

Few contractors are experienced with sweat equity. If you do not explain properly, their bids will include certain tasks that you intend to complete, or they may charge for coordinating with your sweat equity work. To avoid unnecessary contractor costs, include in the rehabilitation specifications a statement that (1) lists sweat equity tasks you specifically exclude from the general contractor's scope of work and (2) exempts the contractor from ordering any of the materials for those tasks and from supervising or coordinating any of your work, except through your sweat equity supervisor.

TRAINING AND SUPERVISION

Most members you will recruit into the co-op are used to being renters. When a problem occurred in their apartments, they called the owner or manager. While a few may be handy at construction tasks, and some may have worked in construction industries, most co-op members are like you and me—unskilled. This does not mean we cannot do sweat equity, just that we need training and supervision.

A sweat equity supervisor is strongly recommended. The supervisor should be an experienced carpenter or craftsperson, preferably one with some supervisory experience. The supervisor becomes responsible for planning and scheduling sweat equity tasks, purchasing sweat equity materials, training the members to do their work, supervising and assisting members so that work gets done on time, and coordinating with the general contractor. This person may also supervise the contractor as clerk of the works.

Training for sweat equity jobs is often an informal process between the supervisor and the members. The supervisor demonstrates the work tasks and helps until individual members are able to do the work themselves. If many or all members are going to do the same task, a training session may be in order. Any training should include a demonstration of the correct and safe use of tools. Many people do not know how to use tools safely; a demonstration spares embarrassment and injuries.

In some cities, local adult education programs, building co-ops, nonprofit developers, institutes of technology, or other institutions offer training in the building trades. If the co-op members decide not to hire a supervisor or want to receive more formal training in construction, such programs may be helpful.

THE VALUE OF SWEAT EQUITY

Since members substitute their labor for dollars, it is only fair that they be paid for their work when they leave the co-op.

Most sweat equity co-ops assign value to the hours of labor contributed, such as $5.00 per hour for common labor tasks and $10.00 per hour for skilled labor tasks. Installing a cabinet may be estimated at two hours of skilled labor, or $20.00.

The Frankie O'Day Co-op in Boston started with the plan to record actual hours worked, but the members soon realized that they had created a negative incentive for efficient work. Members who were fast and efficient received less credit than slow members. To eliminate this negative incentive, they revised their plan by assigning standardized values to tasks. For example, if someone installed a door, he or she was credited $50 regardless of the time it took.

Work out all these details of sweat equity before the first hammer is swung. The sweat equity co-ops in the Cleveland demonstration adopted a membership agreement that formally spelled out the sweat equity requirements of membership. This lessened confusion and disputes about what work was required of the members, how their work was valued, how long members were expected to stay in the co-op, and what they were paid for their sweat equity contributions when they left the co-op.

To minimize future disputes among members, the co-op's sweat equity supervisor should be the only person authorized to inspect completed work and the only one allowed to reject poorly done work. Make sure everyone understands this point: inspection is done to ensure building safety and cost-effectiveness. It is not a forum for acting out personal grudges.

9
HOUSE POLICIES

EVEN THOUGH THE CO-OP is your home, it is also a business and must operate as a business. Financial transactions between the co-op and its members should be conducted in a businesslike fashion, so that each member is treated fairly. We call the standard operating procedures of the co-op its *house policies*.

The co-op bylaws set the rules for making decisions about policies, and they also dictate some policies, but most of the everyday rules of living in the co-op are voted on in co-op meetings by the members or the board of directors. House policies should be decided prior to occupancy so that members know from the start what is expected of them.

House policies need not be excessive or oppressive. Because members set the rules for themselves, they will not impose unnecessary hardships or requirements on themselves, and yet they will understand why some policies are needed. We have chosen to concentrate our discussion of house policies in five major policy areas: carrying charges and collections; management; maintenance; capital improvements; and resale and transfer of memberships. Additional policy issues are listed at the end of the chapter.

Carrying Charges and Collections

Now that you are in the business of operating your housing co-op, you have to pay the co-op mortgage and other operating costs each month. To make these payments, each member is assessed a portion of these costs in the form of a monthly carrying charge, which is based on the member's share of financial interest. For the co-op to be a successful business, it must collect all the carrying charges on time.

A collections policy for carrying charges and special assessments should be adopted prior to occupancy, so that every member's payment to the co-op is governed by the same rules. The collections policy should specify the schedule for collections, penalties for late payment, and procedures for collecting arrears or initiating legal action. Collections should be made by check or money order; cash payments present problems of security and record keeping.

Occupancy by individual members is protected by a proprietary lease, but members are considered to be in violation of the lease if they fail to make payments. The lease should include the legal remedies available to the co-op to pursue payment and to evict the nonpaying member. We do not want to overstate the problem of members who will not pay—they are not common. The typical collections problem is that of the member who has temporary financial difficulties and falls behind on paying the carrying charges. The co-op should have a procedure for assessing interest or late charges in those situations and a fixed standard for when legal action becomes necessary.

Management

Co-ops usually choose one of three management models—management staff, management agents, and self-management. The choice is affected by budget, by member interests, and in large part by the size of the co-op. Large co-ops usually have full-time management staff directly employed by the co-op. Co-ops of moderate size (fewer than fifty units) typically do not have enough work to justify hiring full-time employees, and it is cost-effective for them to subcontract with a management firm that provides management services as needed. Small co-ops (fewer than fifteen units) are more likely to manage the building by sharing the responsibilities among the members.

Each co-op has to make its own decision about the most cost-effective way of managing its building. Cost is obviously a big issue, but looming just as large is the question of whether the members are willing to assume a large part of the management work themselves.

THE MANAGEMENT PLAN

HUD requires a formal management plan for all co-ops it insures. Even if you do not plan to obtain federal mortgage insurance for your cooperative, it is prudent to adopt a formal management plan. The following items should be included in your plan:

- The type of management the co-op will use
- How the management entity will report to the board of directors
- What staff, if any, the co-op will hire directly, and the personnel policies that will apply
- A plan for marketing unfilled memberships
- A maintenance and repair program
- A plan for managing revenue collection, a cash management strategy, and accounting procedures

Because the task of drafting a management plan is large, we think the committee approach is ideally suited to it. The building committee might be asked to do this, or the co-op may nominate a special committee for the task. The committee should work on a draft and report a recommended strategy to the board and the membership within a few weeks.

CHOOSING A MANAGEMENT AGENT

We see two ways of finding a management firm. One is to ask members of surrounding co-ops and condominiums about their management agents and to invite two or three agents to bid. The other approach is to advertise publicly for management proposals and to carefully check references on the most attractive ones. Proposals should include a statement of services and fees, a sample management contract, references for management of similar owner-occupied structures, and a general statement of the capabilities of the firm.

Management agents usually propose to provide actual management and maintenance services as needed for cost plus a management fee, typically from 2 to 6 percent of the total revenue collected by the agent from the co-op members. The fee is the agent's charge for accounting and other administrative services, plus profit. You should examine the fee structure of the proposals, but you also should consider the quality of the services by checking references and meeting with the agents.

Interviews are important for selecting the manager. They should be conducted with a representative group of members present. Ask each prospective manager to discuss previous experiences in managing co-ops or condos and also how he or she would handle regular collections, bookkeeping, maintenance, and relations with the board and the members. Also ask how each would respond to certain difficult situations, such as a member who refuses to pay a special assessment. If you really want to test the agent, try role playing a few difficult situations.

THE MANAGEMENT CONTRACT

Every management agent has a standard contract that it uses for most of its properties. Review that contract to ensure that the following matters are covered to the satisfaction of your board of directors.

1. Inclusive description of property to be managed
2. Exclusive agent clause, which protects both parties by stating that no other party will be designated agent so long as the agreement is in force
3. Procedures for providing instructions to the agent, usually

specifying that only the board and not individual members can instruct the agent

4. Enumerated functions of the agent, including responsibilities of financial management, revenue collection, enforcement of policies, building and grounds maintenance, and emergency repairs and services
5. Spending authorization, which usually includes dollar limits on size of expenditures by the agent without prior approval of the board, except for emergency repairs
6. Instructions and standards for accounting management
7. Requirements for reporting on management activities and finances, typically requiring monthly reporting and attendance at board meetings
8. Duties of the agent, such as relocation and security, in the event of disaster
9. Requirement to maintain inventories necessary for timely maintenance and administration
10. Agent's responsibilities for completing and filing various forms, including tax returns
11. Responsibilities of agent to carry workers' compensation insurance, unemployment insurance, and other employee benefits
12. Duty of agent to carry liability insurance and/or to bond its workers

MANAGING THE MANAGER

Regardless of the quality and completeness of the management plan and contract, the best insurance for high-quality management is close monitoring by the board. The board should require regular reports, regular meetings, audits, or other methods of reviewing the performance of the agent. Management reports are typically provided monthly and usually include income, expenses, maintenance activities and backlog, and occupancy status. The monthly financial information is critical for effective monitoring. The financial report should contain the following exhibits or lists of information:

- The operating account reconciliation, summarizing the flow of funds in and out of the account since the last report
- The status of other accounts, such as reserves
- Listings of accounts receivable and accounts payable
- A report on cumulative expenditures to date compared with budgeted figures

In addition to this financial data, the board might also request an attachment to the reports on maintenance activities, vacancies and turnovers, and correspondence.

If your co-op hires a firm as management agent, bear in mind these two simple principles: (1) The manager works for the co-op; the manager is not the landlord. (2) The manager takes orders from the co-op board, not from the members. These may seem obvious, but most problems between the co-op and its manager develop when the lines of authority are broken. Many new co-op members have been renters; they are used to the manager being, or acting for, the owner. If the board thinks this way, the manager's tasks and responsibilities will probably be ill defined and improperly supervised.

At the other extreme, a co-op member might treat the management firm as if the firm worked directly for the member, defying the manager to enforce the co-op's policy against the individual member's wishes: "You can't tell me what to do. I own this place and you work for me." The agent takes orders only from the board. If the individual member does not like the board's policy, the member must take it up with the board rather than the manager.

As we noted above, the building committee or a special management committee may be assigned responsibility for supervision of the co-op. While the board has ultimate financial responsibility, it need not monitor day-to-day management. A separate committee expands members' involvement in the supervision of building management.

SELF-MANAGEMENT

Many small co-ops are self-managed. To bring down operating costs, individual members assume responsibility for various management tasks including maintenance and repairs. The management tasks are usually concentrated in two areas: bookkeeping and building maintenance. While many small co-ops manage both areas themselves, we have found several examples of co-ops in which members do only maintenance and contract the bookkeeping function to a management firm. A self-managed bookkeeping system is discussed in Chapter 10; here we discuss self-managed maintenance.

When responsible members do the routine maintenance and minor repairs, the results are a clean and well-maintained building in which members can take considerable pride. If the members fail to live up to their maintenance responsibilities, however, the results of negligence will be obvious.

Effective self-management systems have the following characteristics: a clear rotation or other system for dividing work among members; the work is evenly divided; a committee oversees work and credits individuals with completing tasks; and there is a reward structure. Some co-ops issue credits that reduce the members' monthly payments; others add penalty payments for members who fail to complete their assigned tasks.

Maintenance

All co-op members want to see the buildings, grounds, and equipment maintained attractively and in good repair. Physical maintenance is important to the members' sense of well-being and comfort and critical to the financial stability of the co-op. The co-op's building and grounds are its primary assets. Members' investments in these assets must be protected through a systematic approach to both repairs and regular preventive maintenance.

Two things contribute to your co-op's success in maintaining the physical condition of the building: a *maintenance program,* which ensures that both regular and emergency maintenance are handled quickly and efficiently; and a sufficient *maintenance budget* to cover repairs as needs arise. Without them, members will find themselves meeting constantly to talk about minor and irritating repair items and bills, and the co-op's maintenance program will deteriorate into a jumbled mess of stopgap repairs.

COMPONENTS OF A MAINTENANCE PROGRAM

The best maintenance programs provide for quick and effective response to problems as they arise and for regular preventive maintenance to minimize unanticipated repairs.

The repair system. Successful repair programs have a standard set of procedures for addressing all problems. Regardless of the seriousness or size of the problem, certain procedures must be followed: All problems should be immediately reported to the maintenance manager—be it the manager, the building superintendent, one of the building committee members, or whoever is designated by the co-op. This person records the problem or complaint in a maintenance log and decides how the problem will be corrected. The proposed repairs are authorized, and the work is completed and inspected.

The central coordinating function of the maintenance manager is critical. It is the only way in which all repair needs can be sorted and handled in the most efficient manner. This manager is responsible for keeping expenditures within the limits of the budget and often coordinates the repairs so as to minimize costly visits by tradespeople. If your co-op has a management agent, the agent may serve as coordinator for reporting, authorizing, and monitoring repairs.

Preventive maintenance system. Not all repair and upkeep needs of the building and grounds are unpredictable. Some regular maintenance activities can be scheduled, including routine cleaning, landscaping, snow removal, boiler maintenance, painting, and extermination. All regular inspections and maintenance can be planned well in advance. For co-ops that have their own management staff, this planning spreads the work over the course of the year and minimizes the number of staff required. For smaller self-help co-ops, this system helps members schedule well in advance the nights or weekends they must set aside for maintenance, or it helps the co-op locate and schedule a contractor to do tasks the members cannot do.

Records. Records help the co-op keep track of which repairs are finished or still need to be done. They also provide background about problems that may be covered by warranties or that, by their recurrence, may indicate poor-quality service or improper use by members.

We indicated that the co-op should maintain a maintenance log for recording all problems and repairs. This chronological record is important for managing multiple repairs and for monitoring the time between the report and the response. In addition to the maintenance log, two sets of files should be kept so the co-op has a record of repairs by type and location:

1. *Apartment files.* A file should be kept on repairs to each unit, including all reported problems, repairs, and inspection notes. Some repairs must be assessed against the individual member rather than paid out of the co-op budget.
2. *Building systems maintenance files.* Files should contain all information about the condition of and repairs to each of the systems in the building: HVAC, plumbing, electrical, roof, structural, windows and doors, common areas, and grounds.

PRIORITIES

The board of directors, the building committee, the building or maintenance manager, and maintenance contractors all play a role in maintaining the co-op building. But who decides what repairs are to be done? Who makes sure they are done correctly and efficiently?

Although the board must assume ultimate responsibility for the maintenance of the co-op's physical plant, we recommend that the board delegate direct responsibility to a committee. This enables the board to share responsibilities for monitoring the everyday details of maintenance and repairs while it retains the power of financial review. We believe this extra layer of checks and balances is important for financial management.

The committee (or board) oversees a maintenance manager, who is directly responsible for handling repairs. The co-op's maintenance policy and budget set the limits on reasonable repairs and costs, and the building manager should be able to make most repairs within those guidelines. Most co-ops operate with repair cost guidelines: if a repair is under $200, for example, and the maintenance budget has not been exceeded, then the building manager may authorize repairs without approval of the board or building committee. The board or committee should insist upon making repair decisions when the repairs are discretionary or when several repairs are needed and the co-op's cash situation or staff capacity cannot respond immediately to all the problems.

When co-ops cannot pay for all repairs that are needed at a particular time, a set of priorities is needed so that the co-op board or building committee (with the advice of the manager) can determine which maintenance and repairs will be done. Top priority is given to *emergency repairs* and to situations that threaten the lives, health, and safety of the residents. Heating and electrical repairs generally fall into this category, as do repairs from fires or burglaries. Second priority is given to repairs of things that are *damaging to the building* and will be significantly more costly in the long run. Roof leaks, plumbing leaks, and foundation sagging are examples. Lowest priority is given to *cosmetic repairs,* which eliminate building eyesores but do not require immediate attention. Patching and painting work fall into this category.

Emergency repairs should be implemented by the building manager immediately. This is not a category of repairs in which discretion may be exercised. The other categories of repairs do not have the same sense of immediacy or danger to the members. The board or building committee can request that the manager identify and price all options, evaluate their risks, and recommend courses of action. The board or committee can then review and select the options in light of the budget.

RESPONSIBILITY FOR REPAIRS IN APARTMENTS

To this point, we have been talking about repair costs that must be incurred by the co-op. There are, however, a number of repairs that must be made to individual living spaces: garbage disposals and drains become clogged; walls are damaged while moving furniture; windows are broken; closet doors get stuck. Individual members are financially responsible for repairs to their units, except when the repairs are necessary because of a problem outside the unit.

For a variety of reasons, some co-op members do not maintain their units adequately or make timely repairs. In response to this problem, some co-ops have instituted mandatory repair programs. Each member is required to make a repair deposit with the co-op for use by the co-op in making repairs in the units. When a repair is needed, the co-op makes the repair and deducts the cost from the member's account. So that repair needs do not go unreported, co-ops make annual inspections of the units.

Capital Improvements

From time to time, co-op members will decide to make improvements to the property, such as remodeling common areas, landscaping, or purchasing a new boiler. These improvements are paid for out of the co-op's capital reserves, by acquiring second mortgages, or by special assessments charged to members.

Individual members may also wish to make improvements or permanent additions that add to the value of their units but that cannot be taken when they leave the co-op. Members can be reimbursed for such improvements either by direct payment from the co-op or by a higher membership price from the replacement member.

The co-op must ensure that all improvements be done properly and tastefully, so that they add to the value of the property rather than detract from it. A unit improvement policy should require that members receive prior board approval of all improvements, that the improvements be inspected and appraised upon completion, and that the improvements be recorded in the member's file. The penalty for failure to comply with the co-op's improvement policy in one co-op is that the member pay for removal of the unapproved improvement and return the unit to its original condition.

Resale and Transfer Value

Inevitably, some members are going to decide to leave the co-op. Reasons include moving to another area, taking a different job, getting married, having children, choosing a different lifestyle, buying a larger home, or even deciding that the co-op is no longer a comfortable living arrangement. Whatever the reason for leaving, the co-op must treat each departing member equitably. This requires guidelines under which the departing member sells the membership, procedures for the approval of a new member, and a formula for calculating the fair value of the membership interest that is being transferred.

The co-op has three basic objectives in restricting resale: it must ensure the continued financial stability of the co-op by controlling turnover; it must ensure that all debts are settled by the departing member; and it must ensure that the new member will be a positive addition to the co-op membership. Some limited-equity co-ops have an additional objective: to ensure that the value of membership is protected from loss or excessive profits.

Co-ops can be put in financial jeopardy by turnover, particularly during the first two or three years, when reserves are still low. Some co-ops have prohibited resales during the early years, except in cases of death, mandatory job relocation, or extreme personal financial hardship. Still other co-ops have designed repurchase schedules that severely penalize the early seller, similar to the way in which a bank penalizes early withdrawal from high-yield accounts.

Prior to a member's leaving the co-op a number of events must transpire: inspection of the unit, return of deposits, approval of a new member, and settlement of all member accounts. It is important that members be aware of these procedures. Above all else, the co-op should require proper notice from a member when the member is going to leave and sell the membership. Notice should be required at least two months prior to departure, although many co-ops simply require that members continue in the co-op until a replacement member is found.

RESALE ALTERNATIVES

Several alternative methods of resale are currently used by co-ops:

1. *Unrestricted resale.* The co-op permits the member to sell the membership interest privately, and the co-op board of directors retains only the right of approval or disapproval of the prospective buyer. This is the most common policy among unsubsidized, market-rate co-ops, such as those in Manhattan.

2. *Right of first refusal.* The co-op permits the member to sell privately but retains the right of first refusal to purchase the membership at a scheduled price, determined either by market value or formula. If the co-op repurchases the membership, it can select a buyer itself. This method is most common among limited-equity and subsidized co-ops.

3. *Automatic repurchase.* The co-op automatically repurchases the membership interest from the departing member and

conducts its own search for a buyer. Many subsidized co-ops use this approach. Although some co-ops legally have only the right of first refusal, in practice they exercise that right with every sale.

The departing member's primary concern is to find someone who is financially capable of paying the best price for the membership. By contrast, the primary interests of the co-op are that the new member be able to make the monthly payments and that the member be willing to be active and cooperative. The highest bidder is not necessarily the person who will make the best member.

SELECTION OF NEW MEMBERS

Regardless of the rules your co-op adopts for transfer of memberships, the co-op should have final approval of new members. New member interviews should be conducted by either the board or a membership committee. During the interviews, prospective members must be made aware of all membership responsibilities, including financial obligations, democratic participation, and sweat equity. Financial investigations can be conducted by the committee or the management agent. The prospective member should be asked for job, bank, credit, and personal references. Check all references.

The Boston Mutual Housing Association (BMHA) helped start a limited-equity co-op in the East Fenway neighborhood, a small residential pocket in the downtown that is occupied predominantly by students attending Boston University, MIT, Northeastern University, Berklee College of Music, and the New England Conservatory of Music. The converted building had a large portion of student tenants, many of whom opted to purchase memberships to assure themselves of housing during their tenure in the tight Boston market. A membership screening committee was established of charter members, and their recommendations went to the BMHA board.

As memberships were filled, the screening committee became concerned about the image of their co-op. In particular, they felt their member selection should not reinforce an image that the co-op consisted of students and gays; rather, they wanted to create the image that the co-op was open to all. The membership committee refused to select any more students or gays until a better balance was achieved. They encountered challenges of discrimination, but since both the membership and the membership committee had substantial representation of both students and gays, they were able to respond satisfactorily to the accusations.

TRANSFER VALUE

When a homeowner decides to sell, the price is determined in the marketplace. In strong markets, the price is usually high enough to provide the owner with a large gain over the owner's direct investments. In a declining market, however, the owner might take a loss. Market-rate co-ops take this free-market approach to housing value.

In limited-equity cooperatives, a different value structure exists, based on two principles. First, a person should receive benefits in proportion to contributions. It is a limited, but stable, return that is unaffected by the risks of the marketplace. Second, part of the return on the co-op investment comes every month in the form of the lowest possible housing costs. Therefore, one does not have to sell in order to profit from the co-op. Consistent with these principles, many co-ops have created schedules that fix the transfer value to the contributions of the member, including the following:

1. The original share price, adjusted for inflation or a fixed interest rate.
2. The value of all preapproved capital improvements made to the unit by the member, adjusted for depreciation, damages, or removal. Each improvement must have been approved and assigned a value at the time of the improvement, and depreciation should be calculated using the IRS Accelerated Cost Recovery Schedule (ACRS).

3. The share of the member's carrying charges that was used to pay mortgage *principal* (but not interest). This is calculated by subtracting the principal balance at the time the person became a member from the principal balance at the time of the sale, and dividing that figure by the member's share of financial interest.
4. The member's contributions to current operating reserves and surpluses (but not replacement reserves). This is calculated by subtracting the operating surplus when the person became a member from the current operating surplus, and dividing that figure by the member's share of financial interest.
5. The value of the member's sweat equity contributions to the building's capital improvements (but not maintenance and repairs).

In addition, if the member established a damage deposit with the co-op, it should be returned with interest, although it should not be considered part of the membership value.

It is this formula approach that defines a co-op as limited equity. Each co-op structures the formula a little differently to reflect the interests of its members. If your co-op decides to provide limited return on equity, the policy and formula should be incorporated in the prospectus to all members before they buy.

NEW MEMBERS' EQUITY

Depending on a co-op's repurchase policy, new members pay either the departing member or the co-op the agreed-upon price for the membership. This price, however, may not be the only up-front commitment the co-op requires of the new member. It is sound policy to require a damage deposit. Since purchases force even financially secure people into tight cash-flow situations, some co-ops will allow members several months to build up their deposit accounts. These deposits should be put in separate escrow accounts and the interest accrues to the individual members.

Other House Policies

The co-op membership may choose to establish as policy a variety of other guidelines for co-op living. Making house rules may deter major confrontations in the future. We suggest a few other areas in which policies can be established:

- *Limits on appliances in units.* In some older buildings, electrical service is inadequate to support modern appliances. Co-ops may have to prohibit washing machines, dryers, air conditioning, or other appliances; or they may charge extra for these appliances if utilities are paid out of the common co-op funds.
- *Supervision of children.* While some co-op members would prefer not to admit members with children, such a policy is illegal in many states. Family co-ops may make policies about supervision of the children, both for the benefit of the parents and the prevention of damage. One co-op requires that families either pay for or repair damages done by their children. Other co-ops have been able to avoid problems by providing activities and supervision for the children. Day-care services are sometimes provided for small children.
- *Garbage and trash.* Living in close proximity necessitates that each family keep its unit clean and remove garbage to proper storage. Complaints about garbage rank high on the list for many co-ops. It is a good idea to make a policy about how garbage is to be handled and to enforce it.
- *Use of common spaces.* Many co-ops are fortunate to have community rooms, lounges, reception areas, patios, roof decks, and other common facilities that must be shared. The co-op needs guidelines for their use: What kinds of activities can be held there, and when? What are the procedures for reserving the space, and is rent or a deposit charged? If the co-op has common storage space, how will space be allocated, and what are the rules for access?
- *Use of laundry facilities.* Many problems between co-op members seem to come out in the wash. Some users leave

a mess, tie up washers and dryers, and otherwise annoy subsequent users. Try to develop some understanding among members about laundry room etiquette. Also, if security is a problem, use keys to gain access to the room and tokens in place of change.

- *Parking.* Buildings usually have limited parking spaces, which must be allocated. You can let the free market determine who gets the space: set a monthly lease price for the spots and rent them on a first-come basis. Special priority may be given to handicapped people or emergency personnel such as medical professionals, fire fighters, or police officers. Sign a contract with a local towing company if illegal parking is a problem; use parking stickers and post towing signs. Even if spaces are available for everyone, the co-op may want to assign individual spots and reserve some spots for guests, to avoid the inevitable problems of people who "hog" spaces or allow their friends to take up other members' spaces.

- *Insurance.* Co-ops carry insurance to cover the building, co-op possessions, and public liability. However, it should be the responsibility of the individual members to insure personal belongings in their units and in common storage spaces. This is not so much a matter of policy as a matter of informing the members.

- *Smoke detectors.* Many states and cities require smoke detectors in every unit, making it the co-op's responsibility to install them. Otherwise, encourage members to install them. Check with the local fire department about city regulations and for advice on where to install detectors.

- *Grounds for immediate eviction.* Certain acts, such as use or threat of use of a deadly weapon and arson, may be grounds for immediate eviction. Make it clear from the start what actions will not be tolerated.

I. S. Cobb once cautioned, "Learn all the rules, every one of them, so that you will know how to break them." The purpose of house rules or policies is not that they should be

House Policies / 167

broken or that the co-op group is setting up obstacles for individual members. Rather, policies create expectations of how the co-op deals with its individual members in certain situations. They replace arbitrary treatment with due process. In a democratic organization—where you help set the rules—they exist for your protection.

10
BOOKKEEPING

WE ALL HAVE A TENDENCY to be a little (or a lot) disorganized, and we all hope to have enough money to pay the bills without keeping the checkbook up to date and without planning which bills get paid with the next check. But just as this luxury is not real for most of us, the co-op cannot expect to avoid careful bookkeeping and bill paying. In this chapter, we assume that everyone has low income when it comes to buying the co-op building and paying the co-op's bills. Every dollar counts, the co-op cannot purchase everything it might like, and someone has to keep very close track of finances.

The five Hispanic families who live in a small five-story walkup apartment building on Tenth Avenue in the Lower West Side of Manhattan are setting up a cooperative. With the assistance of the Urban Homesteading Assistance Board (UHAB), these tenants incorporated their tenant association, established a business checking account, and completed training in operating their cooperative, managing their building, and keeping the co-op's financial records.

Maria, who was voted treasurer by the co-op members, and Jeanette, the UHAB co-op specialist assisting the group, are meeting around Maria's dining room table in her two-bedroom unit on the third floor. Maria is divorced and has an eighteen-month-old daughter. The co-op members selected

Maria as treasurer because they feel she needs the income that the co-op will pay its bookkeeper. "Besides," she says, "it gives me a way of contributing as well as keeping busy."

Maria tries to keep her baby girl quiet and happy at the same time as she goes over the collections and deposits for the first month of operations for the trial co-op. Her records for the month are in order, and Maria is proud that she has learned the bookkeeping system quickly. "I've never done anything like this before," she says.

Maria informs Jeanette that the co-op has one rent-collection problem. The co-op voted to raise the rents of the two commercial tenants in the building's storefront. One of the tenants—an older man who operated the first-floor space as a meat locker—failed to pay his rent and now can't be found. Jeanette describes the legal procedures for evicting the tenant and attaching the property in the storefront if the tenant does not pay. She instructs Maria to read certain sections of the commercial lease and to call a lawyer about legal eviction.

Like all other businesses, a housing co-op must keep accurate records of all its business transactions. The co-op must report its income to state and federal governments for tax reasons, but that isn't the only reason for keeping records. The board of directors and the members have a right and a need to know that the co-op's money is being used efficiently and effectively. After all, it's their co-op business and their money.

The board needs financial records to plan the current and future operations of the co-op. The board must decide such questions as the following: Are the carrying charges adequate to cover the cost of operation? Are any particular expenditures abnormally high? Should the co-op convert its old heating plant to a new, more efficient one? It is just like when you bring your checkbook up to date to see if you can afford new tires for your car: the board can answer its questions about expenditures only if it has accurate financial records.

We should mention two other potential users of the financial data: lenders and prospective members. Lenders invest in the co-op business by making loans for building purchase and improvement. Prospective lenders want to be sure that the co-op's financial plans are sound and that the co-op will have the money to repay the loan. Prospective members want to know that they are investing in a stable business. If it is not stable, they may lose their investment or end up paying more than the specified carrying charges to cover deficits.

Medium-size and large businesses typically employ staff accountants or bookkeepers who have been trained in accounting. Smaller businesses, like small housing co-ops, do not have a volume of financial transactions that justifies employing staff accountants. For the smaller housing co-op, the options are usually to hire an accountant or bookkeeper on a part-time or consulting basis; to use the bookkeepers of its management agent; to share bookkeeping staff with other co-ops; to use the bookkeeping services provided by its bank; or to assign bookkeeping tasks to its members.

In this chapter, we will describe an accounting system that should be adequate for a small co-op. It is not that complex double-entry system that larger businesses use and that requires skilled bookkeepers. Our single-entry record-keeping system is similar to checkbook record keeping and can be managed easily by one diligent co-op member. Even if you don't manage your own books, this chapter will explain some of the basics of accounting and introduce the financial statements that all co-op members should understand. Your management or financial committee should be familiar with the terms in this chapter.

When co-op members keep the records, there are several benefits. The co-op saves money because members maintain the records for free or for a smaller fee than professionals charge. The co-op also benefits because its members learn more about the co-op's operations and finances and can make more informed decisions. Also, individual members can learn valuable accounting and other business skills. A case in point: Maria recently found employment as a bookkeeper for a small business.

Setting Up a Simple Accounting System

This section introduces some of the key concepts of accounting so that co-op members and officers are able to understand how co-op books are kept and how financial reports are constructed. It is not a complete or comprehensive introduction to accounting. We strongly advise the co-op treasurer or bookkeeper to seek out a course in accounting for small businesses. Courses may be available locally through adult education programs, continuing education programs, professional schools, clerical schools, or colleges.

The term *accounting* conjures up visions of a little man in a green visor hovering late at night over growing stacks of receipts and papers in a dingy corner of an office. The single light bulb barely illuminates his work, and the eyes behind the small wire-rimmed glasses squint while the pencil scribbles yet another entry into the books. But accounting is not just something reserved for dark corners of business offices. Everyone practices accounting at some level. Accounting is the systematic practice of maintaining records of all financial transactions for an individual or business. It is the language of business.

Accounting systems can be as simple as your checkbook register. Every time you write a check or make a deposit, you write it in the register so that you can calculate the balance of your account at any given time. Once a month the bank sends you a statement, which you check against your own records. These are the essentials of an accounting system: (1) standard procedures for recording transactions, (2) the capability of calculating the financial position of the business at any point, and (3) documentation sufficient for auditing or checking the numbers.

A system of self-managed accounting for the small co-op can work, provided the co-op sets up the proper procedures. The co-op should design an accounting system with sufficient records and regular examinations to ensure that the books are accurate and up to date. We suggest some of the following ideas:

- The co-op should establish a financial committee to prepare budgets and oversee management of the records. This function can be performed by the board of directors, although we like the idea of a committee preparing budgets for the board to review and adopt because it involves more members in the financial planning.
- The committee or board should select as the bookkeeper a member who is considered to be both reliable and trustworthy. It is preferable that the bookkeeper have some experience with accounting, although any member who is at least unafraid of numbers and willing to learn the basics of bookkeeping can manage. It is important that the co-op designate *one* person with the responsibility for making the entries, because bookkeeping by committee inevitably leads to confusion about who did or did not make entries.
- The co-op should provide the bookkeeper with the opportunity to take a course or training in accounting procedures for small businesses.
- The co-op should hire a professional accountant to do annual audits and financial statements. This accountant can suggest a simple bookkeeping system for the co-op's bookkeeper to use. Be sure that the accountant does not set up a system that is too complicated. If you don't understand the system, it can't work for you.
- The co-op should schedule a regular review of the co-op books by the board or general membership, preferably monthly. The bookkeeper should be required to submit a monthly summary of income and expenses.
- The co-op should designate someone in addition to the

bookkeeper to sign checks. Double signatures on checks are common practice.

The accounting system we suggest is designed to be simple and yet adequate for a small housing co-op. It allows members to manage the co-op's cash and also to maintain sufficient records so that a qualified accountant or a certified public accountant (CPA) can construct year-end statements and prepare the co-op's tax return.

The system is based on a single-entry journal. When you receive income, you make a single entry in a journal; when you make a payment you make a single entry in an expanded checkbook/journal format. Backing up these journal entries are certain files of receipts and records that a professional accountant can use for the audit statements.

The system can be simple because income and expenses for the co-op are fairly fixed and regular. Each month the co-op collects about the same amount of money from its members and pays the bills of a fairly regular group of creditors: banks, utility companies, maintenance services and tradespeople, and employees. Working with similar collections and bills each month makes it easier to plan and track the cash flow.

BANK ACCOUNTS

A co-op is likely to need more than one bank account to hold funds for different purposes. First, the co-op should set up a checking account for operations, depositing co-op income and disbursing cash for expenses from this account. Second, the co-op should maintain an account for capital funds, replacement reserves, and capital for buying and selling member shares. Because these funds are not increased or disbursed regularly, they need not be in a checking account. Checking accounts bear little or no interest, so a reliable money market fund may be the best place to deposit these funds. Third, the co-op may collect security or damage deposits from members. These funds should be accounted separately, since they can be used by the co-op only under certain circumstances.

ACCOUNTING RECORDS

There are two major types of accounting records: journals and ledgers. Journals are chronological records of all transactions by the co-op. Your personal checkbook register is an example of a simple journal. Ledgers classify all transactions by type, recording different types of transactions in different accounts. The accounts are typically the line items on the co-op's financial statements. Examples of ledger accounts might be utilities expense, maintenance expense, and insurance expense. The small co-op can operate a successful bookkeeping system with three journals:

1. *Collections journal.* A monthly record of each member's required and actual contributions to the co-op. The journal page might look like the page depicted in Figure 5. Each

Figure 5
Sample Co-op Collections Journal Page

Always Cooperative
Boston, MA   Collections Journal   April 1983

Unit #	Member Name	Old Arrears	New Charges	Total Due	Amount Paid
1-A	Prince	$ 0	$ 275	$ 275	$ 275
1-B	Smith	0	275	275	
2-A	Kent	320	320	640	640
2-B	Hall	0	320	320	320
3-A	Meyer	0	275	275	275
3-B	Ewing	275	275	550	550
4-A	Hines	0	320	320	320
4-B	Cobb	0	320	320	320
	TOTALS	$595	$2380	$2975	$2700

month, a new journal sheet (or sheets) is started with the columns in the figure, and one line is designated to each unit in the co-op.

2. *Cash receipts journal.* The cash receipts journal is a chronological listing of all money received by the co-op. Such money can be recorded according to the date it is actually received or the date it is deposited in the appropriate account. Figure 6 shows a sample cash receipts journal page. The purpose of the cash receipts journal is to provide an accurate record of the source and destination (account of deposit) of each dollar of co-op income. It may seem like you are duplicating all your records, but such is the nature of bookkeeping. Note that for income category in Figure 6 you may have two columns for income code number and amount allocated, or you may set up a column for each income category, such as monthly charges, parking, special assessments, and so on.

Figure 5

Sample Co-op Collections Journal Page (*cont'd.*)

Date Paid	Date Deposited	Adjustments	New Arrears (Carry Forward)	Explanation
4/7	4/10		$275	Late Fee—
4/1	4/1	$10	10	March
4/3	4/4			
4/8	4/10			
4/3	4/4			
4/1	4/1			
4/9	4/10			
		$10	$285	

Figure 6
Sample Co-op Cash Receipts Journal Page

Cash Receipts Journal

Always Cooperative
Boston, MA

April 1983

Date Received	Source (Name)	Receipt #	Amount	Date Deposited	Income Category
4/1	Kent, Apt. 2-A	051	640	4/1	
	Hines, Apt. 4-A	052	320	4/1	
4/3	Hall, Apt. 2-B	053	320	4/4	
	Ewing, Apt. 3-B	054	550	4/4	
4/5	Laundry Income		25.50	4/10	
4/7	Prince, Apt. 1-A	055	275	4/10	
4/8	Meyer, Apt. 3-A	056	275	4/10	
4/9	Cobb, Apt. 4-B	057	320	4/10	
4/30	Interest Income—Bank		47.28	4/30	
			2772.78		

3. *Cash disbursements journal.* This journal records every expenditure of funds. For each expenditure, the journal might look like the sample in Figure 7. Many co-ops have found that maintaining "one-write" check systems enables them to combine the checkbook and the cash disbursements journal into one step. One-write systems are designed so that

Figure 7
Sample Co-op Cash Disbursements Journal Page

Cash Disbursements Journal

Always Cooperative
Boston, MA

April 1983

Date Paid	Payee (Name)	Check #	Amount	Expense Category/Explanation
4/1	Boston Bank & Trust	209	1437	Mortgage
4/5	Edison	210	272.38	Electric Bill (Feb.–March)
4/5	City Gas Co.	211	326.32	Gas (March)
4/5	Charles Plumbing	212	60	Service (3/11)
4/8	Meyer	213	12.72	Reimburse—Office Supplies
4/9	Lynch	214	350	Accountant (1982 IRS)
4/15	Practical Insurance Co.	215	300	Insurance (April)
4/26	Park Management Co.	216	1200	Janitorial Services (March–April)
4/30	Boston Bank & Trust	—	12.00	Service Charge

the writing of a check is carbon-copied onto appropriate columns on a cash disbursements journal sheet. After the check is written, the treasurer merely has to allocate that expenditure to the proper expense category. One-write check systems are available from most business supply stores.

At the end of the co-op's fiscal year, these journals are summarized to create the income statement for the co-op. The fiscal year can begin and end at any time during the year, but most co-ops find it convenient to operate according to the calendar year, since most banks operate by the calendar year and because the co-op must allocate mortgage interest and real property tax deductions to its members for calendar years.

Depending on the detail of these journals, the co-op may decide to keep a general ledger of accounts. This ledger maintains a running record of each of the income and expense accounts mentioned in the journal. It also maintains accounts on each of the asset and liability categories of the co-op's balance sheet, recording each transaction that may affect these accounts. While the journals typically are summarized once a month, the ledger accounts may be summarized continuously, so that the co-op members can always know the cumulative status of the co-op—what it owns and owes.

FILES

Because the co-op may have to prove its sources and uses of funds, it must maintain files of all receipts. invoices, statements, and other "paper" that can document the transactions that have been recorded. Separate files may be maintained for carbons of receipts issued, deposit slips, unpaid invoices, paid invoices, and bank account reconciliations. These files (with the exception of the unpaid invoices file) may be cleaned out monthly or annually, depending on your limits of file space. Old files should be boxed, labeled, and then stored for several years.

In addition, co-ops should maintain permanent files for important documents and information such as deeds, mortgage papers, the co-op articles of incorporation and bylaws, minutes of meetings, the co-op prospectus, subscription agreements, and proprietary leases.

The Co-op Accounting Cycle

An accounting cycle is the sequence of steps for recording each transaction from the starting point of the journal entry through the end of the accounting period when all accounts are closed. For the co-op, there are two cycles, monthly and annual.

MONTHLY CYCLE

Each month the housing co-op must pay its bills: mortgages, utilities, and other operating expenses. To pay these bills, the members are assessed monthly charges in proportion to their financial interest in the co-op. The monthly cycle begins with collection of these fees from the members.

At the beginning of each month, the bookkeeper prepares the collections journal. This journal contains a line of information on each unit, including any old arrears (uncollected charges from the previous month) and the charges for the current month. Payments by each member are recorded when received.

Payments should be accepted only by check or money order. Cash can be more easily lost or stolen, and cash payments require the use of receipts. Checks, on the other hand, provide an automatic record of the transaction. A canceled check is the member's legal proof of payment, and checks that are lost can be canceled at the bank and new checks issued. Both the member and the co-op are protected.

It is important that checks be deposited quickly, to avoid losing them and to maximize the interest the co-op can earn from the balance of its accounts. When checks are deposited, they should be recorded—check by check—in the cash receipts journal. Bank deposit slips should be placed in a file.

Invoices and bills come into the co-op at all times during the month. Some may have to be paid immediately while others may wait. All invoices should be placed in an unpaid invoice file when they are received.

Checks should be used to make all payments. As invoices and bills are to be paid, the invoice should be removed from the unpaid file, a check issued, the check recorded in the cash disbursements journal, and the invoice marked paid and placed in the paid invoices file.

Once a month on a specified date the co-op receives statements on its various checking, savings, or other accounts. The date statements are issued is determined by the bank, although many banks are willing to shift the date at the request of the account holder. The co-op bookkeeper should compare the cash balance reported by the bank and the balance indicated by the co-op's books. Differences must be explained or reported to the bank for corrections. The reconciliation process can take the form shown in Figure 8.

Figure 8
Sample Reconciliation of Bank Statement

From co-op records:
Account balance—beginning of month	$ 572.16
Add: Deposits	6,740.79
Subtotal: Total cash	$7,312.95
Subtract: Checks issued	6,109.26
Balance from co-op records	$1,203.69

From bank statement:
Subtract: Bank charges	10.00
Subtract: Uncredited deposits	0
Add: Interest paid	27.64
Add: Outstanding checks	$ 685.55
Bank balance—end of month	$1,906.88

Note that reconciling the balance does not resolve differences between your records and the bank's. Uncredited deposits, unless made on the last day of the statement period, should be discussed with your bank. Make sure that you record the bank charges as a cash disbursement.

At the end of the month, the journal pages should be summarized and filed, and new pages started for the following month. Most co-ops require that the bookkeeper submit a monthly report to the board of directors for planning purposes. A sample report is included in Figure 9.

THE ANNUAL CYCLE

At the end of each year of operation, co-ops must "close their books." All accounts are summarized for the year, and income and expense accounts are cleared; that is, they are started over with a beginning balance of zero. Year-end statements are prepared by an independent accountant or a CPA, to check for record-keeping errors and to verify that the books are being managed correctly.

At least two financial statements are done at this time: the income statement and the balance sheet (properly called the statement of financial position). The income statement summarizes the revenues generated and expenses incurred by the co-op during the year. Property managers rely heavily on this information to detect problems of excessive operating costs in certain categories. For example, if heating costs exceed the budget by more than 20 percent, it is a good indication that the system may have some leaks, the boiler may need repairs, or the co-op may have to do some weatherproofing to get costs back in line. An example is given in Figure 10. Note that the statement indicates a net loss. This is because of the substantial depreciation expense, which is not an actual cash outlay. This paper loss demonstrates how real estate investors can gain tax benefits from real estate.

The balance sheet in Figure 11 gives a picture of the co-op at a certain point in time by summarizing the financial resources of the co-op and the claims against those resources.

Figure 9

Sample Co-op Treasurer's Report

Monthly Report for the Always Cooperative
For Month Ending August 31, 1982

Property Summary

Beginning cash	$ 572.16
Receipts	6,740.79
Total cash	7,312.95
Disbursements	6,109.26
Ending cash	1,203.69
Accounts receivable	617.47
Accounts payable	794.39

Cash receipts

Carrying charges	$6,400.00
Parking	325.00
Interest	15.79
Total	$6,740.79

Cash disbursed (actual names are used on report)

Lock shop	$ 55.52
Gas company	147.57
Electric company	685.55
Trash removal	245.00
Pest control	60.45
Advertising	17.90
Accountant	120.00
Maintenance person	356.23
Lawyer	240.00
Mortgage company	4,945.19
Management fee	325.85
	$7,199.26

Accounts Payable	
Gas company	$ 383.91
Electric company	321.76
Pest control	80.00
Management agent	8.72
	$ 794.39
Accounts Receivable (report may contain members' names)	
Carrying charges	$ 267.47
Parking	350.00
	$ 617.47

Each year the co-op may allocate the amounts paid for mortgage interest and real property taxes to individual members based on their financial interest in the co-op. The individual members may use these interest and tax payments as deductions from their income on their federal income tax statements. (See Chapter 5 for a discussion of financial interest and deductions.)

Other Money-Handling Matters

Under most circumstances, expenditure of co-op funds is done by check, which must be approved and signed by the co-op officers. There are some situations, however, in which authorized purchases are small or are made by members other than the officers: a community affairs committee member buys stamps and paper for a mailing about a co-op event; another member buys a plunger for the co-op. The following are some suggestions about handling reimbursement in such situations.

REIMBURSEMENT POLICY

Since it is sometimes easier and faster to purchase some items with cash, the co-op should establish a reimbursement policy. This governs the repayment of members or employees

Figure 10

Sample Co-op Income Statement

ALWAYS COOPERATIVE
Statement of Income and Expenses
For the Year Ended December 31, 1982

Income
Gross potential carrying charges	$80,735
Less: Vacancies	1,948
Net carrying charges	$78,787
Parking	2,065
Interest	491
Laundry	412
Other income	300
Total income	$82,055

Expenses
Gas	$ 2,249
Electricity	5,499
Water	798
Payroll	371
Repair and maintenance	2,510
Supplies	767
Depreciation	29,160
Real estate tax	16,625
Interest expense	18,269
Insurance	8,012
Management fee	4,850
Administrative expense	275
Total expense	$89,415

Net Income (Loss)	($ 7,360)

Figure 11

Sample Co-op Balance Sheet

ALWAYS COOPERATIVE
Balance Sheet
As of December 31, 1982

ASSETS

Current Assets	
Cash	$ 572
Cash security deposits	6,012
Accounts receivable	1,590
Prepaid insurance	1,230
Utility deposits	350
Insurance escrow	5,417
Real estate taxes escrow	2,361
Total current assets	$ 17,532

Buildings and Equipment	
Building improvements	$583,203
Accumulated depreciation	43,555
Net	539,648
Land	663
Total building and equipment	$540,311

LIABILITIES AND FUND BALANCE

Current Liabilities	
Accounts payable	$ 957
Accrued interest payable	1,511
Security deposits	6,983
Prepaid carrying charges	848
Mortgages payable (Due in 1 year)	25,000
Total current liabilities	$ 35,299

Long-Term Liabilities	
Mortgage payable	$507,898
Less: Due in 1 year	21,285
Total long-term liabilities	$482,898
Total Liabilities	$518,197
Fund Balance	
Always Cooperative fund balance	$ 39,646
Total Liabilities and Fund Balance	$557,843

for *authorized* cash purchases for the co-op. The following rules should be used:

- Require store receipts for reimbursement.
- Predetermine the people in the co-op who are authorized to make purchases.
- Set a maximum dollar limit (such as $25.00) for reimbursements without prior approval of the board or officers.
- Do not reimburse members by reducing their monthly charges. It confuses the bookkeeping.

Draw up a *reimbursement form,* which can be completed by the purchaser to provide all the information the bookkeeper needs and to which receipts may be attached. This form should also be filed when cash is advanced to a member for authorized purchases. Make sure you enter these items in the cash disbursements journal.

PETTY CASH

A small amount of cash may be kept on hand for small purchases such as stamps and office supplies. The size of the fund should be small so as not to encourage theft or misuse, but large enough to cover the small cash outlays for the period between visits to the bank. Your co-op may choose an amount that will cover a one-week to one-month period.

11
ROUNDING OUT THE CO-OP EXPERIENCE

IF THERE IS ONE THING that distinguishes co-ops, it's participation. By *participation* we mean that members are active both in the business management of the co-op and in the social activities the co-op may sponsor. We also mean that participation goes beyond the formal decision-making structures. Participation is the social energy for the co-op; it's the members' responsibility.

Participation makes the co-op more democratic. Active members know more about the co-op and are more likely to use their right to participate in co-op decision making. The more members are knowledgeable and involved, the less likely decisions and power will concentrate in a few people.

Co-op members can learn important skills by participating in co-op activities. We have seen examples of co-op members who found new and better jobs as a result of their experiences in learning to manage the co-op business. More often, we found people who simply felt that the experience they gained in the co-op was helpful to them in all kinds of work and social settings. "If only I had known then what I know now" or "If only I had known about co-ops earlier," they say. Knowledge is power to the consumer, and co-ops empower their members.

Participation can save co-ops money. Many co-ops reduce

their costs of operation by substituting the volunteer labor of their members for professional services. Sweat equity not only saves money, but it enables members to make sure things are done right by doing them themselves.

Participation creates social capital. Social capital is the product of the co-op experience, an asset for both the co-op and its individual members. It is the "interest" that members receive for their time invested in the co-op. Co-ops that foster opportunities for growth for their individual members build social capital more quickly than others; they are usually more successful. When hard times come to the co-op, it is this reserve of goodwill that members use to get by. Their feeling is that "because the co-op did something for me, I must make the effort in return."

Of course, we recognize that not everyone can or will participate to the degree we advocate in this chapter. It's a matter of personal preference, and there is room even in the most active co-ops for less-active members. And there certainly are co-ops that are structured for only a minimal amount of member participation, but these co-ops are usually more expensive and in many respects less rewarding. Because of the benefits participation can offer the group and its members, we have chosen to take the high road.

Building Participation

The task of building participation—really the task of encouraging members' willingness to participate—is in part determined by the size of the co-op and the meaningful roles the co-op can create for its members. All co-ops expect formal member participation through general membership meetings and election of the board of directors. All co-ops also must create and maintain co-op membership by communicating with the members and encouraging their attendance at the co-op's business meetings. Beyond that, the needs of the individual co-op dictate the strategy.

Spreading the work is one strategy co-ops use to encourage

participation. They maximize the number and use of committees, work groups, floor captains, and other mechanisms that distribute responsibilities far and wide. The 201-unit Bishop Cooperative in Wyandotte, Michigan, operates with a floor representative system to develop active cooperation among members. Certain problems such as broken floor tiles are handled by the floor reps, and the reps also check regularly on the well-being of members on the floor. The 474-unit Benning Heights Cooperative in Washington, D.C., is spread out in townhouses over a 22-acre site. To organize and represent tenants from all parts of the development, the co-op has twenty-nine court captains to represent clusters of townhouses.

COMMITTEES

The board of directors, at the direction of the general membership, may delegate some or most of its powers to committees. The tasks of co-op management may be too much to expect the few members of the board to shoulder. Committees share the work and expand participation.

Committees may be established to fill a temporary need of the co-op, or they may be permanent. Some of the most common committees we have found in co-ops around the country are listed below with their typical responsibilities:

- *Membership committee* creates a plan for advertising to attract members and for selecting members; it reviews member applications and recommends choices of new members to the board; it also conducts an ongoing program of member education and entertainment.
- *Financial committee* does the financial planning for the co-op; it negotiates loans and other financing; it establishes and monitors budgets; and it directs the co-op accountant and auditor.
- *Building committee* conducts the search for the co-op building and negotiates its purchase; it plans and monitors rehabilitation and improvements; and it develops the maintenance strategy and monitors building management.

- *Improvements committee* sometimes operates independently, while the building committee focuses on maintenance.
- *Activities committee* coordinates all social and member activities, while a separate membership committee screens new members.
- *Community affairs committee* manages the co-op's formal relationships with the community; it monitors and informs members of outside activities in which members may choose to participate; and it handles all public relations and co-op activities that are open to the community.
- *Security committee* plans and implements needed security devices and programs; it also maintains relations with local police and community security programs.
- *Newsletter committee* compiles and distributes a regular newsletter to and about the co-op members. As noted below, it contains a variety of pieces. Who will know about all the good if no one spreads the story?

At the time the co-op establishes committees, it should define the tasks or products of each committee. Establishing an agenda for each committee distinguishes it as one of action. Participation in the committees should be open to all.

Committees can make co-op living very active and rewarding. The 57-unit mixed-income Savo Island Co-op in Berkeley, California, came about as a result of ten years of effort by the neighborhood to convert World War II military base housing. The co-op has five standing committees that handle the various co-op duties. The social committee is allotted $25 per month to hold co-op socials. One month they sponsored a fire safety day. Fire engines arrived at the scene, but instead of putting out fires the firefighters talked with the seventy adults and ninety children about fire prevention. They also distributed warning stickers to mark the children's bedrooms. Another of the committee's social projects is the annual Labor Day get-together.

ASSIGNING WORK TASKS

The three typical systems of allocating voluntary labor are random allocation, rotation, and job-specific allocation. In the random system—which sometimes appears as no system at all—co-op members volunteer for whatever jobs they feel like doing in a particular week or month. They make their choices at meetings, on posted sign-up sheets, or through direct conversations with work coordinators. The members are free to participate at whatever level they choose, although they are sometimes required to meet a minimum level. This system encourages the natural and spontaneous flow of people's energies. It is most functional in small co-ops.

The rotation system is more structured. A listing of the necessary tasks is created, and each member has a turn at every job, according to an established cycle. This system guarantees that most members will learn to do most of the jobs, equalizing the distribution of work and knowledge. The price of the system is its rigidity: it forces people to do jobs they prefer not to do, and at times when they may not be able to do them. This system gives rise to informal—and often unreliable—job switching.

The job-specific allocation system is probably the most efficient method, because people select jobs and become experts at them by staying with the same job over several months or longer. Team tasks work well under this system, as do complex tasks or those that require specific skills. The negative aspect of this system is that members learn only a small part of the co-op work. Co-ops can overcome this by educating members in all the work tasks.

ACCOUNTABILITY

For the co-op's interdependent system to work, each member must be accountable to the co-op and to the other members, and the co-op must be accountable to all its members. Accountability works best when the members know each other and can give and take criticism without personal offense. This is the rule of accountability: criticism must be fair and constructive, offered without personal motive or malice, in the interest of achieving a better co-op environment. It means that you can suggest that the halls be kept cleaner. Be diplomatic in such matters, because a bruised ego heals very slowly. It may also mean that the board can suggest that you curb your dog. Turnabout is fair play: everyone's effort, including yours, is accountable to the members.

Accountability is not just negative feedback. It's saying "thanks" or "good job" when members perform. It's also saying "congratulations" when they excel. Too often we fail to deliver the positive side of the critique.

To deal with the negatives, however, the members must come to an understanding about how complaints are to be handled. Agreeing to the procedures for handling complaints ensures that every complaint is treated fairly and that every party is given due process. Many co-ops prefer to deal with complaints as they arise, and by prior understanding some officer or member of the co-op tries to mediate. Other co-ops, particularly larger ones, have procedures whereby complaints are brought to the board or a special committee. Complaint and response are delivered in a controlled setting that allows confrontation with minimal conflict.

THE PROBLEMS OF PARTICIPATION

Some people are reluctant to participate because they feel they have nothing to contribute. These people need encouragement; they also need to understand that other people began with few skills but that the co-op is a patient organization that exists to help its members learn. Start such people with tasks they feel they can manage.

One member of a mixed-income co-op suggested that many of the lower-income members demonstrated a reluctance to participate because they "got into the co-op from much worse subsidized housing situations." It is a combination of a past in which they have been unable to control their housing and a frustration or resignation that the co-op will present the same situation of helplessness.

At the other extreme are people who overdo it. These people do everything themselves, exhibit impatience with the group, and dominate group discussions. The co-op must control these people with job rotations, limitations on terms in office, and other rules that spread the opportunities around.

Some other members may try to dominate the co-op through coalitions: we have witnessed this in both upper-income and mixed-income co-ops. Controlling such activity is difficult. Diligent effort is required to keep all parties communicating. We refer you to some of our advice in Chapter 4.

RACISM AND SEXISM

Housing co-ops offer women and minorities a special opportunity to become leaders and to gain leadership experience that many other institutions still resist. It is to the co-op's advantage to spread the knowledge of co-op business operations as evenly as possible among the members. Many of the officers and leaders of co-ops began with little or no experience in housing, but with an earnest desire to learn. Experience is something that is gained in the co-op, not brought to it. Throughout the book we have pointed to examples of co-ops where women and minorities run the business and gain valuable skills.

Nonworking women have proved to be major assets to co-ops. They have taken over many of the day-to-day responsibilities of co-op management: bookkeeping, cash-flow management, supplies purchase, employee supervision, and many other things that need to be handled during a working day. As we noted in *The Food Co-op Handbook,* "When time, energy, and commitment become defined as assets, a truly incredible amount of womanpower can be liberated." Co-ops do a better job of recognizing the value of social capital.

Racism, like sexism, has no place in a healthy co-op. Historically speaking, housing co-ops have marched a step ahead of society in adhering to policies of nondiscrimination. The principle of open membership applies to race. Of course, we do not suggest that all co-ops are integrated or that no co-op discriminates. Co-ops unfortunately can only be as good as their memberships. If the members ignore the principle, discrimination can thrive as it does in the rest of society.

Even for well-intentioned groups, adhering to the open membership principle is not easy. The co-op must select members who will be compatible with other members, whose lifestyle accommodates the lifestyle of other members. One member with an excessively loud stereo, or frequent parties, or unclean living habits, can destroy the goodwill and devalue the social capital of the co-op. Co-ops need not be homogeneous, but the lifestyle of the members must be compatible. Unfortunately, some co-op groups lean toward selecting a homogeneous membership as a substitute for a more careful attention to selecting compatible members.

INFORMAL PARTICIPATION AND SPINOFF ACTIVITIES

So far we have been talking about formal participation and mandatory work tasks. Co-ops also foster many informal, enjoyable activities for their members. Co-op members who know each other and who enjoy sharing opportunities to eat, drink, talk, and dance together are more likely to endure the work tasks together. It's a good idea for the social committee to organize picnics, parties, and weekend retreats for the members. Potluck dinners are popular for combining co-op meetings and socializing. In rural New England, co-op square dances are enjoyable occasions.

Your co-op may be able to borrow films from local libraries or buy discounted blocks of tickets to sporting and cultural events. Coed basketball and volleyball games are fun for younger crowds. Finding the right ingredients for a co-op celebration may be a little extra work, but worthwhile.

Co-ops can also undertake activities that provide important social services to their members and the surrounding community. Co-op child-care centers are common, serving members while they work, shop, or attend to their co-op duties. Less expensive alternatives include cooperatively supervised playgrounds and co-op baby-sitting where services rather than dollars are exchanged. Co-ops with large youth or elderly populations provide organized activities. Co-ops should bear in mind that both young and old can contribute to the co-op: children can help clean up the grounds, the elderly can do many of the management tasks.

We are impressed by co-ops that have organized skill-swapping services among the members. "I'll fix your faucet leak if you'll take care of my child next Saturday afternoon" is a common swap. One of the most elaborate systems has been implemented by an Arizona co-op. Members are paid for their services with chits that represent the hours worked and that can be used to buy the services offered by other members. Their skill-exchange service includes 132 skills, from goat husbandry to foot massage. Simpler systems use regularly scheduled tag sales or goods and services exchange boards where members can trade unneeded items and services. Exchange rates are set by the individual parties. These exchanges have been particularly popular among families with young children.

Communication and Education

The original cooperative—the Rochdale Society of Pioneers in Rochdale, England—established a precedent in 1844 when the members decided to set aside 2½ percent of the society's surplus for education. They established a reading room, taught the members the principles of cooperation, and encouraged the members to use the co-op's meeting facilities for evening socializing and discussions.

Today's co-ops still subscribe to the education principle. Democratic decision making requires members that are well informed and regularly updated on business matters. Their active participation helps co-ops control costs, and education improves the quality of volunteer efforts. Education also serves a long-term organizational goal.

Our use of the term *education* is not limited to the formal training that takes place in classrooms. Co-op members learn by doing things such as landscaping and keeping the books. Members learn by investigating cable TV systems for their co-op. They learn by forming food-buying co-ops and searching markets and food wholesalers for good buys.

MEMBER ORIENTATION

We suggest that you start your education program by planning a member orientation package of activities and information. Original members will have received a prospectus that includes many of the legal documents of the corporation. Additional information you can provide in orientation is the names and telephone numbers of the officers and other members, a listing of house policies that have already been adopted, a community information package (if many of the members are new to the neighborhood), and a calendar of co-op events. Choose social activities you know will give the members plenty of opportunities to meet other members.

The purpose of orientation is to prepare the new members for life in the co-op. You want them to stop thinking as tenants and begin acting as responsible owners. For many, this transition occurs gradually over the first several months or year of occupancy.

This is the time to establish the expectations for an active and productive membership. You welcome the members into the group *and its activities;* they are now expected to participate. Spend some time explaining the co-op philosophy of participation, but be sure to work your explanation toward the specifics of participating in your co-op: what members are expected to do and what the benefits are. If you can point to dollar savings, by all means do so.

We like the idea of the weekend retreat for new co-ops. Members assemble at a church or someone's getaway spot for an intensive series of meetings, dinners, volleyball games, discussions, and other activities. For the existing co-op that has to integrate only a few new members, it makes sense to work the orientation into the co-op's regularly scheduled business and social events. One California co-op reported that it has regular potluck dinners for its twenty-five members on the first Sunday of each month, after which the membership meeting is held. When there are new members, they begin orientation sessions in the afternoon, and then they are formally introduced to the membership at the potluck dinner. Informal introductions to individual members continue through dinner. The orientation day culminates in the new members' first membership meeting.

TRAINING PROGRAMS

Orientation is only the start of member education. We like to think of the total co-op living experience as a cumulative set of learning opportunities. Much of the learning is informal, but there are some things that may be shared in training sessions. Training is particularly important for business administration skills in self-help co-ops.

Many co-ops seem to overlook the need to train the members of their board of directors. In co-ops we do not find professional board members like those who make careers of serving on boards of banks, corporations, and foundations. A new co-op board may consist of people who have never before been corporate officers, never managed a business, and never been involved in housing beyond their monthly rent payment and tenant meeting. The director's job is one that can be learned.

The New York City Tenant Interim Lease Program requires all its prospective tenant groups to go through an eleven-month probationary period, during which the officers and members are required to attend several training sessions. These training sessions, offered by the Urban Homesteading Assistance Board, cover topics such as the legal entity of the co-op, estimating rehabilitation needs, and management and bookkeeping for the small co-op. Over fifty small co-ops have participated in these training sessions.

Not every new co-op has the advantage of an Urban Homesteading Assistance Board nearby, but there are a variety of national assistance organizations that may be able to provide materials and information. The groups that have a national reputation for co-op assistance are listed in Appendix 1. In addition to these groups, we urge you to contact local government housing agencies, community development corporations, and especially other co-ops to find people and organizations in your area who may assist you in training.

STUDY GROUPS

Study groups may seem academic, but we mean them in a more practical manner. A study group consists of individuals who have come together to share in the task of exploring a new issue. Study groups are an alternative to training. A study group in one Massachusetts co-op is devoting its time to energy technologies. The group collected documents from the state and federal governments on various energy strategies, and they have visited several alternative energy installations in the Boston area. The study group proposed to the co-op that an energy audit be conducted, and the audit has been arranged through MassSave, a statewide nonprofit energy audit program. The group is now learning how to do cost-benefit analysis of various improvements suggested by the audit results.

The requirements for a study group are simple. A small group of people must be interested in a specific topic, and they must be willing to share in making phone calls, collecting materials, talking with other people, and preparing a report to the board or general membership for discussion of the issue and alternative solutions.

NEWSLETTERS

Many food and housing co-ops consider their monthly newsletter to be their "back fence." It's their way of starting news along the grapevine. An important purpose of the newsletter is to make sure that everyone gets the critical information *accurately,* particularly during the time between co-op meetings. If word of mouth and informal communication alone are used, some will not hear the news and others will

Rounding Out the Co-op Experience / 199

not hear it correctly. When the newsletter goes out to everyone, the records are set straight and rumors are squashed. Newsletters can be used to provide summaries, corporate notices, policy changes, committee activities, and other co-op business matters. Newsletters should also contain more than business news. Fill them with notes on community events, recipes, gardening hints, movie reviews, co-op work schedules, social news, phone numbers, political news and contacts, new jobs, births, and birthday greetings. Ask members to write articles of general interest, poetry, or even editorials. Along the co-op's back fence, all members are welcome to share their bits of information.

POSTERS, SIGNS, AND LEAFLETS

Posters, signs, and leaflets are important ways of communicating quickly with the co-op members. A notice board at the entrance, mailboxes, laundry room, or other commonly used public space in the co-op building will spread information about upcoming meetings and events. The notice board can also serve as the "market basket" for exchange of goods and services between members.

Keep the notice board well organized. Avoid a jumbled mess of signs and crowded lettering on individual signs, because few people will bother to decipher the message. If there are any artists in the co-op, or persons with artistic talents, enlist them for the business signs. Let the co-op set the standard for signs on the notice board. Also keep signs current; remove outdated signs regularly.

If the co-op decides to permit leafleting, request that members dispose of the leaflets properly. Your neighbors will appreciate it.

SPEAKERS

Whether your co-op is interested in the continuing education of the members or in promoting co-ops in the community, you may wish to bring in speakers. The special guests may be experts, members or organizers of other co-ops, or local speakers on a variety of topics from politics to pottery, from taxes to turnips. Establish a small committee or speaker's bureau to poll the members and coordinate appearances of speakers. There's nothing worse than a room full of people waiting for a speaker who doesn't show.

PUBLIC RELATIONS AND MEDIA

The term *public relations* conjures up notions of slick Madison Avenue types with three-piece suits, glasses, and briefcases bulging with private advertising dollars and new ideas for selling the same old soap. In a more modest way, public relations is very useful to the co-op. Co-ops may benefit from a little positive press under certain conditions: more members must be recruited; the co-op wants to get other co-ops started; or the members want to promote some local political issue or campaign. All these things can be accomplished in part through local media.

Large budgets are not necessary for effective public relations efforts; attention to quality and performance is. Dinners, award ceremonies, parties, benefits, yard sales, fairs, art exhibits, and political events—all special co-op events to which the public is invited should be carefully planned, adequately advertised, started and completed on schedule, and followed up with a notice of the success of the event. News releases and public service announcements should be written properly, clearly, and concisely. The media can bring much needed attention to the co-op and its efforts; it can also bring attention to poor administration and negative results. If you are using the media, make sure you have taken every measure to ensure a successful media event. Be sure to give all reporters adequate background on the co-op, and give them a tour.

INFORMAL COMMUNICATION

Most communication occurs informally. All your formal plans and elaborate detail for member education and community relations may be reinforced by informal networks, or

Rounding Out the Co-op Experience / 201

they may be undermined by the same networks. To make informal communication an ally, be aware of how the informal networks operate. Grapevines often are started by only a few people. It is often said that the person on the corner of the block is the opinion leader. Find out who rules the corners in your co-op, and get the information to them next time you need to spread the word fast.

The informal networks play a very important role in welcoming new members. To inform new members is insufficient; to involve them is essential. Try to hook new members into the informal network. Usually this begins with one or two members who are not officers making the effort to talk regularly with new members until they have had time to establish their own set of contacts.

The informal network can also be an important source of feedback and complaints about the co-op, its officers, and its members. We all know that many problems aren't raised in meetings or sent via other formal channels. Tap the grapevine regularly to find out what problems lie beneath the surface of formal co-op interactions and meetings. Of course, provide a suggestion box so people can register complaints or ideas anonymously.

12
VISIONS

VISIONS GROW WHEN they are shared and when they are acted upon. We would like to share with you our visions of the future of co-ops. As you begin to consider co-ops, organize co-op groups, buy a co-op membership, or manage your co-op corporation, you will have some visions of your own to add. The movement will thrive so long as its members continue to build on the ideas that have gone before.

The housing co-op movement is young. Only half a million families now live in co-ops, and many of these are co-ops only in legal form, not in substance. But we sense the rumblings of a growing interest in or—to be more exact—a growing need for co-ops. The 80 million members of the postwar baby boom are just reaching peak buying age at a time when prices and interest rates preclude even more established families from buying. The investment aspect of housing works for those who already own, but it tends to work against those who do not. Co-ops may be the first-time buyer's entrée to homeownership.

There are over 25 million elderly Americans, who are much healthier than their predecessors. They are likely to live longer and are capable of maintaining their own homes longer, but they cannot afford to do so on a fixed income. The elderly need a range of affordable living alternatives between the home and the nursing home. Elderly co-ops—and there are many successful examples—offer one such alternative.

There are more than 10,000 nonprofit housing and community development corporations in this country, many of which have affordable housing as their primary objective. Reductions in public funds for housing have caused many of these groups to turn to self-help housing strategies. Co-ops have recently crept onto the agenda of these groups. Housing co-ops are a way to provide tenant control of housing, to avoid luxury condominium conversions, and to reduce costs through self-management.

There are more than 12,000 food co-ops around the country, from multimillion-dollar supermarkets to small preorder co-ops. The members joined together to control their food costs. But in the last few years, housing costs have surpassed even food costs as the number-one out-of-control family budget item. Now when these groups sit down and talk about co-ops, the focus is likely to be housing.

The baby boom generation, the elderly, the community development industry, and the co-op movement: what do all these groups have in common? How can we envision these diverse groups as the components of a future movement?

Our vision is of a new housing co-op movement emerging through four stages. The first stage has already begun with the consumer groups we noted above. During the second stage, local federations of co-ops form. Isolated co-ops join with other co-ops to deal with mutual problems. Neighborhood issues from Stop signs to joint purchasing of supplies are worked out. In short, the co-op gets involved in the local community. As this occurs, we envision co-op management groups forming for those who need it.

In the third stage, we see the beginning of a proactive phase, where many new co-ops start and grow horizontally. By that we mean that the local model of housing co-ops will be replicated. Finally, the fourth stage is one of vertical growth, where one national voice for housing co-ops becomes real and substantive. A national organization based on neighborhood grassroots organizations will become effective for the many issues that co-op housing will face over the years.

Central to this vision of the co-op movement is the consumer. Millions and millions of average consumers are struggling to buy the best life they can with limited incomes. We believe that the pocketbook issue will draw these people together and that together they will discover participatory solutions to housing problems.

The individual housing co-op acts as a miniature community—a social organization and economic unit in which the members participate to fulfill their needs for economy and for community. They run the co-op business themselves and in doing so become more informed about the economics of housing. In turn, this helps them manage their personal affairs.

In no small part, we envision that more housing co-ops will swell the sea of consumer cooperatives. Food co-ops, worker-run co-ops, day-care co-ops, optical and health co-ops, building and supplies co-ops, and cable TV co-ops—all are necessary and useful to communities. Maybe we will not see more Co-op Cities or self-supporting co-op communities, but we do envision co-ops becoming a larger part of many communities and serving the many needs of consumers of all income levels.

Co-ops are permanent organizations. They are not speculative ventures for profiteering; rather, they are set up to provide housing for as long as the members desire. Co-ops add stability to a community. They are less susceptible to the ups or the downs of neighborhoods and neighborhood housing values, because the co-op building is not for sale and individual membership prices usually are established by formula. Neighborhoods fortified with several co-ops will not rise and fall so dramatically as many urban neighborhoods have in recent decades. Co-ops promote community.

In the long run, we see co-ops becoming a larger and more influential segment of the housing market. Co-ops emphasize the consuming aspect of housing: we need housing and should not pay more than necessary for this good. Co-ops downplay the investment angle of housing.

The original vision of the Rochdale founders was an organization that promoted practical consumer economics and social democracy. It was to be a progressive organization that led society in dealing with problems. Unfortunately, our democracy has yet to achieve some of the principles endorsed by these co-op pioneers in the 1800s. Co-ops must continue to press for the principles of social democracy.

Participation is another word for cooperation. Throughout this book we have talked about the dual principles of participation and sound business practice. The two are interrelated. Participation by the members is a cost-effective means of saving in both the short run and the long run. Participation in the short term means that members do things that the co-op would otherwise pay to have done—sweat equity. For some co-ops, the members merely replace the owner in decision making, and their savings is the landlord's previous profit. For other co-ops, participation means greater savings through self-help maintenance and management.

In the long run, participation is the glue that holds the co-op enterprise together. Participating members are more stable, and losses of turnover are minimized. High levels of participation also produce social capital, the product of the co-op experience. It is an intangible asset that benefits both the co-op and its individual members. People reap financial and emotional rewards from the co-op. Social capital sustains the co-op in hard times because the members remember the good, and they feel a responsibility to the other members to work together and endure the more difficult times.

The Grain of Salt: How to Take Our Advice

We have devoted an entire book to the many issues of choosing, buying, starting, and managing a housing co-op. Though the book may seem encyclopedic in places, we recognize there are many issues we did not explore. Our intention was to present a sequence of steps or tasks that could be used in buying into, owning, or creating a co-op. Each co-op, however, is unique, and only you and the members of your group can decide the best way to shape your co-op. Despite careful planning and scheduling, we know that things, when they happen, happen all at once. Use our tasks as milestones. Every so often, take a breather. Step back and examine how far your group has progressed.

Much of the book has focused on structure. Structure of the organization can help you do what you intend to do, but it alone is insufficient to guarantee results. The truth is that people make the co-op. As Ralph Waldo Emerson observed: "It is not the organization that creates. Man creates: organizations build."

We also concentrated on the issue of empowerment. As we noted above, you know best what kind of co-op is right for you. Our assistance in the book, and our numerous references to the use of experts, are intended to help you. Know how to use this help, but the vision and the effort are yours.

If the book has communicated on no other level, it has at least demonstrated the complexity of issues surrounding affordable housing in our society. This problem will not go away; right now, we see it as becoming more serious. We envision co-ops as a small part of the solution to the housing crisis, and knowledgeable consumers as another part. It is our hope that this book has empowered both.

Appendix 1

Co-op Assistance Organizations

Alternative Realty Center
4273 Montgomery Street
Oakland, CA 94611
(415) 547-6772
   Acts as developer, consultant, and broker in conversions of limited equity cooperatives.

Citizens Housing and Planning Association
7 Marshall Street
Boston, MA 02108
(617) 742-0820
   Consulting in conversions of HUD multi-family properties.

Common Space
2529 Nicollet Avenue South
Minneapolis, MN 55404
(612) 872-0550
   Promotes lower-income co-op conversions through technical assistance, public education, and advocacy.

Community Development Legal Assistance Center
36 W. 44th Street—Rm. 913
New York, NY 10036
(212) 840-1541
   Legal assistance to co-op conversions.

Community Economics, Inc.
1904 Franklin Street—Suite 900
Oakland, CA 94612
(415) 832-8300
   Technical assistance to limited-equity co-ops and non-profit housing; co-op housing publications.

Conference on Alternative State and Local Policies
2000 Florida Avenue, NW—Suite 400
Washington, DC 20009
(202) 387-6030
   Publishes the Co-op Bank *Monitor*.

Cooperative League of the U.S.A.
1828 L Street, NW—Suite 1100
Washington, DC 20036
(202) 872-0550
   Trade association of co-ops.

Cooperative Services, Inc.
7404 Woodward Avenue
Detroit, MI 48202
(313) 874-4000
   Co-op management services.

Co-operative Union of Canada
237 Metcalfe Street
Ottawa, Ontario
Canada K2P 1R2
Executive Director: Bruce Thordarson
(613) 238-6711

Metropolitan Washington Planning and Housing Association
1420 New York Avenue, NW—Suite 300
Washington, DC 20005
(202) 842-1800
   Assists tenant conversions of properties.

Multi Family Housing Services, Inc.
518 North Charles Street
Baltimore, MD 21201
(301) 659-6966
   Housing co-op development, marketing, and management services.

National Association of Housing Cooperatives
2501 M Street, NW—Suite 451
Washington, DC 20037
(202) 887-0706
Association supporting housing co-ops through publications, seminars, and advocacy. Member associations are as follows:

California Association of Housing Cooperatives
300 Valley Street—Suite 301
Sausalito, CA 94965
Executive Director: Lydia Joseph
(415) 332-7021

Cooperative Services, Inc.
7404 Woodward Avenue
Detroit, MI 48202
Housing Development Manager: Martha Sachs
(313) 874-4000

Eastern Cooperative Housing Organization
4530 West 62nd Street
Cleveland, Ohio 44144
President: Ben Lecorchick
(216) 661-6023

Federation of New England Housing Cooperatives
Northridge Homes
81 Northridge Road
Beverly, MA 01915
President: Dean McKennon
(617) 922-6514

Federation of New York Housing Cooperatives
Federation of Section 213's
138-10 Franklin Avenue
Flushing, NY 11355
President: Charles Rappaport
(212) 353-5080

Midwest Association of Housing Cooperatives
343 South Main Street—#208
Ann Arbor, MI 48104
Executive Director: Debra Locke
(313) 994-4314

Mitchell-Lama Council
Room 612
799 Broadway
New York, NY 10003
President: Murray Raphael
(212) 673-5631

Potomac Association of Housing Cooperatives
1418 Fenwick Lane
Silver Spring, MD 20901
President: Edward F. Jesse, C.P.A.
(301) 589-5450

Southeast Association of Housing Cooperatives
405 Fairburn Road, SW—#94
Atlanta, GA 30331
President: Marlene Cooper
(404) 588-3865

National Consumer Cooperative Bank
Office of Technical Assistance
2001 S Street, NW
Washington, DC 20009
(202) 745-4600, (800) 424-2581
   Credit and technical assistance to emerging co-ops of all types.

   Regional offices: Atlanta (404) 525-0759
                     Boston (617) 223-5234
                     Dallas (214) 767-8040
                     Minneapolis (612) 725-2305

New York City (212) 264-8333
Oakland (415) 273-7576

National Federation of Community Development
Credit Unions
577—6th Street
Brooklyn, NY 11215
(212) 768-7859
Technical assistance, advocacy, and training.

New School for Democratic Management
109 Minna Street, Box 296
San Francisco, CA 94105
(415) 566-0221
Management training and technical assistance for community-based organizations.

North American Students of Cooperation (NASCO)
P.O. Box 7293
Ann Arbor, MI 48107
(313) 663-0889
Publications, conferences, consulting, and board trainings on co-ops.

Rural America
1900 M Street, NW—Suite 320
Washington, DC 20036
(202) 659-2800
Provides information and technical assistance on rural housing programs.

Shared Living Project
67 Newbury Street
Boston, MA 02116
(617) 266-2257
Develops intergenerational shared-living housing.

Urban Alternatives Group
4273 Montgomery Street
Oakland, CA 94611
(415) 547-6772
> Educational programs, development consulting, research, and publications to further community self-reliance and cooperation.

Urban Homesteading Assistance Board
Cathedral House
1047 Amsterdam Avenue
New York, NY 10025
(212) 749-0602
> Assists low income co-op conversions and building rehabilitation in New York City.

Appendix 2

HUD Model Documents for Housing Co-ops

Model Form of By-Laws
Model Form of Certificate of Incorporation
Model Form of Occupancy Agreement
Model Form of Subscription Agreement

FHA FORM NO. 3245
Revised June, 1970

U. S. DEPARTMENT OF HOUSING AND URBAN DEVELOPMENT
FEDERAL HOUSING ADMINISTRATION

MODEL FORM OF BY-LAWS
(For use by Cooperatives in Sections 213, 221 and 236 cases)

ARTICLE I. NAME AND LOCATION OF CORPORATION

ARTICLE II. PURPOSE

ARTICLE III. MEMBERSHIP

    Section 1. Eligibility
    Section 2. Application for Membership
    Section 3. Subscription Funds
    Section 4. Members
    Section 5. Membership Certificates
    Section 6. Lost Certificates
    Section 7. Lien
    Section 8. Transfer of Membership
        (a) Death of Member
        (b) Option of Corporation to Purchase
        (c) Procedure Where Corporation Does Not Exercise Option
        (d) Transfer Value
    Section 9. Termination of Membership for Cause
    Section 10. Sales Price

ARTICLE IV. MEETINGS OF MEMBERS

    Section 1. Place of Meetings
    Section 2. Annual Meetings
    Section 3. Special Meetings
    Section 4. Notice of Meetings
    Section 5. Quorum
    Section 6. Adjourned Meetings
    Section 7. Voting
    Section 8. Proxies
    Section 9. Order of Business

ARTICLE V. DIRECTORS

    Section 1. Number and Qualification
    Section 2. Powers and Duties
    Section 3. Election and Term of Office
    Section 4. Vacancies
    Section 5. Removal of Directors
    Section 6. Compensation
    Section 7. Organization Meeting
    Section 8. Regular Meetings
    Section 9. Special Meetings
    Section 10. Waiver of Notice
    Section 11. Quorum
    Section 12. Fidelity Bonds
    Section 13. Safeguarding Subscription Funds

ARTICLE VI. OFFICERS

    Section 1. Designation
    Section 2. Election of Officers
    Section 3. Removal of Officers
    Section 4. President
    Section 5. Vice-President
    Section 6. Secretary
    Section 7. Treasurer

ARTICLE VII. RIGHTS OF FEDERAL HOUSING ADMINISTRATION

ARTICLE VIII. AMENDMENTS

ARTICLE IX. CORPORATE SEAL

ARTICLE X. FISCAL MANAGEMENT

    Section 1. Fiscal Year
    Section 2. Books and Accounts
    Section 3. Auditing
    Section 4. Inspection of Books
    Section 5. Execution of Corporate Documents

ARTICLE XI. COMMUNITY FACILITY PROVISIONS (SALES TYPE PROJECTS)

    Section 1. Applicable Provisions
    Section 2. Membership
    Section 3. Directors

ARTICLE I

NAME AND LOCATION OF CORPORATION

Section 1. The name of this Corporation is _____
_____ . Its principal office is located at _____ ,
_____ .

ARTICLE II

PURPOSE

Section 1. The purpose of this Corporation is to provide its members* with housing and community facilities, if any, on a nonprofit basis consonant with the provisions set forth in its Certificate of Incorporation.

ARTICLE III

MEMBERSHIP

Section 1. <u>Eligibility.</u> Any natural person approved by the Board of Directors shall be eligible for membership, provided that he or she executes a Subscription Agreement and Occupancy Agreement in the usual form employed by the Corporation covering a specific unit in the housing project.**

Section 2. <u>Application for Membership.</u> Application for membership shall be presented in person on a form prescribed by the Board of Directors, and all such applications shall be acted upon promptly by the Board of Directors.

Section 3. <u>Subscription Funds.</u> *** All subscription funds (except funds required for credit reports) received from applicants prior to the endorsement of the mortgage note by the Federal Housing Administration (hereinafter sometimes referred to as the "Administration") shall be deposited promptly without deduction in a special account or accounts of the Corporation as escrowee or trustee for the Subscribers to Membership, which monies shall not be corporate funds, but shall be held solely for the benefit of the Subscribers until transferred to the account of the Corporation as hereinafter provided. Such special account or accounts shall be established with _____
_____ (name of institution) located at _____
_____ , whose deposits are insured by an agency of the Federal Government. Such account or accounts may be interest bearing, with the interest earned to be retained and owned by the Corporation. Such funds shall be subject to withdrawal, or transfer to the account of the Corporation or disbursed in a manner directed by the Corporation only upon certification by the President and Secretary of the Corporation to the above-named institution or institutions that:

(a) The Subscription Agreement of a named applicant has been terminated pursuant to its terms and such withdrawal is required to repay the amount paid by him under such agreement; or

---

* In corporations organized on a stock basis, change the word "members" to "stockholders" and add thereafter the following parenthetical clause: "(hereinafter referred to as 'members')."
** In corporations organized on a stock basis, change the word "membership" to "stock ownership" and add thereafter the following parenthetical clause: "(hereinafter referred to as 'membership')."
*** In view of the fact that certain sponsoring groups such as labor unions, veterans' organizations, church groups, cooperative sponsoring organizations, may wish to use some other method of handling subscriptions or subscriptions funds, this section may be altered, subject to prior approval of the Administration.

(b) Applicants for _____ * dwelling units have not been procured within the effective period of the FHA Commitment, or any extension thereof, and such withdrawal is required to repay to the applicants the amounts paid by them; or

(c) Applicants for _____ * dwelling units (or such lesser number as may be approved by the Administration) have signed Subscription Agreements, have been approved as to their credit by the Administration, and have paid the subscription price in full. If these requirements have been met and the mortgage loan has been scheduled for closing with the approval of the Administration, the entire amount of the funds in the subscription escrow account may be transferred to the corporation, at which time the corporation shall issue and deliver membership certificates to all members.

If more than one mortgage is to be executed by the corporation, this section shall be deemed to be applicable to the specific subscription fund received from applicants with respect to the specific dwelling units to be covered by each mortgage and to require the creation of separate and specific escrow accounts with respect to each mortgage.

Section 4. Members. The members shall consist of the incorporators and such subscribers as have been approved for membership by the Board of Directors and who have paid for their membership and received membership certificates. The status of the incorporators as members shall terminate at the first annual meeting of members unless they have executed Subscription Agreements and, where required by the Administration, Occupancy Agreements. The authorized membership of the Corporation shall consist of _____ regular memberships. **

Section 5. Membership Certificates. Each membership certificate shall state that the Corporation is organized under the laws of the State of _____ , the name of the registered holder of the membership represented thereby, the Corporation lien rights as against such membership as set forth this Article, and the preferences and restrictions applicable thereto, and shall be in such form as shall be approved by the Board of Directors. Membership certificates shall be consecutively numbered, bound in one or more books, and shall be issued therefrom upon certification as to full payment. Every membership certificate shall be signed by the President or Vice President, and the Secretary, and shall be sealed with the corporate seal.

Section 6. Lost Certificates. The Board of Directors may direct a new certificate or certificates to be issued in place of any certificate or certificates previously issued by the Corporation and alleged to have been destroyed or lost, upon the making of an affidavit of that fact by the person claiming the share certificate to be lost or destroyed. When authorizing such issuance of a new certificate or certificates, the Board of Directors may, in its discretion, and as a condition precedent to the issuance thereof, require the registered owner of such lost or destroyed certificate or certificates, or his legal representative, to advertise the same in such manner as the Board of Directors shall require and to give the Corporation a bond in such sum as the Board of Directors may require as indemnity against any claim that may be made against the Corporation.

Section 7. Lien. The Corporation shall have a lien on the outstanding regular memberships in order to secure payment of any sums which shall be due or become due from the holders thereof for any reason whatsoever, including any sums due under any occupancy agreements.

Section 8. Transfer of Membership. Except as provided herein, membership shall not be transferable and, in any event, no transfer of membership shall be made upon the books of the Corporation within ten (10) days next preceding the annual meeting of the members. In all transfers of membership the Corporation shall be entitled to a fee it deems appropriate to compensate it for the processing of the transfer.

---

* Insert number required by the applicable FHA Commitment.
** In cases where FHA control is via ownership of preferred stock, add "and _____ preferred memberships."

(a) <u>Death of Member.</u> If, upon death of a member, his membership in the Corporation passes by will or intestate distribution to a member of his immediate family, such legatee or distributee may, by assuming in writing the terms of the Subscription Agreement and Occupancy Agreement, where required by the Administration, within sixty (60) days after member's death, and paying all amounts due thereunder, become a member of the Corporation. If member dies and an obligation is not assumed in accordance with the foregoing, then the Corporation shall have an option to purchase the membership from the deceased member's estate in the manner provided in paragraph (b) of this Section, written notice of the death being equivalent to notice of intention to withdraw. If the Corporation does not exercise such option, the provisions of paragraph (c) of this Section shall be applicable, the references to "member" therein to be construed as references to the legal representative of the deceased member.

(b) <u>Option of Corporation to Purchase.</u> If the member desires to leave the project, he shall notify the Corporation in writing of such intention and the Corporation shall have an option for a period of thirty (30) days commencing the first day of the month following the giving of such notice, but not the obligation, to purchase the membership, together with all of the member's rights with respect to the dwelling unit, at an amount to be determined by the Corporation as representing the transfer value thereof, less any amounts due by the member to the Corporation under the Occupancy Agreement, and less the cost or estimated cost of all deferred maintenance, including painting, redecorating, floor finishing, and such repairs and replacements as are deemed necessary by the Corporation to place the dwelling unit in suitable condition for another occupant. The purchase by the Corporation of the membership will immediately terminate the member's rights and the member shall forthwith vacate the premises.

(c) <u>Procedure Where Corporation Does Not Exercise Option.</u> If the Corporation waives in writing its right to purchase the membership under the foregoing option, or if the Corporation fails to exercise such option within the thirty (30) day period, the member may sell his membership to any person who has been duly approved by the Corporation as a member and occupant.

If the Corporation agrees, at the request of the member, to assist the member in finding a purchaser, the Corporation shall be entitled to charge the member a fee it deems reasonable for this service. When the transferee has been approved for membership and has executed the prescribed Occupancy Agreement, the retiring member shall be released of his obligations under his Occupancy Agreement, provided he has paid all amounts due the Corporation to date.

(d) <u>Transfer Value.</u>* Whenever the Board of Directors elects to purchase a membership, the term "transfer value" shall mean the sum of the following:

(1) The consideration (i.e. down payment) paid for the membership by the first occupant of the unit involved as shown on the books of the Corporation;

(2) The value, as determined by the Directors, of any improvements installed at the expense of the member with the prior approval of the Directors, under a valuation formula which does not provide for reimbursement in an amount in excess of the typical initial cost of the improvements; and

(3) The amount of principal amortized by the Corporation on its mortgage indebtedness and attributable to the dwelling unit involved as paid by the member involved and previous holders of the same membership.** However, the amount of principal paid by the Corporation for a period of three (3) years after the Corporation has made its first principal payment on the mortgage shall not be included in this computation.

---

* If desired, a provision may be added to the effect that the transfer value otherwise applicable may be increased and decreased pursuant to fluctuations in the economy as evidenced by a Cost of Living Index or a Construction Cost Index. The language of such provision must be cleared with the FHA.

** In Section 221 below market interest rate cases and in Section 236 cases the sentence following the asterisks should be added. (A limitation which further restricts the amount payable to the retiring member in such cases may be imposed subject to the approval of FHA.)

* Whenever a member who has received rent supplement assistance sells his membership, the amount of such assistance shall be deducted from the transfer value to which such member would otherwise be entitled as follows:

   (i) A portion of that amount of principal amortized as determined in (d) (3), above, will not be made available to the member. The amount so withheld shall be determined by multiplying the amortized principal attributable to the unit by the quotient of the total rent supplement assistance to the member divided by the total monthly carrying charges the member was obligated to pay under his occupancy agreement and would have paid if he had not received rent supplement assistance.

   (ii) In the event the corporation exercises its option to purchase the membership pursuant to paragraph (b), above, an amount computed in accordance with (i), above, shall be withheld from the proceeds of such sale and retained by the Corporation.

   (iii) In the event the member sells his membership pursuant to paragraph (c), above, the selling member and the purchaser who purchases from such member shall jointly certify to the Corporation as to the sales price of the membership in such manner and in such form as may be required by the Corporation. An amount equal to the amount computed in accordance with (i), above, shall be paid to the Corporation prior to the Corporation's release of such member's obligation under his occupancy agreement and the transfer of his membership to the new owner; provided, however, that in the event the sales price does not exceed the total paragraphs d(1) and d(2), above, then the selling member shall be entitled to receive the full amount of the sales price.

   (iv) All funds received by the Corporation representing withheld amortized principal attributable to Rent Supplement Payments shall be deposited in a special account by the Corporation and disbursed as directed by the Federal Housing Administration.

Section 9. <u>Termination of Membership for Cause.</u> In the event the Corporation has terminated the rights of a member under the Occupancy Agreement, the member shall be required to deliver promptly to the Corporation his membership certificate and his Occupancy Agreement, both endorsed in such manner as may be required by the Corporation. The Corporation shall thereupon at its election either (1) repurchase said membership at its transfer value (as hereinabove defined) or the amount the retiring member originally paid for the acquisition of his membership certificate, whichever is the lesser, or (2) proceed with reasonable diligence to effect a sale of the membership to a purchaser and at a sales price acceptable to the Corporation. The retiring member shall be entitled to receive the amount so determined, less the following amounts (the determination of such amounts by the Corporation to be conclusive):

   (a) any amounts due to the Corporation from the member under the Occupancy Agreement;

   (b) the cost or estimated cost of all deferred maintenance, including painting, redecorating, floor finishing, and such repairs and replacements as are deemed necessary by the Corporation to place the dwelling unit in suitable condition for another occupant; and

   (c) legal and other expenses incurred by the Corporation in connection with the default of such member and the resale of his membership. In the event the retiring member for any reason should fail for a period of 10 days after demand to deliver to the Corporation his endorsed membership certificate, said membership certificate shall forthwith be deemed to be cancelled and may be reissued by the Corporation to a new purchaser.

** Section 10. <u>Sales Price.</u> Memberships may be sold by the Corporation or the member only to a person approved by the Board of Directors in accordance with the requirements of the Regulatory Agreement, and the sales price shall not exceed the transfer value as provided in this Article, except that in sales effected by the Corporation a service charge not in excess of $100 may be charged by the Corporation. Where the sale is accomplished by a member, a certificate in form approved by the FHA as to the price paid shall be executed by the seller and purchaser and delivered to the Corporation.

---
* Include this paragraph only in projects where rent supplements are contemplated.
** Omit in Section 213 cases and market interest rate cases under Section 221(d) (3).

Appendix 2/223

ARTICLE IV

MEETINGS OF MEMBERS

Section 1. <u>Place of Meetings</u>. Meetings of the membership shall be held at the principal office or place of business of the Corporation or at such other suitable place convenient to the membership as may be designated by the Board of Directors.

Section 2. <u>Annual Meetings</u>. The first annual meeting of the Corporation shall be held on _____ . (Date) Thereafter, the annual meetings of the Corporation shall be held on the _____ (1st, 2nd, 3rd, 4th) _____ (Monday, Tuesday, Wednesday, etc.) of _____ (Month) each succeeding year. At such meeting there shall be elected by ballot of the members a Board of Directors in accordance with the requirements of Section 3 of Article V of these By-Laws. The members may also transact such other business of the Corporation as may properly come before them.

Section 3. <u>Special Meetings</u>. It shall be the duty of the President to call a special meeting of the members as directed by resolution of the Board of Directors or upon a petition signed by twenty (20) percent of the members having been presented to the Secretary, or at the request of the Federal Housing Commissioner or his duly authorized representative. The notice of any special meeting shall state the time and place of such meeting and the purpose thereof. No business shall be transacted at a special meeting except as stated in the notice unless by consent of four-fifths of the members present, either in person or by proxy.

Section 4. <u>Notice of Meetings</u>. It shall be the duty of the Secretary to mail a notice of each annual or special meeting, stating the purpose thereof as well as the time and place where it is to be held, to each member of record, at his address as it appears on the membership book of the Corporation, or if no such address appears, at his last known place of address, at least _____ but not more than _____ days prior to such meeting (the number of days notice to comply with state statute). Service may also be accomplished by the delivery of any such notice to the member at his dwelling unit or last known address. Notice by either such method shall be considered as notice served. Notices of all meetings shall be mailed to the Director of the local insuring office of the Federal Housing Administration.

Section 5. <u>Quorum</u>. The presence, either in person or by proxy, of at least _____ * percent of the members of record of the Corporation shall be requisite for, and shall constitute a quorum for the transaction of business at all meetings of members. If the number of members at a meeting drops below the quorum and the question of a lack of quorum is raised, no business may thereafter be transacted.

Section 6. <u>Adjourned Meetings</u>. If any meeting of members cannot be organized because a quorum has not attended, the members who are present, either in person or by proxy, may, except as otherwise provided by law, adjourn the meeting to a time not less than forty-eight (48) hours from the time the original meeting was called, at which subsequent meeting the quorum requirement shall be _____ * percent.

Section 7. <u>Voting</u>. ** At every meeting of the regular members, each member present, either in person or by proxy, shall have the right to cast one vote on each question and never more than

---

* The figure to be inserted will vary with the size of the cooperative, as follows:

Number of Memberships	Quorum percentage to be inserted in Article IV, Sec. 5	Quorum percentage applicable to adjourned meetings to be inserted in Article IV, Sec. 6
20 or less	50	25
21 - 150	25	15
151 - 300	20	10
301 - 500	15	10
501 or more	10	5

** There will be no objection to including a provision permitting voting by mail, and this may be desirable in the larger cooperatives.

one vote. (Note - If desired, a provision may be included to the effect that where a husband and wife are joint members, each shall be entitled to cast a one-half vote.) The vote of the majority of those present, in person or by proxy, shall decide any question brought before such meeting, unless the question is one upon which, by express provision of statute or of the Certificate of Incorporation or of these By-Laws, a different vote is required, in which case such express provision shall govern and control. No member shall be eligible to vote or to be elected to the Board of Directors who is shown on the books or management accounts of the Corporation to be more than 30 days delinquent in payments due the Corporation under his Occupancy Agreement.

Section 8. Proxies. A member may appoint as his proxy only a member of his immediate family (as defined by the Board of Directors) except that an unmarried member may appoint any other member as his proxy. In no case may a member cast more than one vote by proxy in addition to his own vote. Any proxy must be filed with the Secretary before the appointed time of each meeting.

Section 9. Order of Business. The order of business at all regularly scheduled meetings of the regular members shall be as follows:

(a) Roll Call.
(b) Proof of notice of meeting or waiver of notice.
(c) Reading of minutes of preceding meeting.
(d) Reports of officers.
(e) Report of committees.
(f) Election of inspectors of election.
(g) Election of directors.
(h) Unfinished business.
(i) New business.

In the case of special meetings, items (a) through (d) shall be applicable and thereafter the agenda shall consist of the items specified in the notice of meeting.

If present, a representative of the Administration will be given an opportunity to address any regular or special meeting.

ARTICLE V

DIRECTORS

Section 1. Number and Qualification. The affairs of the Corporation shall be governed by a Board of Directors composed of _____ persons*, a majority of whom shall be members of the Corporation.

Section 2. Powers and Duties. The Board of Directors shall have all the powers and duties necessary for the administration of the affairs of the Corporation and may do all such acts and things as are not by law or by these By-Laws directed to be exercised and done by the members. The powers of the Board of Directors shall include but not be limited:

(a) To accept or reject all applications for membership and admission to occupancy of a dwelling unit in the cooperative housing project, either directly or through an authorized representative;

(b) Subject to the approval of the Administration, to establish monthly carrying charges as provided for in the Occupancy Agreement, based on an operating budget formally adopted by such Board;

---

* Any convenient number of Directors (not less than three nor more than nine) may be provided.

(c) Subject to the approval of the Administration, to engage an agent or employees for the management of the project under such terms as the Board may determine;

(d) To authorize in their discretion patronage refunds from residual receipts when and as reflected in the annual report;*

(e) To terminate membership and occupancy rights for cause;

(f) To promulgate such rules and regulations pertaining to use and occupancy of the premises as may be deemed proper and which are consistent with these By-Laws and the Certificate of Incorporation;** and

(g) ***Pursuant to a plan approved by the Administration, to prescribe additional monthly carrying charges to be paid by families whose incomes exceed the limitations for continuing occupancy established from time to time by the Administration; or, at the Board's option, to terminate the membership and occupancy of such families.

Section 3. Election and Term of Office. The term of the Directors named in the Certificate of Incorporation shall expire when their successors have been elected at the first annual meeting or any special meeting called for that purpose. At the first annual meeting of the members the term of office of two Directors shall be fixed for three (3) years. The term of office of two Directors shall be fixed at two (2) years, and the term of office of one Director shall be fixed at one (1) year. At the expiration of the initial term of office of each respective Director, his successor shall be elected to serve a term of three (3) years. The Directors shall hold office until their successors have been elected and hold their first meeting. (If a larger Board of Directors is contemplated, the terms of office should be established in a similar manner so that they will expire in different years.)

Section 4. Vacancies. Vacancies in the Board of Directors caused by any reason other than the removal of a Director by a vote of the membership or by the vote of the preferred members **** shall be filled by vote of the majority of the remaining Directors, even though they may constitute less than a quorum; and each person so elected shall be a Director until a successor is elected by the members at the next annual meeting to serve out the unexpired portion of the term.

Section 5. Removal of Directors. At any regular or special meeting duly called, any Director may be removed with or without cause by the affirmative vote of the majority of the entire regular membership of record and a successor may then and there be elected to fill the vacancy thus created. Any Director whose removal has been proposed by the members shall be given an opportunity to be heard at the meeting. The term of any Director who becomes more than 30 days delinquent in payment of his carrying charges shall be automatically terminated and the remaining Directors shall appoint his successor as provided in Section 4, above.

Section 6. Compensation. No compensation shall be paid to Directors for their services as Directors. No remuneration shall be paid to a Director for services performed by him for the Corporation in any other capacity, unless a resolution authorizing such remuneration shall have been unanimously adopted by the Board of Directors before the services are undertaken. No remuneration or compensation shall in any case be paid to a Director without the approval of the Administration. A Director may not be an employee of the Corporation.

Section 7. Organization Meeting. The first meeting of a newly elected Board of Directors shall be held within ten (10) days of election at such place as shall be fixed by the Directors at the meeting at which such Directors were elected, and no notice shall be necessary to the newly elected Directors in order legally to constitute such meeting, providing a majority of the whole Board shall be present.

---

* Delete in Section 236 cases.
** Add " and the Regulatory Agreement" where Regulatory Agreement is executed by the Corporation.
*** Include this provision only in Section 221 below market rate cases.
**** Delete "or by a vote of the preferred members" where Corporation has executed Regulatory Agreement.

Section 8. *Regular Meetings*. Regular meetings of the Board of Directors may be held at such time and place as shall be determined, from time to time, by a majority of the Directors, but at least four such meetings shall be held during each fiscal year. Notice of regular meetings of the Board of Directors shall be given to each Director, personally or by mail, telephone or telegraph, at least three (3) days prior to the day named for such meeting.

Section 9. *Special Meetings*. Special meetings of the Board of Directors may be called by the President on three days notice to each Director, given personally or by mail, telephone or telegraph, which notice shall state the time, place (as hereinabove provided) and purpose of the meeting. Special meetings of the Board of Directors shall be called by the President or Secretary in like manner and on like notice on the written request of at least three Directors.

Section 10. *Waiver of Notice*. Before or at any meeting of the Board of Directors, any Director may, in writing, waive notice of such meeting and such waiver shall be deemed equivalent to the giving of such notice. Attendance by a Director at any meeting of the Board shall be a waiver of notice by him of the time and place thereof. If all the Directors are present at any meeting of the Board, no notice shall be required and any business may be transacted at such meeting.

Section 11. *Quorum*. At all meetings of the Board of Directors, a majority of the Directors shall constitute a quorum for the transaction of business, and the acts of the majority of the Directors present at a meeting at which a quorum is present shall be the acts of the Board of Directors. If, at any meeting of the Board of Directors, there be less than a quorum present, the majority of those present may adjourn the meeting from time to time. At any such adjourned meeting, any business which might have been transacted at the meeting as originally called may be transacted without further notice.

Section 12. *Fidelity Bonds*. The Board of Directors shall require that all officers and employees of the Corporation handling or responsible for corporate or trust funds shall furnish adequate fidelity bonds. The premiums on such bonds shall be paid by the Corporation.

Section 13. *Safeguarding Subscription Funds*. It shall be the duty of the Board of Directors to see to it that all sums received in connection with membership subscriptions prior to the closing of the mortgage transaction covering the housing project of the Corporation, are deposited and withdrawn only in the manner provided for in Article III, Section 3 of these By-Laws.

ARTICLE VI

OFFICERS

Section 1. *Designation*. The principal officers of the Corporation shall be a President, a Vice President, a Secretary, and a Treasurer, all of whom shall be elected by and from the Board of Directors. The Directors may appoint an assistant treasurer, and an assistant secretary, and such other officers as in their judgment may be necessary. (In the case of a corporation of one hundred members or less the offices of Treasurer and Secretary may be filled by the same person).

Section 2. *Election of Officers*. The officers of the Corporation shall be elected annually by the Board of Directors at the organization meeting of each new Board and shall hold office at the pleasure of the Board.

Section 3. *Removal of Officers*. Upon an affirmative vote of a majority of the members of the Board of Directors, any officer may be removed, either with or without cause, and his successor elected at any regular meeting of the Board of Directors, or at any special meeting of the Board called for such purpose.

Section 4. *President*. The President shall be the chief executive officer of the Corporation. He shall preside at all meetings of the members and of the Board of Directors. He shall have all of the general powers and duties which are usually vested in the office of president of a corporation, including but not limited to the power to appoint committees from among the membership from time to time as he may in his discretion decide is appropriate to assist in the conduct of the affairs of the Corporation.

Section 5. <u>Vice President</u>. The Vice President shall take the place of the President and perform his duties whenever the President shall be absent or unable to act. If neither the President nor the Vice President is able to act, the Board of Directors shall appoint some other member of the Board to so do on an interim basis. The Vice President shall also perform such other duties as shall from time to time be imposed upon him by the Board of Directors.

Section 6. <u>Secretary</u>. The Secretary shall keep the minutes of all meetings of the Board of Directors and the minutes of all meetings of the members of the Corporation; he shall have the custody of the seal of the Corporation; he shall have charge of the stock transfer books and of such other books and papers as the Board of Directors may direct; and he shall, in general, perform all the duties incident to the office of Secretary.

Section 7. <u>Treasurer</u>. The Treasurer shall have responsibility for corporate funds and securities and shall be responsible for keeping full and accurate accounts of all receipts and disbursements in books belonging to the Corporation. He shall be responsible for the deposit of all moneys and other valuable effects in the name, and to the credit, of the Corporation in such depositaries as may from time to time be designated by the Board of Directors.

ARTICLE VII

RIGHTS OF FEDERAL HOUSING ADMINISTRATION

Section 1.* The management, operation and control of the affairs of the Corporation shall be subject to the rights, powers, and privileges of the Federal Housing Administration pursuant to a Regulatory Agreement between the Corporation and the Federal Housing Administration. The Corporation is bound by the provisions of the Regulatory Agreement which is a condition precedent to the insurance of a mortgage of the Corporation on the project.

ARTICLE VIII

AMENDMENTS

Section 1. These By-Laws may be amended by the affirmative vote of the majority of the entire regular membership of record at any regular or special meeting, provided that no amendment shall become effective unless and until it has received the written approval of the Administration. Amendments may be proposed by the Board of Directors or by petition signed by at least twenty (20) percent of the members. A description of any proposed amendment shall accompany the notice of any regular or special meeting at which such proposed amendment is to be voted upon.

ARTICLE IX

CORPORATE SEAL

Section 1. <u>Seal</u>. The Board of Directors shall provide a suitable corporate seal containing the name of the Corporation, which seal shall be in charge of the Secretary. If so directed by the Board of Directors, a duplicate of the seal may be kept and used by the Treasurer or any assistant secretary or assistant treasurer.

---

* Delete the language of this Section where FHA regulation is exercised through ownership of preferred stock rather than by Regulatory Agreement and substitute the following:

"Section 1. Rights of Federal Housing Administration. The rights and privileges of the regular memberships of the Corporation and the management, operation and control of the affairs of the Corporation shall be subject to the rights, powers and privileges of the preferred memberships of the Corporation registered in the name of the Federal Housing Administration as provided in the Certificate of Incorporation."

ARTICLE X

FISCAL MANAGEMENT

Section 1. <u>Fiscal Year.</u> The fiscal year of the Corporation shall begin on the _____ day of _____ every year, except that the first fiscal year of the Corporation shall begin at the date of incorporation. The commencement date of the fiscal year herein established shall be subject to change by the Board of Directors should corporate practice subsequently dictate, but not without the prior written approval of the Administration.

Section 2. <u>Books and Accounts.</u> Books and accounts of the Corporation shall be kept under the direction of the Treasurer and in accordance with the Uniform System of Accounts prescribed by the FHA Commissioner. That amount of the carrying charges required for payment on the principal of the mortgage of the Corporation or any other capital expenditures shall be credited upon the books of the Corporation to the "Paid-In Surplus" account as a capital contribution by the members.

Section 3. <u>Auditing.</u> At the closing of each fiscal year, the books and records of the Corporation shall be audited by a Certified Public Accountant or other person acceptable to the Administration, whose report will be prepared and certified in accordance with the requirements of the Administration. Based on such reports, the Corporation will furnish its members with an annual financial statement including the income and disbursements of the Corporation. The Corporation will also supply the members, as soon as practicable after the end of each calendar year, with a statement showing each member's pro rata share of the real estate taxes and mortgage interest paid by the Corporation during the preceding calendar year.

Section 4. <u>Inspection of Books.</u> Financial reports such as are required to be furnished to the Administration and the membership records of the Corporation shall be available at the principal office of the Corporation for inspection at reasonable times by any members.

Section 5. <u>Execution of Corporate Documents.</u> With the prior authorization of the Board of Directors, all notes and contracts, including Occupancy Agreements, shall be executed on behalf of the Corporation by either the President or the Vice President, and all checks shall be executed on behalf of the Corporation by (1) either the President or the Vice President, and countersigned (2) by either the Secretary or Treasurer.

ARTICLE XI[*]

COMMUNITY FACILITY PROVISIONS

Section 1. <u>Applicable Provisions.</u> Notwithstanding any provision herein to the contrary, upon the payment in full of each FHA-insured mortgage executed by the Corporation and the release of the dwelling units included therein to the respective members, the following provisions of these By-Laws shall not be applicable to such members:

(a) Article III; and

(b) Sections 2 and 13 of Article V; and

in lieu thereof the following provisions shall apply to such members, and to all members upon payment in full of all FHA-insured mortgages executed by the Corporation:

Section 2. <u>Membership.</u>

(a) <u>Members.</u> Members shall consist of the owners of the dwelling units listed in Appendix B of the Articles of Incorporation, a copy of which is attached hereto, who have been approved for membership by the Board of Directors, and who have paid for their membership and received membership certificates, and such other persons to whom memberships have been transferred as provided herein.

---

[*] This Article to be included only in Sales Type projects where community facilities are to be owned by the Corporation.

(b) **Transfer of Membership.** Except as herein provided, memberships are not transferable or assignable:

1. The Board of Directors shall determine the membership value (hereinafter called the "Membership Fee") at which same may be transferred.

2. Subject to the prior approval of the Board of Directors, memberships may be permanently transferred by members to any of the following, in the order listed:

   a. To the purchaser or lessee of the member's home if same is listed in Appendix B of the Articles of Incorporation.

   b. To the owner or lessee of any of the other houses listed in Appendix B of the Articles of Incorporation who does not already own a membership.

   c. To the applicant for membership at the top of a waiting list maintained by the Board of Directors, who is a resident of the area, the confines of which shall be as determined by the Board of Directors.

   d. To a non-resident of the area.

(c) **Temporary Transfers.** Subject to the prior approval of the Board of Directors, a member may temporarily assign his membership to his lessee for a designated period of time provided, however, that the member making the temporary assignment remains obligated to the Corporation for the payment of all assessments and other charges approved by the membership, and for the payment of the lessee's dues. Any delinquency in payment of dues, assessment and such other charges shall be subject to the provisions of paragraph (d) hereof.

(d) **Termination of Membership.** Any member failing to pay annual dues, assessments or other charges duly approved by the Board of Directors within thirty (30) days after notification of delinquency has been mailed to him at the address appearing on the records of the Corporation shall be suspended by the Board of Directors. Any person thus suspended shall be notified promptly in writing by the Secretary of his suspension, and if the amounts due and payable are not paid within fifteen (15) days after the sending of such notice he shall cease to be a member of the Corporation and shall not be entitled to the privileges accorded to members. The Corporation shall be obligated, after reassignment and sale of said membership to return the Membership Fee less amounts due. (The Board of Directors, in its discretion, may reinstate any member upon request and payment of all amounts in arrearage.) The Board of Directors, at its discretion, may cancel the membership of any member upon the return of the Membership Fee provided, however, that the member may be reinstated upon appeal and approval of reinstatement by the majority of the members present at a regular or special meeting. The Corporation shall not be obligated to refund any membership fee to any member except as provided herein.

Section 3. **Directors.** The Board of Directors shall have the powers and duties necessary for the administration of the affairs of the Corporation and may do all such acts and things as are not by law or by these By-Laws directed to be exercised and done by the members. The powers of the Board of Directors shall include but not be limited:

(a) To promulgate such rules and regulations pertaining to the use and operation of the community facilities which are consistent with these By-Laws and the Certificate of Incorporation.

(b) To establish the annual dues, assessments and charges for the operation and maintenance of the community facilities and any other property, real or personal, owned by the Corporation.

230 / *GOING CO-OP*

FHA FORM NO. 3234-B
Rev. Feb. 1969

U. S. DEPARTMENT OF HOUSING AND URBAN DEVELOPMENT
FEDERAL HOUSING ADMINISTRATION

MODEL FORM OF CERTIFICATE OF INCORPORATION

(For Use by Cooperative Corporations in Section 213, 221 and 236 cases where a Regulatory Agreement is Used.)

FIRST: This is to certify that we,

Name	Address

all being of full legal age, do, under and by virtue of the laws of the State of associate ourselves with the intention of forming a corporation to provide housing on a nonprofit cooperative basis.

SECOND: The name of the corporation is
The corporation shall commence business with the filing of these Articles, and have perpetual existence. The principal office of the corporation will be located at
The resident agent of the corporation is
, whose post office address is

THIRD: The purpose for which the corporation is formed, and the business and the objects to be carried on and promoted by it, are as follows:

*(a) (To provide under the provisions of Section 221 of Title II of the National Housing Act, as amended, dwelling accommodations on a cooperative basis for families displaced from urban renewal areas or as a result of governmental action and to assist further the provision of housing for moderate and low income families.)

*(To provide housing on a cooperative basis, in the manner and for the purposes provided in Section 213 of Title II of the National Housing Act, as amended.)

*(To provide housing on a cooperative basis, in the manner and for the purposes provided in Section 236 of Title II of the National Housing Act, as amended.)

(b) To construct, operate, maintain and improve, and to buy, own, sell, convey, assign, mortgage or lease any real estate and any personal property necessary or incident to the provision of such housing.

(c) To borrow money and issue evidences of indebtedness in furtherance of any or all of the objects of its business; to secure the same by mortgage, pledge or other lien.

(d) To apply for and obtain or cause to be obtained from the Federal Housing Commissioner, hereinafter called the "Commissioner", a contract or contracts of mortgage insurance pursuant to the provisions of the above cited Section of the National Housing Act, as amended.

(e) To enter into any kind of activity, and to perform and carry out contracts of any kind necessary to, or in connection with, or incidental to the accomplishment of the non-profit purposes of the cooperative corporation.

(f) To make patronage refunds to members, stockholders, occupants of dwelling units, or others as provided by the by-laws and/or occupancy agreements.**

FOURTH: Notwithstanding any other provision contained herein the corporation formed hereby is authorized to enter into a contract (Regulatory Agreement) with the Federal Housing Commissioner and shall be bound by the terms thereof to enable the Commissioner to carry out the provisions of the National Housing Act, as amended. Upon execution, the contract (Regulatory Agreement) shall be binding upon the corporation, its successors and assigns, so long as a mortgage is outstanding, unpaid and insured or held by the Federal Housing Commissioner.

FIFTH: The Corporation shall have_____ ***directors, elected by the *(common stockholders) (members), who shall act as such until their successors are duly chosen and qualified. Officers shall be elected as provided for in the by-laws.

SIXTH: *(The total amount of the capital stock of the corporation shall be_____ shares of common stock ****having a par value of $_____ per share.)

*(The corporation is organized on a non-stock basis. The consideration for membership shall be $ _____ each.)

SEVENTH: Unless otherwise required by law, no dividend shall be paid at any time upon any *(class of stock) (membership) issued by this corporation.

EIGHTH: No contract or other transaction between this Corporation and any other corporation, and no act of this Corporation, shall in any way be affected or invalidated by the fact that any of the directors or officers of this Corporation are pecuniarily or otherwise interested in, or are directors or officers of, such other corporation; any directors individually, or any firm of which any director may be a member, may be a party to, or may be pecuniarily or otherwise interested in, any contract or transaction of this Corporation, provided the fact that he or such firm is so interested, shall be disclosed on the minutes of this Corporation; and any director of this Corporation who is also a director or officer of such other corporation or who is so interested may be counted in determining the existence of a quorum at any meeting of the board of directors of this Corporation, which shall authorize any such contract or transaction, provided, however, such director may not vote thereat to authorize any such contract or transaction.

Signed by the incorporators this_____ day of_____, 19_____.

THE INCORPORATORS

NOTE:

Must be signed, acknowledged and recorded in compliance with the laws of the State of incorporation. An attorney's opinion and title insurance will be required prior to closing.

---

* Delete inapplicable parenthetical provision.
** Delete clause (f) in Section 236 cases.
*** Any convenient odd number of directors (not less than 3 nor more than 11) may be provided.
**** The "common stock" may be par or no par and may provide for such classes or preferences as are deemed appropriate.

Appendix 2/233

FHA FORM NO 3237
Revised Sept. 1970

U. S. DEPARTMENT OF HOUSING AND URBAN DEVELOPMENT
FEDERAL HOUSING ADMINISTRATION

MODEL FORM OF OCCUPANCY AGREEMENT

(For use by Sec. 213, Sec. 221 and Sec. 236 Cooperatives composed of one mortgage parcel. (Multi-Section cooperative should use FHA Form 3237-B.))

THIS AGREEMENT, made and entered into this _____ day of _____, 19___, by and between _____ (hereinafter referred to as the Corporation), a corporation having its principal office and place of business at _____ and _____ (hereinafter referred to as Member);

WHEREAS, the Corporation has been formed for the purpose of acquiring, owning and operating a cooperative housing project to be located at _____, with the intent that its members [in stock corporations change "members" to "stockholders" and add the following parenthetical clause "(hereinafter called members)"] shall have the right to occupy the dwelling units thereof under the terms and conditions hereinafter set forth; and

WHEREAS, the Member is the owner and holder of a certificate of membership [or _____ shares of common capital stock] of the Corporation and has a bona fide intention to reside in the project;

*WHEREAS, the Member has certified to the accuracy of the statements made in his application and family income survey and agrees and understands that family income, family composition and other eligibility requirements are substantial and material requirements of his initial and of his continuing occupancy.

NOW, THEREFORE, in consideration of One Dollar ($1.00) to each of the parties paid by the other party, the receipt of which is hereby acknowledged, and in further consideration of the mutual promises contained herein, the Corporation hereby lets to the Member, and the Member hereby hires and takes from the Corporation, dwelling unit number _____, located at _____;

TO HAVE AND TO HOLD said dwelling unit unto the Member, his executors, administrators and authorized assigns, on the terms and conditions set forth herein and in the corporate Charter and By-laws of the Corporation and any rules and regulations of the Corporation now or hereafter adopted pursuant thereto, from the date of this agreement, for a term terminating on _____ 19___, **renewable thereafter for successive three-year periods under the conditions provided for herein.

ARTICLE 1. MONTHLY CARRYING CHARGES

Commencing at the time indicated in ARTICLE 2 hereof, the Member agrees to pay to the Corporation a monthly sum referred to herein as "Carrying Charges", equal to one-twelfth of the Member's proportionate share of the sum required by the Corporation, as estimated by its Board of Directors to meet its annual expenses, including but not limited to the following items:

(a) The cost of all operating expenses of the project and services furnished.
(b) The cost of necessary management and administration.
(c) The amount of all taxes and assessments levied against the project of the Corporation or which it is required to pay, and ground rent, if any.
(d) The cost of fire and extended coverage insurance on the project and such other insurance as the Corporation may effect or as may be required by any mortgage on the project.
(e) The cost of furnishing water, electricity, heat, air conditioning, gas, garbage and trash collection and other utilities, if furnished by the Corporation.
(f) All reserves set up by the Board of Directors, including the general operating reserve and the reserve for replacements.
(g) The estimated cost of repairs, maintenance and replacements of the project property to be made by the Corporation.
(h) The amount of principal, interest, mortgage insurance premiums, if any, and other required payments on the hereinafter-mentioned insured mortgage.
(i) Any other expenses of the Corporation approved by the Board of Directors, including operating deficiencies, if any, for prior periods.

The Board of Directors shall determine the amount of the Carrying Charges annually, but may do so at more frequent intervals, should circumstances so require. No member shall be charged with more than his proportionate share thereof as determined by the Board of Directors. That amount of the Carrying Charges required for payment on the principal of the mortgage of the Corporation or any other capital expenditures shall be credited upon the books of the Corporation to the "Paid-In Surplus" account as a capital contribution by the members.

***Notwithstanding the above provisions it is understood and agreed by the Member and the Corporation that where the annual family income of the Member is such that he is entitled to the benefit of the interest reduction payment made by the Secretary of Housing and Urban Development (hereinafter referred to as secretary) to the mortgagee, the monthly Carrying Charges for the member shall be reduced to the extent required by the Secretary as set forth in the Regulatory Agreement.

Until further notice from the Corporation the Monthly Carrying Charges for the abovementioned dwelling unit shall be $_____

***It is understood and agreed that if the annual family income of the Member is hereafter increased, his monthly Carrying Charges will be increased to the extent required by the Secretary as set forth in the Regulatory Agreement.

---

* Required only in Sec. 236 cases and in Sec. 22(d)(3) below market interest rate cases.
** The termination date to be inserted should be three years from the date of the Occupancy Agreement.
*** Required only in Section 236 cases.

234/GOING CO-OP

*The Member agrees, however, that if during the term of this agreement the total income of his family exceeds the limitations for occupancy which may be established from time to time by the Secretary of Housing and Urban Development (hereinafter referred to as Secretary) he will pay to the Corporation, at the option of the Corporation and upon 90 days' written notice, additional Monthly Carrying Charges in an amount commensurate with the amount of his family income in excess of the income limitations, pursuant to a plan previously developed by the Corporation and approved by the Secretary. In no event shall the total Monthly Carrying Charge, including such additional charges for excess income, exceed that which would have been applicable had the mortgage of the Corporation borne interest at the rate of 6 percent per annum and a mortgage insurance premium of ½ of 1 percent been required.

**The Member agrees that his family income, family composition and other eligiblity requirements are substantial and material condition with respect to the amount of monthly carrying charges he will be obligated to pay and with respect to his continuing right of occupancy. The Member agrees to make a recertification of his income to the Corporation at least every two years from the date of this Agreement so long as he is receiving the benefit of interest reduction payments made by the Secretary to the mortgagee. The Member further agrees that the monthly carrying charges are subject to adjustment by the Corporation to reflect income changes which are disclosed on any of the Member's recertifications, as required by the Regulatory Agreement. Immediately upon making such adjustment, the Corporation agrees to give 30 days written notice to the Member stating the new amount the Member will be required to pay, which, until further notice shall then be the Member's monthly carrying charge.

**The Member agrees to pay to the Corporation any Carrying Charge which should have been paid but for (a) Member's misrepresentation in his initial income certification or recertification, or any other information furnished to the Corporation; or (b) Member's failure to supply income recertifications when required or to supply information requested by the Corporation.

ARTICLE 2. WHEN PAYMENT OF CARRYING CHARGES TO COMMENCE.

After thirty days' notice by the Corporation to the effect that the dwelling unit is or will be available for occupancy, or upon acceptance of occupancy, whichever is earlier, the Member shall make a payment for Carrying Charges covering the unexpired balance of the month Thereafter, the Member shall pay Carrying Charges in advance on the first day of each month.

ARTICLE 3. PATRONAGE REFUNDS.***

The Corporation agrees on its part that it will refund or credit to the Member within ninety (90) days after the end of each fiscal year, his proportionate share of such sums as have been collected in anticipation of expenses which are in excess of the amount needed for expenses of all kinds, including reserves, in the discretion of the Board of Directors.

ARTICLE 4. MEMBER'S OPTION FOR AUTOMATIC RENEWAL.

It is covenanted and agreed that the term herein granted shall be extended and renewed from time to time by and against the parties hereto for further periods of three years each from the expiration of the term herein granted, upon the same covenants and agreements as herein contained unless; (1) notice of the Member's election not to renew shall have been given to the Corporation in writing at least four months prior to the expiration of the then current term, and (2) the Member shall have on or before the expiration of said term (a) endorsed all his (stock) (membership certificate) for transfer in blank and deposited same with the Corporation, and (b) met all his obligations and paid all amounts due under this Agreement up to the time of said expiration, and (c) vacated the premises, leaving same in good state of repair. Upon compliance with provisions (1) and (2) of this Article, the Member shall have no further liability under this agreement and shall be entitled to no payment from the Corporation.

ARTICLE 5. PREMISES TO BE USED FOR RESIDENTIAL PURPOSES ONLY.

The Member shall occupy the dwelling unit covered by this agreement as a private dwelling unit for himself and/or his immediate family and for no other purpose, and may enjoy the use in common with other members of the corporation of all community property and facilities of the project so long as he continues to own a [membership certificate] [share of common stock] of the Corporation, occupies his dwelling unit, and abides by the terms of this agreement. Any sublessee of the Member, if approved pursuant to Article 7 hereof, may enjoy the rights to which the Member is entitled under this Article 5.

The Member shall not permit or suffer anything to be done or kept upon said premises which will increase the rate of insurance on the building, or on the contents thereof, or which will obstruct or interfere with the rights of other occupants, or annoy them by unreasonable noises or otherwise, nor will he commit or permit any nuisance on the premises or commit or suffer any immoral or illegal act to be committed thereon. The Member shall comply with all of the requirements of the Board of Health and of all other governmental authorities with respect to the said premises. If by reason of the occupancy or use of said premises by the Member the rate of insurance on the building shall be increased, the Member shall become personally liable for the additional insurance premiums.

ARTICLE 6. MEMBER'S RIGHT TO PEACEABLE POSSESSION.

In return for the Member's continued fulfillment of the terms and conditions of this agreement, the Corporation covenants that the Member may at all times while this agreement remains in effect, have and enjoy for his sole use and benefit the dwelling unit hereinabove described, after obtaining occupancy, and may enjoy in common with all other members of the Corporation the use of all community property and facilities of the project.

ARTICLE 7. NO SUBLETTING WITHOUT CONSENT OF CORPORATION.

The Member hereby agrees not to assign this agreement nor to sublet his dwelling unit without the written consent of the Corporation on a form approved by the Department of Housing and Urban Development (hereinafter referred to as HUD). The liability of the Member under this Occupancy Agreement shall continue notwithstanding the fact that he may have sublet the dwelling unit with the approval of the Corporation and the Member shall be responsible to the Corporation for the conduct of his sublessee. Any unauthorized subleasing shall, at the option of the Corporation, result in the termination and forfeiture of the member's rights under this Occupancy Agreement. Non-paying guest of the Member may occupy Member's unit under such conditions as may be prescribed by the Board of Directors in the rules and regulations.

ARTICLE 8. TRANSFERS.

Neither this agreement nor the Member's right of occupancy shall be transferrable or assignable except in the same manner as may now or hereafter be provided for the transfer of memberships in the By-Laws of the Corporation.

* Required only in Sec. 221 below market interest rate cases.
** Required only in Section 236 cases.
*** Omit this paragraph in Section 236 c

Appendix 2/235

The Member hereby certifies that neither he nor anyone authorized to act for him will refuse to sell his membership, after the making of a bona fide offer, or refuse to negotiate for the sale of, or otherwise make unavailable or deny the membership to any person because of race, color, religion, or national origin. Any restrictive covenant or cooperative property relating to race, color, religion, or national origin is recognized as being illegal and void and is hereby specifically disclaimed. Civil action for preventive relief may be brought by the Attorney General in any appropriate U.S. District Court against any person responsible for a violation of this certification.

ARTICLE 9. MANAGEMENT, TAXES AND INSURANCE.

The Corporation shall provide necessary management, operation and administration of the project; pay or provide for the payment of all taxes or assessments levied against the project; procure and pay or provide for the payment of fire insurance and extended coverage, and other insurance as required by any mortgage on property in the project, and such other insurance as the Corporation may deem advisable on the property in the project. The Corporation will not, however, provide insurance on the Member's interest in the dwelling unit or on his personal property.

ARTICLE 10. UTILITIES.

The Corporation shall provide water, electricity, gas, heat and air conditioning in amounts which it deems reasonable. (Strike out any of the foregoing items in this Article which are not applicable.) The Member shall pay directly to the supplier for all other utilities.

ARTICLE 11. REPAIRS.

(a) By Member. The Member agrees to repair and maintain his dwelling unit at his own expense as follows:

    (1) Any repairs or maintenance necessitated by his own negligence or misuse;
    (2) Any redecoration of his own dwelling unit; and
    (3) Any repairs, maintenance or replacements required on the following items:

    (Insert the items desired, subject to HUD approval.)

(b) By Corporation. The Corporation shall provide and pay for all necessary repairs, maintenance and replacements, except as specified in clause (a) of this Article. The officers and employees of the Corporation shall have the right to enter the dwelling unit of the Member in order to effect necessary repairs, maintenance, and replacements, and to authorize entrance for such purposes by employees of any contractor, utility company, municipal agency, or others, at any reasonable hour of the day and in the event of emergency at any time.

(c) Right of Corporation to Make Repairs at Member's Expense. In case the Member shall fail to effect the repairs, maintenance or replacements specified in clause (a) of this Article in a manner satisfactory to the Corporation and pay for same, the latter may do so and add the cost thereof to the Member's next month's Carrying Charge payment.

ARTICLE 12. ALTERATIONS AND ADDITIONS.

The Member shall not, without the written consent of the Corporation, make any structural alterations in the premises or in the water, gas or steampipes, electrical conduits, plumbing or other fixtures connected therewith, or remove any additions, improvements, or fixtures from the premises.

If the Member for any reason shall cease to be an occupant of the premises, he shall surrender to the Corporation possession thereof, including any alterations, additions, fixtures and improvements.

The Member shall not, without the prior written consent of the Corporation, install or use in his dwelling unit any air conditioning equipment, washing machine, clothes dryer, electric heater, or power tools. (Strike out any of the foregoing items which are not applicable.) The Member agrees that the Corporation may require the prompt removal of any such equipment at any time, and that his failure to remove such equipment upon request shall constitute a default within the meaning of Article 13 of this agreement.

ARTICLE 13. DEFINITION OF DEFAULT BY MEMBER AND EFFECT THEREOF.

It is mutually agreed as follows: At any time after the happening of any of the events specified in clauses (a) to (i)* of this Article the Corporation may at its option give to the Member a notice that this agreement will expire at a date not less than ten (10) days thereafter. If the Corporation so proceeds all of the Member's rights under this agreement will expire on the date so fixed in such notice, unless in the meantime the default has been cured in a manner deemed satisfactory by the Corporation, it being the intention of the parties hereto to create hereby conditional limitations, and it shall thereupon be lawful for the Corporation to re-enter the dwelling unit and to remove all persons and personal property therefrom, either by summary dispossess proceedings or by suitable action or proceeding, at law or in equity or by any other proceedings which may apply to the eviction of tenants or by force or otherwise, and to repossess the dwelling unit in its former state as if this agreement had not been made:

(a) In case at any time during the term of this agreement the Member shall cease to be the owner and legal holder of a membership [or share of the stock] of the Corporation.
(b) In case the Member attempts to transfer or assign this agreement in a manner inconsistent with the provisions of the By-Laws.
(c) In case at any time during the continuance of this agreement the Member shall be declared a bankrupt under the laws of the United States.
(d) In case at any time during the continuance of this agreement a receiver of the Member's property shall be appointed under any of the laws of the United States or of any State.
(e) In case at any time during the continuance of this agreement the Member shall make a general assignment for the benefit of creditors.
(f) In case at any time during the continuance of this agreement any of the stock or membership of the Corporation owned by the Member shall be duly levied upon and sold under the process of any Court.
(g) In case the Member fails to effect and/or pay for repairs and maintenance as provided for in Article 11 hereof.
(h) In case the Member shall fail to pay any sum due pursuant to the provisions of Article 1 or Article 10 hereof.
(i) In case the Member shall default in the performance of any of his obligations under this agreement.

---

* Change "(i)" to "(k)" in Section 236 cases and in Section 221 below market interest rate cases.

236 / GOING CO-OP

*(j) In case at any time during the term of this agreement the limitations for occupancy which may be established from time to time by HUD are exceeded.

*(k) In case at any time during the term of this agreement, the Member fails to comply promptly with all requests by the Corporation or HUD for information and certifications concerning the income of the Member and his family, the composition of the Member's family and other eligibility requirements for occupancy in the project.

The Member hereby expressly waives any and all right of redemption in case he shall be dispossessed by judgment or warrant of any Court or judge;the words "enter", "re-enter", and "re-entry", as used in this agreement are not restricted to their technical legal meaning, and in the event of a breach or threatened breach by the Member of any of the covenants or provisions hereof, the Corporation shall have the right of injunction and the right to invoke any remedy allowed at law or in equity, as if re-entry, summary proceedings, and other remedies were not herein provided for.

The Member expressly agrees that there exists under this Occupancy Agreement a landlord-tenant relationship and that in the event of a breach or threatened breach by the Member of any covenant or provision of this Agreement, there shall be available to the Corporation such legal remedy or remedies as are available to a landlord for the breach or threatened breach under the law** by a tenant of any provision of a lease or rental agreement.

The failure on the part of the Corporation to avail itself of any of the remedies given under this agreement shall not waive nor destroy the right of the Corporation to avail itself of such remedies for similar or other breaches on the part of the Member.

ARTICLE 14. MEMBER TO COMPLY WITH ALL CORPORATE REGULATIONS.

The Member covenants that he will preserve and promote the cooperative ownership principals on which the Corporation has been founded, abide by the Charter, By-Laws, rules and regulations of the Corporation and any amendments thereto, and by his acts of cooperation with its other members bring about for himself and his co-members a high standard in home and community conditions. The Corporation agrees to make its rules and regulations known to the Member by delivery of same to him or by promulgating them in such other manner as to constitute adequate notice.

ARTICLE 15. EFFECT OF FIRE LOSS ON INTERESTS OF MEMBER.

In the event of loss or damage by fire or other casualty to the above-mentioned dwelling unit without the fault or negligence of the Member, the Corporation shall determine whether to restore the damaged premises and shall further determine, in the event such premises shall not be restored, the amount which shall be paid to the Member to redeem the (membership) (common stock) of the Member and to reimburse him for such loss as he may have sustained.

If, under such circumstances, the Corporation determines to restore the premises, Carrying Charges shall abate wholly or partially as determined by the Corporation until the premises have been restored. If on the other hand the Corporation determines not to restore the premises, the Carrying Charges shall cease from the date of such loss or damage.

ARTICLE 16. INSPECTION OF DWELLING UNIT.

The Member agrees that the representatives of any mortgagee holding a mortgage on the property of the Corporation, the officers and employees of the Corporation, and with the approval of the Corporation the employees of any contractor, utility company, municipal agency or others, shall have the right to enter the dwelling unit of the Member and make inspections thereof at any reasonable hour of the day and at any time in the event of emergency.

ARTICLE 17. SUBORDINATION CLAUSE.

The project, of which the above-mentioned dwelling unit is a part, was or is to be constructed or purchased by the Corporation with the assistance of a mortgage loan advanced to the Corporation by a private lending institution with the understanding between the Corporation and the lender that the latter would apply for mortgage insurance under the provisions of the National Housing Act. Therefore, it is specifically understood and agreed by the parties hereto that this agreement and all rights, privileges and benefits hereunder are and shall be at all times subject to and subordinate to the lien of a first mortgage and the accompanying documents executed by the Corporation under date of _____, (or to be executed by the Corporation) payable to _____ in the principal sum of $ _____ with interest at _____ per centum, and insured or to be insured under the provisions of the National Housing Act, and to any and all modifications, extensions and renewals thereof and to any mortgage or deed of trust made in replacement thereof and to any mortgage or deed of trust which may at any time hereafter be placed on the property of the Corporation or any part thereof. The Member hereby agrees to execute, at the Corporation's request and expense, any instrument which the Corporation or any lender may deem necessary or desirable to effect the subordination of this agreement to any such mortgage, or deed of trust, and the Member hereby appoints the Corporation and each and every officer thereof, and any future officer, his irrevocable attorney-in-fact during the term hereof to execute any said instrument on behalf of the Member. The Member does hereby expressly waive any and all notices of default and notices of foreclosure of said mortgage which may be required by law.

In the event a waiver of such notices is not legally valid, the Member does hereby constitute the Corporation his agent to receive and accept such notices on the Member's behalf.

ARTICLE 18. LATE CHARGES AND OTHER COSTS IN CASE OF DEFAULT.

The Member covenants and agrees that, in addition to the other sums that have become or will become due, pursuant to the terms of this Agreement, the Member shall pay to the Corporation a late charge in an amount to be determined from time to time by the Board of Directors for each payment of Carrying Charges, or part thereof, more than 10 days in arrears.

If a Member defaults in making a payment of Carrying Charges or in the performance or observance of any provision of this Agreement, and the Corporation has obtained the services of any attorney with respect to the defaults involved, the Member covenants and agrees to pay to the Corporation any costs or fees involved, including reasonable attorney's fees, notwithstanding the fact that a suit has not yet been instituted. In case a suit is instituted, the Member shall also pay the costs of the suit, in addition to other aforesaid costs and fees.

ARTICLE 19. NOTICES.

Whenever the provisions of law or the By-Laws of the Corporation or this agreement require notice to be given to either party hereto, any notice by the Corporation to the Member shall be deemed to have been duly given, and any demand by the Corporation upon the Member shall be deemed to have been duly made if the same is delivered to the Member at his unit or to the Member's last known address; and any notice or demand by the Member to the Corporation shall be deemed to have been duly given if delivered to an officer of the Corporation. Such notice may also be given by depositing same in the United States mails addressed to the Member as shown in the books of the Corporation, or to the President of the Cooperative, as the case may be, and the time of mailing shall be deemed to be the time of giving of such notice.

---

* Required only in Section 236 cases and in Section 221 below market interest rate cases.
** In some States it may be desirable to include reference to a particular State statute on this subject.

Appendix 2/237

ARTICLE 20. ORAL REPRESENTATION NOT BINDING.

No representations other than those contained in this agreement, the Charter and the By-Laws of the Corporation shall be binding upon the Corporation.

ARTICLE 21. RENT SUPPLEMENT (Insert only in cases involving Rent Supplements)

The Corporation has entered into a Rent Supplement Contract with the Secretary which provides that the Secretary will pay a portion of the rent on behalf of qualified members. Pursuant to said Contract, the Secretary has approved the monthly Carrying Charge specified in Article I for the unit and has determined that the member is eligible for rent supplement payments in the amount of $_____ per month. In addition, to the conditions recited above, the member agrees that the following special conditions shall be applicable so long as he receives the benefit of rent supplement payments:

(a) Of the monthly Carrying Charge, Member agrees to pay, as Member's share, the sum of $_____ being the difference between the monthly Carrying Charge and the amount of monthly rent supplement payment to be made by the Secretary pursuant to the Rent Supplement Contract.

(b) Member agrees in the event the amount of monthly rent supplement payment is adjusted by the Secretary to reflect income change of the Member, to pay in lieu of the amount specified in the preceding paragraph, the difference between the monthly Carrying Charge and the adjusted amount of rent supplement payment. The Corporation agrees to give written notice to Member, by an addendum to be made a part of this Agreement, immediately upon such adjustment made by the Secretary, stating the new amount the Member will be required to pay as Member's share of the monthly Carrying Charge.

(c) Member agrees that the family income, family composition and other eligibility requirements shall be deemed substantial and material obligations of his occupancy with respect to the amount of rent supplement benefits for which Member is eligible and in determining Member's share of the monthly Carrying Charge.

(d) Member agrees to comply promptly with all requests by the Corporation or the Secretary for information and certifications concerning the total current family income of the Member, the composition of the Member's family and other requirements for occupancy.

(e) Member agrees to report immediately to the Corporation if his monthly income increases to or is more than $_____ (this amount is equal to four times the basic monthly Carrying Charge for the unit).

(f) Member, except in the case of Members who are 62 years of age or older, agrees that a recertification of income shall be made to the Secretary each year from the date of the original certification by the Secretary.

(g) Member understands that the rent supplement payment and Member's share of the monthly Carrying Charge is subject to adjustment to reflect income changes and agrees to be bound by such adjustment.

(h) Corporation and Member understand that, where by reason of an increase in income, Member is no longer entitled to rent supplement benefits, Member may continue to occupy the unit by paying increased monthly Carrying Charges established by the Corporation with the approval of the Secretary.

(i) Member agrees to reimburse the Secretary for any excess rent supplement payments made by the Secretary during any period when an appropriate adjustment or termination of payments was not made:

(1) because of Member's failure to report an increase in income to the Corporation, as required by paragraph (e), above;

(2) because of Member's misrepresentation of statements made in Member's application for rent supplement payments, recertification of income or any other information furnished to Corporation or Secretary; or

(3) because of Member's failure to supply information requested by the Corporation or the Secretary.

IN WITNESS WHEREOF, the parties hereto have caused this agreement to be signed and sealed the day and year first above written.

_____
Corporation

By _____(SEAL)

_____
Member and Stockholder

TO BE DULY ACKNOWLEDGED

238 / GOING CO-OP

FHA FORM NO. 3232
Rev. February 1969

U. S. DEPARTMENT OF HOUSING AND URBAN DEVELOPMENT
FEDERAL HOUSING ADMINISTRATION

MODEL FORM OF SUBSCRIPTION AGREEMENT
(For use by all Cooperative Corporations under Sections 213, 221 and 236 of the National Housing Act)*

Application No. _____

Dwelling Unit No. _____

Date _____

1. **Subscription Amount**

    (a) I/We _____, a legal resident of _____, hereinafter called the "Subscriber", in consideration of the mutual promises of other subscribers and other good and valuable considerations, hereby subscribe for membership in _____, a cooperative housing corporation hereinafter called the "Corporation", and hereby subscribe for

    (OMIT INAPPLICABLE PARTS)

    (i) One share of common capital stock, Class _____, of said Corporation having a par value of $ _____ per share.

    (ii) _____ shares of common capital stock of said Corporation having a par value of $ _____ per share.

    (iii) Membership Certificate in said Corporation having a par value of $ _____ .

    (b) I/We hereby agree to pay the subscription price of $ _____, as follows:**

    (i) $ _____ upon signing this Agreement;

    (ii) $ _____ on written demand by the Corporation. (Such demand will constitute notification of subscriber's acceptability for membership; provided that, if full payment is made of the subscription price without a written demand therefor, the Subscriber's acceptability for membership shall not occur until written notification thereof is sent to the Subscriber.)

2. **Ratification of Other Provisions**

    I/We hereby ratify the provisions contained in the Certificate (Articles) of Incorporation, By-Laws, Regulatory Agreement, Information Bulletin,*** and Occupancy Agreement, copies of which are attached hereto and receipt of which is hereby acknowledged.

3. **Priority of Mortgage Lien**

    This Agreement and all rights hereunder are and at all times shall be subject and subordinate to the lien of the mortgage and accompanying documents to be executed by the Corporation to a lending institution and to be insured under (Section 213) (Section 221) (Section 236)**** of Title II of the National Housing Act; and to any and all modifications, extensions, and renewals thereof; and to any mortgage or deed of trust made in place thereof; and to any mortgage or deed of trust which may at any time thereafter be placed on the property of the Corporation or any part thereof.

---

* In Sales Type Corporations under Section 213, FHA Form 3231 or 3233 should be used.
** The total of all subscription prices should be in an amount determined by the sponsors to be sufficient to cover the difference between the mortgage loan and the total cost of the project plus the amount required for working capital deposit specified in the FHA Commitment for Insurance. Normally, the amount of stock subscribed by each member should be equivalent to his "down payment". Where this is not the case and the stock subscription amounts or membership fees are to be augmented by paid in capital in some other form, the applicable facts should be clearly spelled out in the Subscription Agreement. As to the small fee to be paid by the subscriber for a credit report, which is in addition to the subscription price, this may be conveniently covered by a separate receipt bearing the statement, if desired, that such fee is not refundable.
*** Insert at this point "Cooperative Agency Agreement" in cases where the cooperative has retained an organizing agent, and add "Sales Agreement" where such form is required by the FHA Commitment for Insurance.
**** Delete inappropriate references.

4. Occupancy Agreement

The subscriber, if approved for membership, will be entitled to occupancy of the above dwelling unit under the terms of the Occupancy Agreement. It is estimated that the initial carrying charge per month for said unit will be $_____, but it is to be emphasized that this is only an estimate, subject to fluctuations as provided for in the Occupancy Agreement. I/We agree to execute the Occupancy Agreement on demand and to comply with all the terms thereof. (In Section 236 cases the following language should be added.) The basis for calculating the carrying charges is described in the Information Bulletin. The estimated carrying charge amount shown above is a tentative amount computed by the cooperative's sales representative based upon income and other information supplied by the subscriber and is subject to verification by the Federal Housing Administration. The effective carrying charge figure may therefore be increased, decreased or remain the same. If the figure is increased the subscriber will be notified in writing and be given the option to accept same, but if he does not wish to do so he may request that this agreement be cancelled, whereupon he will be entitled to a return of all sums paid hereunder. In order to cancel the agreement and obtain such refund, however, he must give written notice to this effect to the corporation within 15 days after the date of the notification to him of the increased monthly charges.

5. Cancellation Provisions

(a) By Corporation: The Corporation reserves the right at any time before it has notified the subscriber of his acceptability for membership, for reasons deemed sufficient by the Corporation, to return the amount paid by the subscriber under this Agreement, or in the event the subscriber shall have died prior to becoming a member the Corporation reserves the right to return same to subscriber's estate or legal representative, and thereupon all rights of the subscriber shall cease and terminate without further liability on the part of the Corporation.

If the subscriber shall default in any of the obligations called for in this Agreement, and such default shall continue for fifteen (15) days after notice sent by registered mail by the Corporation to the Subscriber at the address given below, then, at the option of the Corporation, the subscriber shall lose any and all rights under this Agreement, and any amount paid toward the subscription price may be retained by the Corporation as liquidated damages, or may at the option of the Corporation be returned less the subscriber's proportionate share of expenses incurred by the Corporation, such proportionate share of expenses to be determined solely by the Corporation. The Corporation may, at its option, release the obligations of the subscriber under this Agreement in the event the subscriber shall secure an assignee of this Agreement who has assumed the obligations herein contained and is satisfactory to the Corporation and the Federal Housing Administration. This Agreement is not otherwise assignable.

(b) (USE ONLY IN SECTION 213 CASES AND SECTION 221 MARKET RATE CASES) By Federal Housing Administration: It is understood that the subscriber's credit is subject to approval by the Federal Housing Administration. In the event the Federal Housing Administration determines that the subscriber does not meet FHA credit requirements for participation in this project, then the subscriber will be entitled to a return of all sums paid hereunder. Upon such return this Agreement shall be deemed null and void and all of the subscriber's rights shall cease and terminate without further liability on the part of the Corporation.

(b) (USE ONLY IN SECTION 236 CASES AND SECTION 221 BELOW MARKET INTEREST RATE CASES) By Federal Housing Administration: It is understood that the subscriber's credit is subject to approval by the Federal Housing Administration and that said subscriber's family income and composition must be consistent with the limitations for initial occupancy established by the FHA.* The subscriber agrees to furnish information as required by FHA concerning his family income and composition. In the event the FHA determines that the subscriber does not meet FHA credit and/or family income and composition requirements for participation in this project, then the subscriber will be entitled to a return of all sums paid hereunder. Upon such return this Agreement shall be deemed null and void and all the subscriber's rights shall cease and terminate without further liability on the part of the Corporation.

(c) By Subscriber: If the subscriber within five (5) days after the execution of this Subscription Agreement notifies the Corporation in writing that he wishes to withdraw from the Agreement, the amounts paid by him under this Agreement will be returned to him and thereupon all rights and liabilities of the subscriber hereunder shall cease and terminate. The right of the subscriber to so withdraw shall, however, terminate unless exercised within such 5-day period, except that if membership is not achieved to the extent required by the Federal Housing Administration or construction of the project

---

* In certain cases involving the conversion of existing rental projects to cooperative ownership, this language may be modified with FHA approval to reflect that existing over-income tenants may become cooperative members but will be required to pay higher carrying charges than would otherwise be applicable.

240 / GOING CO-OP

has not commenced within one year from the date of execution of this Agreement, subscriber shall again have the right to withdraw and obtain such refund. ** (In Section 236 cases the following language should be added.) Subscriber shall also have the right to withdraw under the circumstances described in Paragraph 4 above.

6. (USE ONLY IN SECTION 221 BELOW MARKET INTEREST RATE CASES) Income Limitations:

It is understood as provided in the By-Laws and Occupancy Agreement, that if subscriber's total family income exceeds the income limitations for continuing occupancy which may be established from time to time by the FHA, the subscriber will as determined by the Corporation, either (a) quit and deliver up the premises or (b) pay such additional monthly carrying charges as have been established by the Corporation with FHA approval.

(USE ONLY IN SECTION 236 CASES) Income Limitations:

It is understood as provided in the Occupancy Agreement, that if subscriber's total family income exceeds the income limitations which may be established from time to time by the FHA, the subscriber will pay such additional monthly carrying charges as have been established by the Corporation with FHA approval.

7. Oral Representations Not to be Relied Upon

This Agreement will supersede any prior understandings and agreements and constitutes the entire agreement between us, and no oral representations or statements shall be considered a part hereof.

WITNESS

_____
Subscriber

_____
Subscriber

_____
Address

_____
Telephone

** In projects composed of existing rather than new construction, delete the words "construction of the project has not commenced" and substitute in lieu thereof the following "title to the project has not been acquired by the Corporation". In Investor Sponsor cases and in cases where Commitment Form 3208 is used, delete "construction of the project has not commenced within one (1) year from the date of execution of this Agreement" and substitute in lieu thereof the following "title to the project has not been acquired by the Corporation within one (1) year after the date estimated by the FHA for completion of the project."

Index

Index

A

Accountability, 191–192
Accounting: cycle, co-op, 179–183; system, setting up simple, 171–179
Activities, informal participation and spinoff, 194–195
Administrative costs, 111
Affordability, 28–29, 76–77; analysis, 78–79, 93–98, 104–113
Air conditioning, 87
Allocation, of voluntary labor: job-specific, 191; random, 191
Alternative Realty Center (ARC, Oakland, California), 81
American Institute of Architects (AIA), 133
Apartment, inspecting, before buying, 28, 34–40
Appliances, limits on, 165
Architect: final plans and specifications from, 135–136; hiring, 132–133; working with, 133–134
Assignment, task, 54–55, 191

B

Baby boom generation, 2–3, 202, 203
Balance sheet, 181, 185–186
Balloon payments, 43
Bank accounts, 173–174
Banks, 122, 124–126
Bargain buildings, finding, 81–82
Bathrooms, inspection of, 40
Beneficial interest, *see* Financial interest
Benning Heights Cooperative (Washington, D.C.), 18–19, 50–51, 102, 131, 189
Best's Insurance Reports, 109
Bids, seeking, 137–138
Bishop Co-op (Wyandotte, Michigan), 9–10, 189
Bonding: payment, 138; performance, 138
Bookkeeping, 168–171. See *also* Accounting
Boston Mutual Housing Association (BMHA), 162–163
Brainstorming, 53, 55
Bricks, missing, 86
Buckingham Village (Arlington, Virginia), 8–9
Budgets, 42–43; estimating co-op operating, 105–107
Building: conditions, 28, 40; inspecting, 83–89; management, 40; questions related to kind of, 76; selecting, 76–83. See *also* Affordability; Inspection; Rehabilitation
Business plan, 121, 125–126
Buyer protections, 47–48
Bylaws, 41, 65–66, 67, 69, 149

C

Capital: improvements, 159–160; social, 188; working, 121–122
Carrying charge(s): assessments, 72; and collections, 149–150
Certificate (or articles) of incorporation, 41, 65
Change orders, 142
Children, policies about supervision of, 165
Closing, 46–47, 103
Cobb, I. S., 166
Collections, carrying charges and, 149–150
Commercial space, leasing, 114
Committee(s): building assessment, 58; building participation with, 189–190; financial planning, 58; legal, 58, 63; setting up, 58–59, 69–70; of the whole, 65
Common Space, Inc. (Minneapolis), 5, 22–23
Common spaces, policies about use of, 165
Communication and education, 195–201
Community development industry, 203
Community Reinvestment Act (CRA, 1977), 6, 124
Condominiums, 7, 8, 20; compared with co-ops, 12–14
Construction, 136; contract, 138–140; meetings, 141–142; monitoring, 140–143; schedules, 140–141. *See also* Contractor, general
Contractor, general, 115–116; change orders requested by, 142; hiring, 136; negotiations with, 138–140; progress payments to, 142–143; seeking bids from, 137–138. *See also* Construction

Co-op City (New York), 17, 19, 204
Co-ops, housing: basics of, 14–17; characteristics of members of, 23–26; size of, 17–19; types of, 19–23
Corporation, co-op, 27–28, 64–65. *See also* Incorporation
Cost(s): capital, 77–78; operating, 77–78; picture, total, 77–79; reducing operating, 116–118; ways of achieving lowest possible, 7, 27. *See also* Expenses
CPM (co-op path method), 50, 59, 60–62, 63; chart, 61, 75
Critical path method (CPM), 50, 59. *See also* CPM (co-op path method)

D

Debs, Eugene, 54
Debt service, 107
Decision making: consensual, 54; democratic, 15; factors involved in, 11–14
Directors, board of, 67, 189; and officers, 68–70
Disclosure requirements, 47
Displacement, 102
Diversification, 125
Documents, inspecting, 40–44
Dodge Reports, 132
Doors, 39
Drywall, 38–39

E

Economic Recovery Tax Act (1981), 91
Education, communication and, 195–201
Elderly, advantages of co-ops for, 9–10, 23–24, 202, 203

Electrical system, 44; condition of, 87; safety and adequacy of, 34–36
Electric heating systems, 37
Emerson, Ralph Waldo, 206
Energy: audit, 198; conservation, 87, 110, 116–117
Equity, new members', 164. *See also* Sweat equity
Eviction, grounds for immediate, 166
Expenses, estimating operating, 107–113. *See also* Costs
Experts, housing, 55–56

F

Fair Access to Insurance Rates (FAIR) Plan, 109
Federal Home Loan Mortgage Corporation ("Freddie Mac"), 123
Fenway Cooperative: First, 6–7, 83; Second, 6; Third, 6; Fourth, 6; Fifth, 6
Files, 178–179; apartment, 157; building systems maintenance, 157
Financial interest, 16, 70, 72, 183
Financial statements, 42–43
Financing, 104–105; choosing different sources of, 117; cutting rehabilitation costs, 115–116; different type of co-op, 118–120; estimating operating budget, 105–107; estimating operating expenses, 107–113; estimating revenue needs, 113; increasing income, 114–115; and lenders, 124–126; putting together loan application package, 120–124; reducing operating costs, 116–118; sources of, 122–124
Fire damage, 86
Floor plan, 34, 36

Floors, sloping, 85–86
Food co-ops, 203
Forced hot air systems, 36
Frankie O'Day Co-op (Boston), 148
Full-service co-ops, 23
Fund raising, 51

G

Garbage and trash, policies about, 165
Goldman, Eric F., 25
Gravity systems, 36
Greenboard, 39
Group anemia, 57

H

Heating systems, 44; condition of, 87; kinds of, 36–38
Historic preservation, 90–91
Hot water systems, 37
House policies, 149; capital improvements, 159–160; carrying charges and collections, 149–150; maintenance, 155–159; management, 150–155; miscellaneous, 165–167; resale and transfer value, 160–164
Housing and Urban Development (HUD), U.S. Department of, 7, 21, 48, 66; finding bargain buildings through, 82; insurance program of, 123; management plan required by, 151; and occupancy agreements, 71; and sweat equity, 143, 144
HVAC (heating, ventilation, and air conditioning), 87

I

Income: portion of, for housing, 28–29; sources, additional, 114–115; statement, 181, 184

Incorporation, 63, 64–66; certificate (or articles) of, 41, 65. *See also* Corporation, co-op
Inspection, building, 83–84; condition of systems, 87; general conditions, 87–89; by professional vs. building committee, 84–85; structural conditions, 85–87
Inspection Checklist, Co-op, 35. *See also* Apartment, inspecting, before buying
Insulation, 38–39, 87
Insurance, 108–110, 166; companies, cooperative, 110; fire or hazard, 108–109; public liability, 108, 109
Intensive repair, 89–90
Interior, U.S. Department of the, 91
Internal Revenue Service (IRS), 14, 44, 113; Accelerated Cost Recovery Schedules (ACRS) of, 163; co-ops and, 72–74, 114, 115
Internal subsidy, 72
Investment-oriented co-ops, 8, 19–20

J

Journal(s), 173; cash disbursements, 176–178; cash receipts, 175, 176; collections, 174–175

K

Kitchen, inspection of, 39

L

Labor costs, reducing, 116
Landscaping, 88
Laundry facilities, policies about use of, 165–166
Leaflets, 199

Lease, proprietary, 15, 42, 71–72, 150
Leasing co-op, 119–120
Ledgers, 174, 178
Legal fees, 111
Lenders, 124–126
Limited-equity co-op, 6, 16–17, 160, 162, 163
Limited partnership, 118
Lintels, inspecting, 85
Loan application package, 120–124
Locations, co-op, 31–32, 79–80

M

Maintenance, 155–156; budget, 156; priorities, 157–159; program, components of, 156–157; and repairs, 112. *See also* Management, building
Management, building, 40, 150–151; agent, choosing, 151–152; contract, 152–153; monitoring of, 153–154; plan, 151; self-management, 117, 155. *See also* Maintenance
Management fees, 111
MassSave, 198
Materials, reducing costs of, 116
Mechanical systems, condition of, 87
Media, public relations and, 200
Member(s), co-op: characteristics of, 23–26; dual role of, 70–73; meeting, before buying into co-op, 28, 33; orientation, 196–197; participation of, 15–16; relations between board, management, and, 67; selection of new, 162–163; services, charging for, 115
Middle class, co-ops for, 25–26
Minutes of meetings, 43–44

Mixed-income co-ops, 26, 72
Moderate rehabilitation, 90
Mortar, crumbling, 86
Mortgages, 43, 95, 122
Mother-daughter societies (Sweden), 22
Multifamily homesteading concept, 143, 145. *See also* Sweat equity
Mutual housing associations, 21–23

N

National Association of Housing Cooperatives, 31
National Consumer Cooperative Bank (NCCB), 32, 51, 120, 123
National Park Service, 91
Negotiations and purchase, 45–47, 99–100
New Beginning Cooperative, 5
Newsletters, 198–199
New York City Tenant Interim Lease Program, 197
Nixon, Richard, 20
North American Students of Cooperation (NASCO), 24
Notes, keeping, 32–33

O

Occupancy agreement, 15, 42, 71–72
Officers, board of directors and, 68–70
Operating reserve, 113, 118
Operators' Manual, Co-op, 66–72
Options, 100
Organization chart, 67
Orientation, member, 196–197
Owner, contacting, 82–83, 99
Ownership: advantages of, 11; forms of, 12–14; responsibilities of, 11–12; shared, 14–15

P

Parking: policies about, 166; spaces, leasing, 114
Participation, 15–16, 187–189, 205; accountability and, 191–192; assigning work tasks for, 191; committees for, 189–190; informal, and spinoff activities, 194–195; problems of, 192–193; and racism and sexism, 193–194
Personal Finances Worksheet, 30–31
Petty cash, 186
Pine Grove Village (Lexington, Massachusetts), 21
Pipes: brass, 38; copper, 38; plastic (PVC), 38; steel, 38
Plans and specifications, final, for rehabilitation, 135–136
Plumbing systems, 38, 44; condition of, 87
Policies, *see* House policies
Portfolio, 125
Posters, 199
Preservation, historic, 90–91
President, responsibilities of, 69
Progress payments, to contractor, 142–143
Proprietary lease, 15, 42, 71–72, 150
Prospectus, 47, 48
Protections, buyer, 47–48
Proxies, 71
Public relations and media, 200
Purchase, 98–99; closing, 103; final days before, 102–103; negotiations and, 45–47, 99–100; and options, 100; and sales contract, 100–102
Purchase-and-sale agreement, *see* Sales contract

R

Racism and sexism, 193–194
Radiant systems, 37
Radiators, 37
Real estate taxes, 107–108
Realtors, using, 80–81
Reconciliation process, 180–181
Records, *see* Files
Registry of Deeds, 45
Rehabilitation, 75, 84, 127–128; under construction, 136–143; costs, cutting, 115–116; deciding to repair or replace, 128–131; defined, 89; essential, 87; estimating cost of, 91–93; historic preservation, 90–91; intensive repair, 89–90; moderate, 90; nonessential, 87–88; planning for, with architect, 131–136; substantial, 90. *See also* Construction; Contractor, general; Sweat equity
Reimbursement policy, 183–186
Repairs, maintenance and, 112, 155–159
Replacement reserves, 89–90, 112, 118, 127, 128–131
Resale and transfer value, 160–164
Revenue needs, estimating, 113
Rochdale Society of Pioneers (Rochdale, England), 16, 195, 204–205
Rogers, Will, 3
Roman Catholic Archdiocese of Boston, 6, 21
Roof, faulty, 86
Rotation, of voluntary labor, 191

S

Sales contract, 45–46, 100–102
Savo Island Co-op (Berkeley, California), 190
Schumacher, E. F., 17
Season, best, for co-op buying, 29–31
Secretary/clerk, responsibilities of, 69
Security, building, 88–89, 112
Self-maintenance, 117
Self-management, 117, 155
Sexism, racism and, 193–194
Shared ownership, 14–15
Shareholders, 15. *See also* Member(s), co-op
Signs, 199
Simon, Robert, 50–51
Size, co-op, 17–19
Smith, Henry, 10
Smoke detectors, policies about, 166
Social capital, 188
Solar systems, 37
Speakers, 199–200
Specifications and plans, final, for rehabilitation, 135–136
Starting own co-op, 49–51; co-op conversions, 57–58; generating ideas and making decisions, 53–54; getting work done, 54–55; organizing co-op tasks, 58–62; preparing for first meeting, 52; pulling up roots, 56–57; using experts, 55–56
Steam systems, 37
Stockholders, co-op, 67, 71. *See also* Member(s), co-op
Streisand, Barbra, 20
Structural conditions, 85–87
Structured co-ops, 20–21
Student co-ops, 24, 162–163
Study groups, 198
Subcontractors, 136
Subscription agreement, 41–42, 70–71
Subsidy, internal, 72
Substantial rehabilitation, 90
Supplies, 111

Sweat equity, 7, 88, 116, 143–144; co-op members, selecting, 144–145; scope of, 145–146; training and supervision, 147; value of, 147–148; work, budgeting, 146

T

Tasks: assignment of, 54–55, 191; management, 59; organizing co-op, 58–62
Tax(es): abatement, applying for, 117–118; credit, investment, for historic preservation, 91; deductions, for co-op members, 29; personal income, 7–8; property, 7, 8; real estate, 107–108; requirements for co-ops, 72–74
TBC (to be called) list, 51, 55
TBD (to be done) list, 55
Tenant association, 51, 57
Tenants, protections for, against displacement, 102
Termites, 86
Thermopane glass, 39
Title transfer, 103
Training programs, 197–198
Transfer value, resale and, 160–164
Treasurer: report of, 181, 182–183; responsibilities of, 69

1210 Massachusetts Avenue Cooperative (Washington, D.C.), 119–120
Types, co-op, 19; full-service co-ops, 23; investment co-ops, 19–20; mutual housing associations, 21–23; structured co-ops, 20–21

U

Upper Americans, co-ops for, 25
Urban Homesteading Assistance Board (UHAB), 17–18, 168, 197
Utilities, 110

V

Ventilation, 87
Vice-president, responsibilities of, 69
Visions, of future of co-ops, 202–206
Voting, 54, 70–71

W

Walls, inspection of, 38–39, 85
Water damage, 86
Wetwall construction, 39
Windows, 39; storm, 87
Working class, co-ops for, 25–26

William Coughlan, Jr., has been an active participant in the co-op movement for over a decade and is the author of *The Organizer's Manual* and *The Food Co-op Handbook*.

Monte Franke, a housing expert, is a consultant with federal agencies, including HUD, the Federal Reserve, and the Federal Home Loan Bank Board. Currently he is renovating a co-op building in Boston's Fenway area.